ECONOMIC GROWTH AND POLITICAL CHANGE IN ASIA

Economic Growth and Political Change in Asia

Graham Field

First published in Great Britain 1995 by
MACMILLAN PRESS LTD
Houndmills, Basingstoke, Hampshire RG21 6XS
and London
Companies and representatives
throughout the world

A catalogue record for this book is available
from the British Library.

ISBN 0–333–59954–3

First published in the United States of America 1995 by
ST. MARTIN'S PRESS, INC.,
Scholarly and Reference Division,
175 Fifth Avenue,
New York, N.Y. 10010

ISBN 0–312–12696–4

Library of Congress Cataloging-in-Publication Data
Field, Graham.
Economic growth and political change in Asia / Graham Field.
p.   cm.
Includes bibliographical references and index.
ISBN 0–312–12696–4 (cloth)
1. Asia—Economic conditions—1945-   —Case studies.   2. Asia-
-Economic policy—Case studies.   3. Asia—Politics and
government—1945-   —Case studies.   I. Title.
HC412.F44   1995
338.95—dc20   95–12496
                                                          CIP

---

10   9   8   7   6   5   4   3   2   1
04   03   02   01   00   99   98   97   96   95

Printed and bound in Great Britain by
Antony Rowe Ltd, Chippenham, Wiltshire

To the memory of my father

Contents

Acknowledgements

This book owes a great deal to the close attention given to the manuscript by Patrick Heenan and Monique Lamontagne, whose insightful criticism and comments did much to shape its development. The author would also like to thank all those people who gave their time and thoughts in interviews as well as his *Asiamoney* colleagues who guided his first steps in the region.

GRAHAM FIELD

List of Abbreviations

ABRI	*Angkatan Bersenjata Republik Indonesia*
ADB	Asian Development Bank
AFTA	ASEAN Free Trade Area
ASEAN	Association of South East Asian Nations
BJP	Bharatiya Janata Party
BN	*Barisan Nasional*
BSF	Border Security Force
BNP	Bangladesh National Party
BSPP	Burma Socialist Programme Party
CCP	Chinese Communist Party
CFD	Campaign for Democracy
CITIC	China International Trust and Investment Corporation
CPB	Communist Party of Burma
CPF	Central Provident Fund
CPP	Communist Party of the Philippines
DAP	Democratic Action Party
DPP	Democratic Progressive Party
EU	European Union
EPB	Economic Planning Board
EPZs	Export processing zones
FDI	Foreign direct investment
FUNCINPEC	*Front Uni National pour un Cambodge Indépendent, Neutre, Pacifique et Coopératif*
GATT	General Agreement on Tariffs and Trade
GDP	Gross domestic product
GLCs	Government-linked corporations
GNP	Gross national product
HCI	Heavy and chemical industries
HDB	Housing Development Board
HPAEs	High performing Asian economies
ICMI	*Ikatan Cendekiawan Muslim Indonesia*
IMF	International Monetary Fund
ISA	Internal Security Act
JVP	*Janatha Vimukthi Peramuna*
KCIA	Korean Central Intelligence Agency
KMT	Kuomintang
KPNLF	Khmer People's National Liberation Front
LNG	Liquefied natural gas

LPRP	Lao People's Revolutionary Party
LTTE	Liberation Tigers of Tamil Eelam
MCA	Malaysian Chinese Association
MIC	Malaysian Indian Congress
MNLF	Moro National Liberation Front
MQM	Mohajir Qaumi Movement
MRD	Movement to Restore Democracy
NBFIs	Non bank financial institutions
NEP	New Economic Policy
NIEs	Newly Industrialising economies
NPA	National People's Army
NPC	National People's Congress
NSP	National Security Planning agency
NTUC	National Trade Union Congress
NU	*Nahdlathul Ulama*
OECD	Organisation for Economic Cooperation and Development
PAP	People's Action Party
PAS	*Parti Islam*
PBS	*Parti Bersatu Sabah*
PDI	*Partai Demokrasi Indonesia*
PDP	Palang Dharma Party
PLA	People's Liberation Army
PPP	*Partai Persatuan Pembangunan*
PPP	Pakistan People's Party
PRC	People's Republic of China
R&D	Research and development
SAR	Special Administrative Region
SBSI	*Serikat Buruh Sejahtera Indonesia*
SEZs	Special enterprise zones
SLFP	Sri Lanka Freedom Party
SPSI	*Serikat Pekerjaan Seluruh Indonesia*
SLORC	State Law and Order Restoration Council
SMIs	Small and medium sized industries
SOC	State of Cambodia
TDRI	Thailand Development Research Institute
UMNO	United Malays National Organisation
UNDP	United Nations Development Programme
UNESCAP	United Nations Economic and Social Commission for Asia and the Pacific
UNP	United National Party
UNTAC	United Nations Transitional Authority for Cambodia
USDA	Union Solidarity and Development Association
UUCA	Universities and University Colleges Act
WTO	World Trade Organisation

Introduction

In a single generation, Asia's economies have undergone a transformation that has been more rapid and extensive than anyone could have imagined. From a collection of predominantly agricultural economies, linked to the world economy chiefly by colonial exploitation of natural resources and plantation agriculture, has emerged a group of vigorous exporting nations enjoying a commanding position in several industries. This has been a shift of global importance. As each fresh segment of the world has industrialised – North West Europe in the eighteenth and early nineteenth centuries; the United States, Germany and Japan in the latter half of the nineteenth century; the Soviet Union in the 1920s and 1930s – it has had global implications for the distribution of income and power. The process unfolding today in Asia is of comparable dimensions, and the internal dynamics of that change are as complex and varied as were those in the earlier periods of industrialisation.

Attempts to shoehorn these changes into an exclusive 'Asian' model or even 'family of models'[1] are misleading. The same analytical tools which gave us an understanding of European or North American industrialisation are as appropriate to economic and political change in Asia. Those changes are driven today by the same motor of capitalist accumulation, the search for the profits extracted from human labour applied to raw materials. Whether in the form of Hong Kong companies manufacturing fluffy toys in Southern China, the world's largest privately-owned power station being built in Pakistan, state companies producing helicopters in Indonesia or the food-processing industry turning out millions of tons of shrimps in Thailand, the same forces are at work as were apparent in iron smelting in Britain, railway construction in the United States or, tellingly, the repeated incorporation of non-Western techniques and ideas in Western societies.

Japan was part of this earlier phase of industrialisation and has now reached a higher level of economic development, having reconstructed its industrial base after the setbacks of the Second World War. For the Japanese people acclimatisation to industrialisation and its social consequences has extended over generations, while the long stretch of post-war prosperity has enabled the state to meet popular demands without having recourse to the brutal methods of the inter-war period. Japan's economic and political problems consequently have far more in common with those of other OECD members struggling to cope with restructuring advanced economies than they do with those of other Asian nations, which confront either the questions posed by the social and political consequences of rapid economic growth over the last

1

ten or twenty years, or the problems of economic stagnation and decline.

Although Japan's influence as a major source of investment in Asia cannot, of course, be ignored, the intricacies of Japan's domestic development fall outside the scope of this study. Our concern here will be with those parts of Asia now being drawn into the regional economy and the world economy. It was this intra-regional dynamic which helped Asia to weather the recession of the early 1990s without, contrary to expectations, experiencing a significant dip in levels of output growth. Trade flows have extended far beyond sales to the US, or to the region's own natural magnet in Japan. Investment, too, whether direct or portfolio, is allocated on a regional basis, weighing the respective merits of Sri Lanka against Laos or Bangladesh for garment factories, or the Philippines against Malaysia or Pakistan for high returns from the stock market. Policymakers have become aware of the need to sell their countries as investment locations in the context of regional competition for funds; and Asia has witnessed the tentative emergence of a series of regional bodies concerned with securing the economic benefits of growth while trying to dispel some of the attendant regional political tensions.

In the regional economy we include firstly the newly industrialising economies (NIEs)[2] of East Asia, by which we refer to South Korea, Taiwan, and Hong Kong. The fourth NIE or 'tiger' economy in Asia is Singapore, which is a member of the Association of South East Asian Nations (ASEAN) along with Brunei, the Philippines, Indonesia, Malaysia and Thailand. The last three of these are sometimes referred as the next 'little dragons' although this term has also been applied to the 'tiger' economies. However they are described, all these economies have become part of a common trading and investment network in Asia, much of it supplying and supplied by Japan. Within this network the NIEs are now increasingly supplementing Japan's role as a provider of capital and markets.

More recently, the economies of South Asia – Bangladesh, India, Pakistan and Sri Lanka – have begun to mesh with the East and South East Asian economies, providing growing markets, cheap labour and investment opportunities. The Himalayas are no longer an economic watershed and governments in South Asia now look to East Asia as well as to North America and Western Europe as sources of capital for their expansion, tailoring their policies to solicit investment from the region. It is these economic linkages which define South Asia as part of Asia for our purposes. The same applies to what we shall refer to here as the market-Stalinist economies: Communist or, in the case of Burma, military, states in which economic reforms are being implemented to allow private capitalist development, including foreign investment, but which have until recently been characterised by state control of industry and collectivised agriculture. Besides Burma, these are Cambodia, China, Laos, North Korea and Vietnam, all of which have 'opened up' economically with varying degrees of success, while a single party or military junta has retained a monopoly of political power. Only Cambodia, under UN auspices, has conducted multi-party elections which have been honoured.

Central Asia, on the other hand, has to date constructed only superficial economic links to the remainder of the region. Transport and communications remain limited, investment conditions have not yet attracted significant interest, and domestic markets are small or difficult to serve. Tentative interest in developing links has been expressed in the form of diplomatic and trade overtures and three of the Central Asian republics have been admitted to the Asian Development Bank. In the longer term the attraction of the substantial raw materials of Central Asia may draw it within the Asian ambit, although there are competing ties to Turkey, Iran and Russia. For the moment, however, it remains outside the region for our purposes. So do Mongolia, the Russian Far East and West Asia, which have no significant economic links to the rest of Asia. Certainly Mongolia and Siberia have raw material endowments that make them potentially an important part of an integrated Asian economy but as yet very few concrete steps have been taken towards realising that potential.

Acceptance of the rules of a market economy is crucial for admission to the regional economy. As a result of programmes of economic reform, often implemented as conditions for receiving financial assistance from the International Monetary Fund (IMF) or the World Bank, the role of direct state controls of the economy has been reduced and the conditions for private capitalist accumulation have been established. Reform of this kind does not necessitate the abandonment of all state-owned industry, but it typically includes devaluation, corporate tax cuts, the elimination of price subsidies, the opening of sectors previously restricted to particular companies and other measures to provide more competition. Besides acceptance of this kind of programme, in many other countries the possession of an abundant supply of cheap labour disciplined by a repressive political system is an important element in admission to the regional economy. It is the pursuit of cheap labour by capital which helps tie the economies of the Asian region together and unites them with Western investors. Capital's search for exploitable labour is the force which is breaking down the isolation of Burma and North Korea, stripping away the regulations that have insulated workers in state industries in China from the full force of the market, pulling down restrictions on foreign participation in the Indian economy and impeding the functioning of free trade unions in Indonesia. Capital's search for labour is the true dynamic element – though it is absent from the World Bank's extensively-publicised analysis of *The East Asian Miracle* – that carries industrialisation from Japan to the next tier of 'tiger economies' and then to 'the little dragons' and the latest newcomers.

As the World Bank's study shows, many Asian countries have demonstrated an outstanding record of economic achievement. *The East Asian Miracle* takes as its starting point the growth of the 23 economies of East Asia which were the fastest-growing in the world over the period 1965–90[3] (this list includes some of the Pacific island states). Among these it singles out eight high-performing Asian economies (Japan, South Korea, Taiwan, Singapore, Hong Kong, Thailand, Malaysia and Indonesia) which grew at more than twice the rate of the rest of East Asia. In face of what the World Bank believes to be an 'infinitely elastic'[4] demand for the products of individual developing countries, the message is clearly that there is more of the same to come. A string of other analysts and commentators have elaborated the argument, predicting, for instance, that 'China is following a model of development that can continue to generate 7 per cent growth indefinitely'.[5] They seem oblivious to the danger of abandoning the scepticism which history should teach us to apply to statements of that nature, or of falling into the kind of hubris apparent on the cover of *Asiaweek* magazine at the start of 1994. 'Can anything go wrong?', the 1994 *Asiaweek* business forecast asked rhetorically. 'It doesn't look it' was the reply.[6]

The cautionary tale of Latin America is surely one to take to heart. Between 1965 and 1980 Brazil achieved growth in excess of 8 per cent while Mexico's was over 6 per cent. Brazil, it was predicted in the 1970s, was set to emerge as one of the world's largest economies in a relatively short period. Whereas China is now acclaimed as the next economic superpower, partly as a result of its ability to promote economic growth over and above political reform, 15 years ago Brazil's broad social strengths were praised in contrast to the 'rigid, obsessive and exclusive focus on economic values characteristic of Korea and Japan'.[7] In the event the Brazilian and Mexican 'miracle economies' delivered growth in the 1980s of just over 2 per cent and barely 1 per cent respectively, while those Asian 'economic values' are now lauded as a prime factor in growth. Such comparisons would be unreasonable were it not for the suspicion that some forecasts of indefinite high growth rest on little more than the assertion that growth has occurred at a rapid rate for a certain period and can therefore be expected to continue, shored up by short-term predictions of demand. John Wong's essay on 'Asean Economies: Continuing Dynamic Growth in the 1990s'[8] is a case in point. He cheerfully supposes that the relocation of investment to ASEAN will continue in the 1990s and that political and social institutions can continue to avoid strife, having done so for a long time. What has undoubtedly been a remarkable transformation has blinded observers to the problems which growth creates and to their own past enthusiasms.

As the case of Latin America should suggest, the future for Asian economies is by no means as secure as predictions of indefinite 7 or 8 per cent growth would indicate. Chapters 1 and 2 set out the various difficulties which the Asian economies will face in sustaining growth and look at the range of policy tools available to them. For some the challenge lies in securing their foothold at the next level of industrialisation, in making the transition from low or medium technology industries to high technology and service sector employment, without at the same time seeing too much of their industrial base cut from under them by cheaper competitors starting up in low-cost production. Where raw materials and agriculture have played important roles in growth, depletion and the limits of growth present different challenges. For others it is handling chronic infrastructure problems, coping with growing obstacles to market access in the developed economies, addressing labour and skill shortages or managing a deregulated economy with the bureaucratic tools of a centrally planned system. For all these reasons it is likely to become progressively harder, rather than easier, to achieve high levels of growth.

According to *The East Asian Miracle*, Asia's achievement has been to combine rapid growth with equity. The statistical evidence of this is itself debatable (as we shall argue in Chapter 3) and it conceals dimensions of worsening inequality, some of which give grounds for questioning the desirability of growth itself, as well as instances of contested inequality. The proliferation of arguments over distribution arising out of rapid growth is recognised not only by Marxists but by mainstream political scientists. Samuel Huntington's book *Political Order in Changing Societies*, which was first published in 1968 and was an attempt to come to terms with the revolutionary upheavals of the 1960s, provided a long list of the politically destabilising effects of economic growth. Traditional social groups are disrupted; a stratum of *nouveaux riches* emerges; geographical mobility increases; the gap between rich and poor may widen; some incomes rise absolutely but not relatively; consumption is restricted to promote investment; education expands and aspirations grow; regional, ethnic and historical conflicts over the distribution of income are aggravated; and the capacity for group organisation improves. These predictions can be mapped with uncanny accuracy onto contemporary Asia, where we shall find exact examples of the effects outlined by Huntington. His underlying thesis is that 'if poor countries appear to be unstable, it is not because they are poor, but because they are trying to become rich'.[9]

Chapters 4 to 7 look at questions of political change in Asia. The 'Asian model' assumes that political liberalisation will follow in each country as an eventual result of economic growth, but only after a decent interval. Asian politicians and sympathetic Western analysts argue that successful economic management is proof that Asian governments have the ability to make timely political reforms. This model ascribes political liberalisation and change to the kindness of benevolent leaders, as the Taiwan government spokesman Shaw Yu-Ming explains in describing the changes introduced by President

Chiang Ching-Kuo after 1985: 'as the people's socio-economic status rises so does their desire to participate in the political process. At first a pluralistic social order emerges in which competing interests vie for political power. Interest groups, as well as the man on the street, seek more power through the political process. The late President saw that Taiwan had clearly reached this stage of development and made policy decisions that brought major changes to Taiwan's social and political environment'.[10] Political liberalisation becomes, therefore, not a right to be taken but a reward for mature behaviour to be claimed at the appropriate moment.

On this argument there are dangers in granting a greater measure of political freedom too soon, if ever. We use the term political freedom here rather than democracy, as opponents of freedom seize upon the term democracy to argue that Western critics are trying to foist a Westminster or Jeffersonian model onto them and insist that such critics are better employed removing the undemocratic flaws in their own countries. If we use instead the term political freedom, we can place all societies at some point on the same continuum. None enjoys perfect freedom, some enjoy very little, but we can at least decide which are becoming more free, and which less so. In this way, it is possible to say that even the ideal of greater freedom is explicitly rejected by several Asian leaders (Lee Kuan Yew, the former Prime Minister and now Senior Minister of Singapore, and Prime Minister Mahathir Mohamad of Malaysia being prime examples – see Chapter 4).

They do so on the grounds that democracy in North America and Western Europe has brought in its train all kinds of social problems from drug abuse and crime to sexual deviance and single parenthood. Moreover, they point out that those regions have seen a decline in economic growth rates which, they argue, can be attributed in part to the workings of the political system and increases in social spending. Critics of greater freedom will point to India or Australia or, as Lee Kuan Yew did quite memorably while speaking alongside President Ramos in Manila, the Philippines, to demonstrate the debilitating effects of greater freedom on economic performance. As practised in the Philippines, Lee argued, democracy leads to powerful self-serving interest groups entrenching themselves in decision-making, to corruption, 'general disorder' and lack of confidence.[11] No one would deny the shortcomings in the Philippine political system, but just as Lee supposes the cure for it lies in greater authoritarianism and discipline, this can also be sought in greater equality and freedom. Yet, with barely concealed self-satisfaction, other advocates of 'delayed' freedom compare the former Soviet Union unfavourably with China for having attempted simultaneously to introduce economic and political reform. How much better, say China's apologists, to delay the latter until the former is accomplished and let *per capita* income serve as the ultimate test of a political system.

Spurious cultural factors are also cited to justify the denial of freedoms.

Asians, the argument goes, are culturally different from Westerners and their overriding concern with the stability and future of the family, inherited from and upheld by Confucian values (at least in China and the countries and communities influenced by it) focuses their attention principally on the family's livelihood and survival. This matters far more than abstract notions of rights which Westerners have imbibed from the individualism of their culture. Add to this an ingrained respect for authority, also often attributed to Confucianism, and the result is the perfect cultural justification for authoritarianism and its supposed concomitant, stability. Moreover, it is one which Westerners are not entitled to challenge, given their inability to perceive the true meaning of the Confucian paradigm or its alleged equivalents elsewhere in Asia. Sociologists of the calibre of Max Weber may have tried to fathom its meaning, but Weber's conclusion that Confucianism would retard economic growth as much as Protestantism had stimulated it in the West is held up as an example of just how wrongheaded their conclusions are when they try.[12] Nevertheless, say the authoritarians, greater political freedom will come in the fullness of time. China, Burma and North Korea alike will liberalise, helped by the sympathetic understanding of 'friends', the 'constructive engagement' of trading partners and gentle nudges through the aid budget (especially from Japan).

The reality is that political change is inextricably linked to economic change, not through the medium of wise or profligate leaders, but through the class forces which it generates. The resistance to greater political freedom exhibited, for example, in Malaysia and Singapore is bound up with the strategy of accumulation and the structure of the ruling class in those two countries. Dependence on foreign investment and a highly unequal distribution of income have meant the need to control labour and, consequently, the squeezing out of dissent from the formal political system. In the same way it is the economic development of classes which leads to demands for change, whether it is the commercial and entrepreneurial bourgeoisie – the class which owns the new private industries that have arisen out of economic growth and which competes with landlords, the civil service or the military for a bigger share of political power – or whether it is workers joining with students in South Korea to demand direct presidential elections and better pay. The ways in which these different classes become engaged in the political process cannot be neatly controlled by Asian leaders with a gift for statecraft, though, as in Burma and China, leaderships can retain power by crushing upheavals which challenge them. Nor are Confucian cultures insulated from savage political conflicts – in China itself for much of the century, in the battles for greater democracy in South Korea or in the behaviour of the KMT in establishing its rule on Taiwan. Where the Confucian ethic is used as a justification for refusing any political concessions it serves only to bottle up demands for change until they appear in less manageable forms than in the bourgeois democracies of the West, where the institutions of representative government allow these demands to be articulated in a manner that does not fundamentally challenge the economic and political power of the ruling class – the owners of the means of production and those other groups which draw off a share of the surplus from production and which guarantee its extraction.

Given the economic growth of the last 20 years, the rise of the Asian bourgeoisie has been the most important change in the class dynamics of these countries. This is not a unified class and, as Chapter 2 shows, different relationships with the state have created business classes with varying degrees of dependence on government assistance. We shall therefore talk of 'fractions' of the bourgeoisie – including foreign capital – which compete for control of the state to appropriate the flow of patronage and influence policy.

By 'the state', we refer to those institutions responsible for guaranteeing the conditions of accumulation: repressive apparatuses (the armed forces and police), the judicial system, institutions which manage the economy and dispense patronage and the ideological state apparatuses – whether religious or educational or among the media – which shape the formation of opinion. Where the state itself owns substantial parts of the productive and financial base of the economy, the bureaucracy itself becomes a 'state bourgeoisie' and a competing fraction of the bourgeoisie in its own right; where it lacks this kind of economic base, it is subservient to dominant fractions of the ruling class. In the course of the contest among different ruling class fractions they will use different ideological guises under which they try to present their interests as 'national' interests and build – within the limits of systems they are themselves fearful of upsetting completely – popular support. The creation of an industrial working class as economic development proceeds across the region means the presence of another potential political actor, although it is one which, in the early stages of industrialisation, plays a subordinate role in change.

The rise of the bourgeoisie is most far advanced in what we will term the 'emerging bourgeois democracies' – Hong Kong, South Korea, Taiwan and Thailand. In South Korea and Taiwan military dictatorship has been cast off and in Thailand the influence of the military receded after the Bangkok uprising of May 1992, even if it is creeping back in. The relationship between the bourgeoisie and the other fractions of the ruling class varies from one economy to another, and the changing interplay of these relations in the emerging bourgeois democracies is considered in Chapter 6. The greater degree of political freedom which these societies now permit can be linked to the development of the economy: a strategy of accumulation which rests principally on the repression and exploitation of labour has been superseded by one in which technology is of greater importance and in which the greater creativeness of a free society assumes a positive economic value. Labour-

intensive industry is relocating, particularly to China, where repressive reserve powers remain very much in being, and the emerging bourgeois democracies have more of the economic leeway they need to accommodate
the demands for increased social spending that grow out of greater political
freedom.

In the 'veiled authoritarian' states of Indonesia, Malaysia and Singapore,
discussed in Chapter 4, the structure of the bourgeoisie and the underlying
economic and political fragility have led the ruling class to resist any greater
measure of political freedom. Heavy dependence on foreign investment in
Malaysia and Singapore, and a fear of rapid erosion of labour cost competitiveness in Malaysia and Indonesia, have contributed to political repression.
So have close ties between the state and favoured businessmen in Malaysia
and Indonesia, which they prefer to obscure from public scrutiny.

In the market-Stalinist economies a bourgeoisie is only just taking root
and allying itself to elements of a decaying state. This is just one aspect of
an increasing polarisation of the state apparatus, described in Chapter 5, as
the political consequences of economic reform make themselves felt. Plant
managers, army officers, local cadres and Central Committee members alike
are increasingly forced to identify with economic reform and the opportunities it presents or to cling to the economic and political power bases
they established under Stalinism. This division of interests extends down
into the peasantry and the industrial working class, creating natural constituencies for opponents and supporters of the regime.

In South Asia and the Philippines, which we term 'élite democracies'
(Chapter 7), the bourgeoisie has historically been relatively unsuccessful as
a class, reflecting the generally poor performance of these economies, and
other fractions of the ruling class have been much stronger. Again, economic change – reform inspired by the pressure of the international agencies
and investors on these relatively weak economies – is creating new alliances
between sections of the local bourgeoisie and elements of the state apparatus which see opportunities from those reforms, while a coalition of opposed interests also emerges. The strength of these opposed interests tends
to mean that governments have been forced to pursue reform policies in a
cautious manner and that these policies could still be reversed.

The development of a new Asian 'middle class' is a widely discussed
phenomenon. Several commentators have seen it as the originator of political change in the region, arguing for instance that 'the main obstacle to
democratisation in most developing countries is the absence of a large middle
class to make strong demands for democratic reforms and to give sustained
support to such reforms, once they are made. This assumption is probably
correct'.[13] The ascription of a separate political role to the middle class
rests on sociological differences in status, income, job security, consumption habits and aspirations. These are taken to distinguish it from the rest of

the working class, in the industrial and primary sectors. These distinctions mean that the middle class does not instinctively identify objective common interests with the working class, even though, with the exception of those managers whose income is tied to profits, it lives, just as much as other workers do, by the sale of its labour. Indeed, distinctions of status and aspiration are played upon precisely in order to impede such an identification. The result is that, as a political actor, the middle class occupies a floating position, siding sometimes with the mass of the working class, sometimes with the bourgeoisie and sometimes with the military or the bureaucracy. Its emergence does, however, provide a wider social base for bourgeois democracy, particularly in supplying the leadership and membership of political parties which seek gradualist change within legislative institutions that does not intrude deeply on the interests of the ruling class. Although in this sense a middle class may be an enabling factor in political change, it is not the dynamic element, as is apparent from those societies like Malaysia and Singapore in which a substantial middle class exists but in which the political system has become more repressive.

In the end economic growth often becomes almost a race against itself. As it generates more expectations growth leads to ever more extravagant promises as the basis for continuing political legitimacy. From Deng Xiaoping's coarse 'to get rich is glorious', or the Vietnamese Prime Minister's ambition of doubling living standards between 1992 and 2000, to the poverty eradication targets of Philippines 2000! or Singapore's goal of a 'Swiss' standard of living, Asian leaders see yet more growth as the panacea to the problems which growth creates. The more the economy expands, however, the more difficult it becomes to extract yet more growth and the more social and political pressures it creates.

Table 1 Annual GDP growth rates (%)

	1989	1990	1991	1992	1993	1994	1995(F)	1996(F)
Bangladesh	2.5	6.6	3.4	4.2	4.5	4.6	5.0	5.3
Burma	3.7	2.8	−0.6	9.3	6.0	6.4	*	*
Cambodia	3.5	1.2	7.6	7.0	4.3	4.9	*	*
China	4.3	3.9	8.0	13.2	13.4	11.8	9.8	8.9
Hong Kong	2.6	3.4	5.1	6.3	5.8	5.5	5.6	5.6
India	6.9	5.4	0.9	4.3	4.3	5.1	6.1	6.5
Indonesia	7.5	7.2	7.0	6.5	6.5	7.4	7.1	7.1
Laos	13.0	6.7	4.0	7.0	5.9	8.0	*	*
Malaysia	9.2	9.7	8.7	7.8	8.3	8.5	8.5	8.0
Pakistan	4.8	4.6	5.6	7.7	2.3	4.0	4.6	6.0
Philippines	6.2	3.0	−0.6	0.3	2.1	4.3	5.0	5.5
Singapore	9.2	8.8	6.7	6.0	10.1	10.1	9.0	8.5
South Korea	6.4	9.5	9.1	5.1	5.5	8.3	7.3	6.8
Sri Lanka	2.3	6.2	4.6	4.3	6.9	5.7	6.0	7.0
Taiwan	8.2	5.4	7.6	6.7	6.3	6.5	6.7	6.8
Thailand	12.2	11.6	8.4	7.9	8.2	8.5	8.6	8.0
Vietnam	7.8	4.9	6.0	8.0	8.1	8.8	8.5	9.0

Source: Asian Development Bank

Table 2 Share of industry in GDP

	1980	1993
Bangladesh	14.8	18.1
Burma	12.3	12.9
Cambodia	*	17.0
China	51.7	52.0
Hong Kong	32.0	22.6
India	25.9	28.1
Indonesia	41.3	42.1
Laos	*	17.5
Malaysia	35.8	44.2
Pakistan	25.6	26.7
Philippines	40.5	34.4
Singapore	38.8	36.5
South Korea	37.8	46.1
Sri Lanka	27.2	29.3
Taiwan	46.0	41.8
Thailand	30.1	40.9
Vietnam	26.3	24.7

Source: Asian Development Bank

1 Factors in Economic Growth

Late in 1991, the scatter-gun of recession hit the Japanese economy, having already struck Western Europe and North America. As Japan followed the world's two other largest markets into a prolonged slump, economists in their observation posts expected to see the rest of the Asian flying geese formation dragged down. Singapore looked particularly exposed, with trade more than three times the size of GDP and 27 per cent of exports to the US in 1991 depending on sales of disk drives alone.[1] Such fears proved groundless when demand for disk drives boomed as the US responded to recession by accelerating the replacement of staff with computers. More importantly for Asia as a whole, intra-regional trade proved highly resilient. As the Asian Development Bank pointed out in its *Asian Development Outlook 1994*, trade within the region grew faster than trade with the rest of the world between 1992 and 1993. Singapore, for instance, was swift to take advantage of new trading opportunities, emerging in 1991 as Vietnam's largest trading partner. Prime Minister Goh Chok Tong has also been seeking commercial opportunities in Burma at a time when many Western governments have been reluctant to associate themselves openly with the State Law and Order Restoration Council (SLORC) regime. Although Singapore's GDP growth was restrained to 5.8 per cent in 1992 it rose to 9.9 per cent in 1993 as the financial services industry expanded rapidly. China's two consecutive years of double digit GDP growth in 1992 and 1993 (13.2 per cent and 13.4 per cent) bolstered regional trade substantially while the four 'newly industrialising economies' (South Korea, Taiwan, Singapore and Hong Kong) provided a growing market to those at a lower level of development. As the OECD floundered, Asia's economies capped the expansion of the 1980s with further strong growth.

China's outstanding growth rates have arguably refuted the view that large economies cannot emulate the rapid expansion of the more compact newly industrialising economies (NIEs). Even India broke out of the confines of the so-called 'Hindu' rate of growth (a steady 3.5 per cent[2]) in the 1980s to move to a 5–6 per cent growth path, while neighbouring Pakistan and Sri Lanka have been growing at similar rates (though Pakistan dipped to growth of 2.6 per cent in 1993). Malaysia remains one of the most consistent economic performers in the region with growth averaging more than 8 per cent over the four years from 1990 to 1993. After a decade of expansion in the

1980s, punctuated by a downturn in 1986, Indonesia came through a credit crunch imposed in late 1991. Growth fell only slightly to 6.4 per cent in 1992 and stayed at that level in 1993. South Korea and Thailand both experienced a moment of excess around the start of the 1990s, when growth exceeded 10 per cent and, even though South Korea came close to what would have been characterised domestically as recession in 1993, growth never fell below 4.7 per cent. Thailand achieved a 'soft landing', dampening growth to 7.6 per cent in 1992 and 7.8 per cent in 1993. Alongside China, Vietnam has reaped considerable benefit in growth terms from its reforms in the second half of the 1980s, registering an 8.3 per cent expansion in 1992 and 8.0 per cent in 1993, its strongest in recent years. Laos too has been pulled along by the rest of the region and its GDP climbed 7.3 per cent in 1992 after rising 4.3 per cent in 1991, though it slipped back to 4 per cent in 1993. In South East Asia the Philippines has been, as in other respects, the oddity in growth terms. The Aquino administration (1986–92) presided over a growth blip which fizzled out into a recession in 1991–2, from which a modest recovery began in 1993 and quickened at the start of 1994.

The immediate history of strong growth rates is expected to be replicated over the period 1994–5 in forecasts from the OECD and the Asian Development Bank. The background of the 1980s was not just a quantitative expansion of Asia's production numbers but a qualitative transformation in its production base. A welter of new industries has arisen, catapulting individual countries into prominence in particular fields of activity. One of the best known examples is Malaysia's rise to become the world's third largest producer of semi-conductors. At the same time South Korea has established from scratch what is now the world's sixth largest automobile industry and become the world's third largest steel maker; Indonesia's IPTN builds satellites while India plans to compete with China for business in launching them; and Taiwan's petrochemicals industry is to build a single US$9.5 billion plant that could add 1 per cent annually to its GDP.[3]

The transformation is reflected in the rise of industry's share in GDP across the region. Agriculture now accounts for a larger share of GDP than industry in just six economies in the region: Cambodia, Laos, Vietnam, Burma, India and Nepal. South Korea has seen one of the most dramatic increases in industry's share in output, nearly doubling as a percentage of GDP from 23.8 per cent in 1970 to 46.3 per cent in 1993. Indonesia and Malaysia have likewise seen industry displace agriculture as the dominant sector and it now accounts for 42.1 per cent and 44.3 per cent of output respectively.[4] With the exception of Hong Kong and the micro-states of Brunei and Singapore, agriculture nevertheless remains the largest employer in most Asian economies, accounting for comfortably in excess of 50 per cent in India, Pakistan and China. But the industrial sector is now taking the lead in output and growth, most emphatically in China where industrial output rose

20.8 per cent in 1992 and 23.6 per cent in 1993. Industrialisation has also meant massive urbanisation and a consequent change in living patterns. The UN now predicts that 13 of the world's 21 mega-cities in the year 2000 will be in Asia. Besides Tokyo, the list includes rapidly emerging cities like Jakarta and Dhaka that were little more than colonial backwaters in 1945, as well as the great entrepôts of Bombay, Calcutta and Shanghai.

Changes in consumption have been equally revealing. In China, the 'three bigs' of the Mao Zedong era – bicycles, watches and sewing machines – have been replaced in the consumers' pantheon by televisions, refrigerators, washing machines, stereos and, for those willing to defy an official ban, air-conditioners. European luxury-car makers are starting assembly operations across the region; Rolls-Royce is hunting out distribution premises in Jakarta; and another 450 cars a day join the traffic jams in Thailand. Indian car makers are enjoying record sales as a burgeoning middle class graduates from scooters, the vehicle of the 'common man'. McDonalds restaurants have mushroomed in Taiwan and Hong Kong and are hugely popular in China. Fast food in the shape of Pizza Hut has reached Sri Lanka, where local executives monitor the movement of the country's four sensitive consumption indicators: sewing machines, cigarettes, stout and Coca-Cola. And for the Philippines, President Ramos sketches out a future in which it will be possible 'maybe, for "Mr and Mr Juan de la Cruz" to make a trip to Hong Kong or a nearby foreign destination'.[5]

There are exceptions to this picture of a dynamic, rapidly industrialising and increasingly free-spending Asia. Cambodia, devasted by the effects of a prolonged civil war that began in earnest in 1970 and was rekindled in 1994, has yet to rebuild its infrastructure, bring 500–600 000 hectares of land back into use[6] and restore rubber production before it can begin to consider industrial development. But the two economies with the gravest problems are the imploding dictatorships of Burma and North Korea. Of the two, Burma has been more successful in inducing foreigners to invest in the economy, rehabilitating tourist facilities and exploring for oil. But a study by the United Nations Development Programme in early 1993[7] highlighted the severe inflation problems Burma is suffering and the near-stagnation in production since 1988. Figures from Burma's Ministry of Planning and Finance claim that the 1992–3 year saw GDP growth of 5.8 per cent, after 1.3 per cent and 2.7 per cent in the preceding two years. Even on these figures, however, growth has barely recouped the losses of the disastrous 11.4 per cent drop in economic activity in 1988–9 as political protest racked the country.[8]

North Korea is in a more parlous state. Precise statistical data cannot be provided but estimates of the contraction in North Korea's economy are of the order of 5 per cent a year since 1989, according to sources in South Korea. More alarming reports deriving from diplomats in the North Korean capital Pyongyang suggest the 1992 shrinkage may have been as large as 30 per cent.[9] By the end of 1993 it was admitted that the third Seven Year Plan had missed virtually all its targets (except in construction). Industry may now be operating at just 45 per cent of capacity as chronic fuel shortages bite into production, while ordinary citizens face food shortages and exhortations to 'eat two meals a day instead of three'.[10]

Although Burma and North Korea are the exceptions, the question for the rest of Asia is one of the sustainability of growth rates of 7 per cent. There is no doubt that the region has a momentum which will propel it forward at or close to this rate over the short to medium term. As Indonesia, South Korea, Taiwan and the other high performing Asian economies (HPAEs) praised by the World Bank demonstrated in the 1960s, 1970s and 1980s, it has been possible to maintain high growth rates even over the medium to long term. To assess the chances of a prolongation of this achievement during the 1990s and beyond, however, we need to ask whether ceilings on growth will begin to appear. To do this means examining the factors which have underpinned the growth recorded so far and analysing their replicability in the future. How big a slice of luck did the Asian economies have in their factor endowments and their achievements? And, we shall ask in the following chapter, what were governments able to do to maximise the returns from the factors at their disposal?

AGRICULTURE

Thirty years ago economists and political scientists were alarmed by the growth of Asian populations relative to the expansion of agricultural production. The spectre of insufficient food supplies and rapid population increases provoked a pessimism that now seems luridly far-fetched – with the possible exception of Bangladesh. Given its absolute size as a sector and its preponderant weight in employment it is clearly important to get agriculture 'right' in achieving sustained growth. But the sector represents far more than a potential problem to be averted: it can provide valuable resources to assist in industrialisation.

This is demonstrated in its purest form in Thailand, where subsequent industrialisation has been built on a platform of agriculture-based growth. Thailand's international economic role for much of the twentieth century has been as an exporter of agricultural produce. It is the world's largest exporter of rice, shrimps and tinned tuna, as well as selling sugar, maize and tapioca (which has been an important component in animal feedstuffs). As recently as 1980, 50 per cent of Thailand's exports were of crops and processed agricultural goods. In 1990, these still comprised 34 per cent of exports.[11] Several of Thailand's leading corporations, such as Charoen Pokphand, have expanded through food processing and agribusiness. By generating a surplus in agriculture and ploughing it back into the development of the sector Thailand was able to grow during the 1960s and 1970s without a heavy reliance on foreign investment.

The surplus extracted from agriculture was also directed into self-sustaining industrial growth in South Korea and Taiwan. South Korea, which continues to accept foreign investment only as an unavoidable necessity, was able to squeeze the agricultural sector to mobilise resources for its industrial development. Grain prices were held down in the cities to help depress wages as part of South Korea's export drive under the administration of President Park Chung-Hee (1961–79). The need to accumulate resources quickly in the first stage of industrialisation in the 1960s depressed rural incomes sharply from a rough parity with urban incomes in 1965 to around 67 per cent by 1970.[12] As a result, 6.7 million people left agriculture between 1967 and 1976, creating the reserve army of industrial labour which South Korea also needed.[13] There were measures to redress the balance in favour of farmers in the 1970s, but after the mid-1970s, rural incomes went back into decline relative to urban levels. Taiwan, likewise, extracted resources from agriculture to subsidise its industrial development from the mid-1960s onwards, partly through the mechanism of an unequal fertiliser/rice barter arrangement between the government and farmers. This scheme lasted until 1972, after which the rice price could still be periodically depressed by use of the substantial stocks accumulated by the Provincial Food Bureau. As in South Korea, 'the government has intentionally held down the peasants' income so as to transfer these people – who originally engaged in agriculture – into business',[14] according to Lee Teng-hui, then an agricultural policy expert (quoted in Bello and Rosenfeld, *Dragons in Distress*).

During the 1980s and 1990s, the market-Stalinist economies achieved big one-off gains in agriculture from decollectivisation and associated reforms. Most dramatically in China and Vietnam but also in Laos the restoration of market incentives and greater responsibility amongst smaller production units has secured a sharp rise in agricultural output and created resources that provide the basis of urban and industrial expansion. Decollectivisation of land placed under the control of collective farms from the 1950s onwards is, in many ways, what Gordon White refers to as the 'easier'[15] kind of economic reform to implement. Rewarding peasant households with a greater share of their produce, or an unlimited amount once a state contract has been fulfilled (as in China's 'production responsibility system'), achieves quick results. Within just three years of the '*Doi Moi*' ('new thinking') reforms, approved in 1986, Vietnam went from being a net rice importer to the world's third largest exporter. Production grew 40 per cent from 1988 to 1992 and rice now accounts for 40 per cent of exports.[16] Land reforms introduced in 1993 have underpinned change by giving farmers the right to hold land for 20 years for annual crops and for 50 years for long-term crops.

Laos has followed the same reform path and saw agricultural output rise by more than 8 per cent in 1992 as paddy production grew by 20 per cent.[17]

Rapid and impressive as these changes have been, the impact of China's agricultural reforms has been more far-reaching. Launched by Deng Xiaoping, soon after he secured his position in the Chinese leadership in 1978, the first stage of reforms was intended to help restore the Chinese Communist Party's badly dented political prestige after the disasters of the Great Leap Forward and the Cultural Revolution as well as to stimulate rural growth. The second objective was soon realised and reforms were applied across China. This reversed the flow of resources out of agriculture and transferred some 243 billion yuan to peasants between 1979 and 1984.[18] A bumper harvest in 1984 confirmed the success of price increases and the production responsibility system, reinforced by the visible growth in rural consumer spending and construction. Encouraged by the kickstart to the economy, the Chinese leaders embarked on further agricultural reforms which (see below) began to demonstrate the limits to this kind of growth, as well as being emboldened to pursue reform in other sectors of the economy. Had agriculture not yielded these initial benefits the economic and political tasks of further change would have been much more difficult for the Chinese leadership.

Outside those Communist countries where decollectivisation has been the most effective means of boosting agriculture the methods of the Green Revolution – the use of more inputs, particularly fertilisers, higher-yielding varieties of seeds, and improved irrigation – have been the key to improved output. A large part of Asian agriculture has now applied these methods, from the Philippines, where the International Rice Research Institute pioneered the development of new rice strains and the Marcos administration encouraged their adoption in the late 1960s and 1970s with credit and irrigation schemes, through Indonesia, where rice self-sufficiency was achieved in the mid-1980s after years as the world's largest importer, to Bangladesh and the Punjab in India's North West. Not every region has been affected: Nepal is still awaiting its Green Revolution, and so are parts of India. Further gains are yet to be made from the application of these new, more capital-intensive methods to the remaining untouched regions of Asia, among which should be included Burma, where agricultural mechanisation is minimal, fertiliser inputs have been reduced as a result of foreign exchange shortages and a bungled procurement system has hampered agriculture.[19]

The distributional effects of these changes are often invidious (as we shall see in Chapter 3) but the contribution they make to overall economic performance cannot be denied. Both decollectivisation and the Green Revolution have, it should be noted, added to the displacement of workers from the land and the consequent creation of a surplus labour force which is drawn to towns and cities.

As well as gains from new methods, the agricultural sector's contribution to GDP can be greatly enhanced by development of food-processing industries. While Thailand has been a leader in this industry, in many other countries failures in transport and marketing systems mean that much food production is wasted: up to US$1 billion of fruit and vegetables annually in Pakistan and as much as 25–30 per cent of produce in India where, despite recent investments, only 0.6 per cent of output is processed.[20] Absurdities arise, such as Bangladeshi farmers feeding pineapples to their cattle because they cannot reach a market outlet. Food processing needs capital and technology, particularly if farmers in the Philippines, for instance, are to satisfy stringent health requirements set by Japan, or investment in air transport if Sri Lanka's aquaculture industry or flower producers are to get fresh produce into the hands of consumers outside the country.

Plantation agriculture has traditionally played a large part in production in Asia, particularly in Malaysia, Sri Lanka, Indonesia and, to some extent, India. Thailand is now an important producer of plantation crops such as rubber. Commercially organised production has been a highly competitive international business from its adoption on a large scale around the turn of the century. The competition is now driven by wages and technology, with the former often assuming a critical importance. After years of nationalised control Sri Lanka's tea estates were put under private fixed-term management in 1992, and wages quickly became the front line of a battle to reduce costs and increase productivity in order to compete more effectively with the rival Indian industry. In Malaysia palm oil has replaced rubber (in which production is falling) as the most important plantation crop and Malaysia is the world's largest palm oil exporter, accounting for 55 per cent of world supply.[21] However, rising domestic wages have led to the expedient of importing cheap labour from Indonesia and other neighbouring countries to maintain competitive advantage and keep tea, rubber and palm oil plantations in business. As many as 1.5 million workers have slipped into Malaysia illegally, dozens of them drowning en route.[22] Nevertheless, both Thailand and Indonesia have already surpassed Malaysia's volume of rubber output. In the longer term Malaysian economists question whether the plantation sector will be viable and suggest that its future may lie in exporting production methods to low wage economies like Vietnam, from which palm oil, for instance, could then be shipped back to Malaysia for processing. Low-wage, relatively labour-intensive activity is transferred to less industrialised countries as costs rise, further reducing the importance of agriculture.

If Malaysia does withdraw more from the plantation sector it will be part of a general tendency to neglect agriculture once take-off has been accomplished. South Korea has progressively abandoned protective support for its agricultural sector, often in face of pressure for market access from low-cost US producers, culminating in the opening of its rice market under the auspices of GATT and over the broken campaign promises of President Kim

Young-sam. With growth being generated by a dynamic industrial sector, however, the consequences of a controlled scaling-down of agriculture are of greater political than economic significance in Malaysia or South Korea.

More worrying is the drying-up of the gains in agricultural production in those economies in which the industrial sector is not yet so large as to enable the economy to continue moving briskly forward and where a greater proportion of the population still depends on agriculture for its livelihood. The gains of decollectivisation are prone to a tailing-off in just this way. In both Vietnam and China the neglect of previously communal responsibilities for irrigation, pumping systems and other infrastructure under a system of household responsibilities has already eroded the rate of production increase. The area of irrigated land in China actually fell from 45 million hectares in 1979 to 44.5 million in 1988.[23] Investment by peasants to substitute for collective investment is discouraged by the absence of land ownership rights in China and by an uncertain policy environment affecting agriculture. Other effects of market developments compound this. One is the demand for land created by growth, whether for construction or for the golf courses springing up across China and Vietnam. This is a particular hazard in China, where average productive land area *per capita* is only one quarter to one third of the world average.[24] More problematic in the short term have been the workings of the price reforms introduced under the second stage of China's agricultural reforms from 1985 onwards. Prices were decontrolled except for grain, cotton and oil-bearing products, which were put onto a 'dual track' mechanism of market and state quota purchase prices. When the dual tracks diverged peasants tried to avoid fulfilling contracts, controls were then reimposed and production was consequently discouraged or distorted. Deregulated prices of other goods sucked resources away from production of staples and out of agriculture altogether into rural industries. The rate of Chinese agricultural output growth between 1985 and 1991 was only half of what it had been from 1979 to 1984.[25]

The shift to cash crops and reliance on market price indicators can also have adverse effects in economies which have depended on market mechanisms for much longer than China. There are basic problems with access to market information and the responsiveness of small-scale producers to changes in world market patterns. Aquaculture, for instance, has become a very significant source of export-led expansion in several poorer Asian countries,[26] yet this has exposed producers to over-reliance on the sometimes volatile Japanese market.[27] For small-scale producers, particularly those with limited access to credit, it is difficult to respond to a market which requires the ability to interchange output swiftly. Nor are they able to maximise use of increasingly expensive fertilisers or to acquire irrigation technology.

At the macro-economic level there are constraints on further gains from the Green Revolution. Although some areas have yet to experience the changes, in others the limits to irrigation are becoming apparent. For Bangladesh these are partly financial, while the scope for large-scale schemes is diminishing elsewhere and pressure from international environmental groups is becoming a bigger and bigger obstacle to implementation. Indian agriculture is close to the limits of what can be gained by further extensive cultivation. Environmental degradation, too, imposes its own limitations on agricultural growth, as in Pakistan, where salinity and waterlogging have now affected up to 40 per cent of the soil.[28] Intensive coastal aquaculture elsewhere is destroying mangroves and fish-spawning grounds and draining the land of fresh water. Logging was finally banned in Thailand in 1989 only after floods and landslides wrought havoc with farms, a problem that is becoming increasingly common as a result of the extensive deforestation elsewhere in the region.

The principal role of agriculture in development must be to feed the population and in this respect Asia has made great strides. As a source of surplus resources to assist development it can play an important part, although it is a helpful rather than necessary condition. Indonesia, for example, has concentrated on the first objective for its agriculture while turning to the exploitation of its abundance of non-agricultural natural resources to provide the initial surplus for investment. In the absence of non-agricultural natural resources – in South Korea and Taiwan – agriculture had to be squeezed hard to generate that surplus, exactly as Taiwan was used to provide cheap agricultural inputs to the Japanese economy when it was under colonial rule. In much of the Indian subcontinent agriculture has striven to meet domestic consumption requirements, while the absence of other readily exploitable natural resources has made the search for an investible surplus considerably harder. It is to that natural resource endowment that we now turn.

NATURAL RESOURCES

Natural resource endowments vary widely in Asia, from the riches of the Indonesian archipelago to the unyielding mountains of Taiwan. The fact that Taiwan and South Korea have been able to follow an equally poorly-endowed Japan along the development path is testament to the reduced importance of natural resource extraction in the modern industrial age. Yet for those who have them natural resources are still a great boon. As a source of foreign exchange earnings they can provide the funds needed for infrastructure and essential imports to construct a more enduring industrial base. Indonesia's use of its oil wealth demonstrates the more farsighted approach to the bounty that resources can generate. As the oil price rose after the 1973 oil shock Indonesia's GNP doubled almost overnight between 1973 and 1977. The share of oil and gas in export revenues rose from 37 per cent in 1970 to 82 per cent in 1981.[29] The windfall receipts were used in infrastructure projects that absorbed 40 per cent of government budgets in the 1970s[30] and helped lay the foundations for sustained growth in the 1980s. Without this expenditure Indonesia would have been far less well-equipped to face the effects of the sharp drop in oil prices in the first half of the 1980s. Its oil supplies are being depleted rapidly and in the absence of major new finds Indonesia is expected to become a net oil importer around the year 2000. However, gas – including the giant Natuna offshore field with its 45 million cubic feet of recoverable reserves – is projected to last much longer. Indonesia's medium-term energy plans are being based on the assumption that gas will be used much more widely in domestic energy supply. Its liquefied natural gas (LNG) exports now account for around 60 per cent of the market in Japan and it has developed long-term contracts to sell other commodities, such as timber, to Japan. Reliability as a supplier has both encouraged and been sustained by Japanese investment.

Malaysia has many of the same advantages as Indonesia in its natural resource endowment. Having accounted for around 10 per cent of the total value of exports in recent years, oil and gas are likely to continue to be valuable resources for Malaysia, as gas reserves are projected to last for over 100 years while oil has perhaps 15 to 20 years to run from the mid-1990s.[31] Malaysia is the world's largest exporter of tropical timber, many of the logs coming from Sabah and Sarawak, the Malaysian states which share the resource-rich island of Kalimantan (Borneo) with Indonesia and Brunei. In 1993, timber exports were worth M$12.2 billion, around 10 per cent of total export earnings.[32] Timber, oil and gas and, earlier, rubber and tin helped generate the funds needed in Malaysia's drive to build its industrial base in the 1970s and 1980s. Natural resource exports are now dwarfed by the 70 per cent of exports produced by the manufacturing sector.

Massive oil royalties have made Brunei a rentier state similar to the Gulf emirates. Its *per capita* income places it as the second richest country in Asia, deriving 98 per cent of export revenues from oil.[33] The government's effort to promote industrial diversification has met with a half-hearted response. More than two thirds of the indigenous workforce are employed in the state sector and much of Brunei's accumulated wealth has gone into overseas investment, partly into blue chip stock market portfolios and occasionally into the idiosyncratic opportunities offered to the state's absolute ruler, the Sultan.[34]

Oil-rich states in South East Asia have been the most obvious beneficiaries of natural resource exploitation. The most recent discoveries in Vietnam and the Philippines may also allow them to gain an important development boost from this source. Offshore oil exploration in Vietnamese waters was under way when the country was reunified in 1975 after more than 30 years of war. Western companies then left Vietnam and limited development of

Vietnam's oil resources was conducted by the Soviet Union in the following years. Oil now ranks as the second largest export earner for Vietnam and reserves could be of the order of 1.5–3 billion barrels.[35] Production-sharing agreements signed with Western oil companies since 1988 will ensure that exploitation of new commercial finds happens quickly. For the Philippines energy shortages have been a binding constraint on economic growth and have added to an already heavy debt burden through expensive attempts to bypass the problem, including the construction of a (non-functioning) nuclear power station. Oil finds off the coast of the western island of Palawan now hold out the hope of 50 per cent self-sufficiency in oil by 1995.[36] This would free the Philippines from some of the balance of payments problems which imported energy requirements have imposed and give more leeway for development.

In self-sustaining development no state has outdone North Korea, where the principle of *juche* (self-reliance) has been elevated since 1966 into an unquestionable credo inextricably entwined with the vision and leadership of the late President Kim Il Sung. Fortunately for Kim, if not for his people, *juche* was kept alive partly because North Korea came off far better at the end of the Korean War, with the lion's share of the peninsula's natural resources. Coal, iron ore and copper all helped fuel the North's drive towards industrialisation, which was led by heavy industry on the Soviet model, and which prompted economists such as Joan Robinson to talk of the North Korean 'miracle' of the 1960s.[37]

For others among Asia's poorest people, the bad luck has been in having either too few resources or in having them in the wrong place. Cambodia has relatively little oil while exploration for offshore gas is hampered by territorial disputes with Vietnam and Thailand.[38] Bangladesh drew the short straw in the form of an economy heavily dependent on the natural fibre, jute. Apart from the fact that jute processing was concentrated around Calcutta, over the Indian border since 1947, worldwide demand for jute has been badly affected by competition from artificial fibres. Bangladesh's other major natural resource is gas, though domestic utilisation has been hindered by the costs of constructing pipelines to get it to consumers and by the extensive commercial and political delays that have impeded the biggest fertiliser plant intending to use it as a feedstock. More encouraging news comes from the signing of coal production and exploration deals in 1994 and from the start of construction on the long-discussed Jamuna bridge, which will join transport and utility services in Bangladesh's East and West.

Transporting raw materials to areas of industrial growth is also a problem in China and India, where industrial development, particularly in a market system, often occurs in different regions to those in which resources are available. Coal mines in China's North East or in Bihar in North Eastern India are ill-placed to serve industry growing rapidly in Southern China or in Gujarat and Maharashtra in India's North West. China's transport systems mostly run West–East rather than North–South and are already overburdened. The output from the major oilfield in China's North East, Daqing, is peaking and, despite a 1978 plan which called somewhat wishfully for the opening of ten similar fields, it was only in 1993 – when China became a net oil importer for the first time since the mid-1970s – that serious exploration contracts began to be signed with foreign companies for the Tarim Basin area in the far West. This could hold several' tens of billions of barrels of oil, but supplies will have to be linked to the consuming areas in the East by a lengthy pipeline.[39] India is also at the stage of trying to exploit its oil and gas industry more vigorously, but the opening of potentially more attractive areas to foreign investment has become a matter of serious contention between the Indian government and international agencies. Besides lignite deposits, Pakistan also has a geology which suggests further gas finds may be possible in addition to existing fields, although difficulties in access are aggravated by the presence of tribal groups who, unlike the indigenous peoples brushed aside by loggers in Sarawak or the Philippines, are armed with modern weapons and control their own affairs through tribal law.

In other cases natural resource exploitation remains rooted at the level of potential. In Burma this is because foreign companies resented government exactions, such as insisting on the employment of expensive staff whose pay ended up in officials' pockets, and had little luck with finds, while output from the undercapitalised state oil and gas industry has been falling. But it applies particularly to the development of hydroelectric power. It is ironic that its greatest potential lies in the mountainous terrains of Laos and Nepal, the two countries least able to invest the US$2 billion which would be needed to enable them to produce each 1000 megawatts of hydroelectric power. Potential is the word most frequently used in relation to Laos, as in the countless studies which talk of turning the tributaries of the Mekong into the 'battery' of Indochina, selling energy to power-hungry consumers in Thailand and Vietnam. Concentrations of iron ore are also dense, so much so that they affected the magnetic instrumentation of US bombers during the Vietnam War. Gems and timber are already being extracted by Thai interests, although the benefits to the Lao economy of this kind of pillaging are few. As for Nepal, the financial constraints on even attempting to meet the enormous energy demand in India's northern industrial belt are aggravated by water-sharing disputes with India which hydroelectric dams would only exacerbate.

Extracting the maximum possible benefit from natural resources depends on the development of processing industries. These ensure that more of the value added to the raw material in its transformation into a finished product is retained in the country of origin. Development of processing industries has been far from uniform and there has been a tendency for refining and petrochemicals, for instance, to emerge in Singapore, South Korea and Taiwan which do not have a natural feedstock but which do have the capital to construct this kind of industry. Indonesia has, however, made significant progress in the expansion of its petrochemicals industry. Japanese funding tied to long-term contracts has backed the construction of LNG processing facilities and a controversial plant which would inaugurate Indonesia's olefin industry, drawing on naphtha feedstock from the state oil company Pertamina.[40] At a less capital-intensive level Indonesia and Malaysia have both been trying to capture more value added by encouraging wood processing. The Indonesian scheme seems to have served largely to generate more profits for certain individual businessmen but Malaysia has witnessed an appreciable change in the composition of exports towards more sawn timber. Furniture exports are also being encouraged, with the Philippines, which has very little rattan of its own left and has come to rely on Indonesian raw materials, suffering as a result of Indonesia processing more of its rattan into furniture.

Besides the successes there are puzzling failures. Pakistan is one of the world's largest producers of cotton yet its garments industry is smaller than those in Sri Lanka and Bangladesh. Thailand has failed to utilise its natural gas fields for development of a fertiliser industry. These remain, however, chiefly problems of capital inadequacy or bad planning rather than resource depletion, which is the gravest threat to growth based on natural resources. The rapid exhaustion of resources and the desire for a broader base of growth have accelerated the policy of shifting production into manufacturing in Malaysia, Indonesia and Thailand. Depletion of the forest in Thailand has been described as 'one of the worst records in the world',[41] estimated at 2.6 per cent annually between 1981 and 1985. The logging ban in Thailand has simply transferred the rapacious methods of Thai loggers to neighbouring countries, where their behaviour has been all the more frenetic because of the uncertain duration of concessions. Similarly, 'sluice mining' techniques were used to recover gems in Cambodia in the period before the UN-supervised elections of May 1993. In the Philippines, plundering of all resources vies for the title 'fastest in the world'.[42] Of the 6–7 million hectares of forest remaining, between 120 000 and 200 000 hectares are disappearing annually. Indonesia is losing as much as 1 million hectares a year, 30 per cent more than is sustainable, while Sarawak is allegedly logging at four times the sustainable rate.[43] Tibetan sources estimate that China has stripped Tibet of $33 billion worth of timber since 1959[44] and incidentally destroyed much of its wildlife. China's hold on Tibet remains firm as it sees further profit from uranium, borax and iron ore. Meanwhile, in India and Nepal deforestation continues as the poor draw on firewood as the principal source of energy.

These figures are strenuously rebutted by governments and logging companies alike and the issue is easily sidetracked into definitions of what is or is not forest cover (palm oil plantations, for instance). In the absence, however, of accountable political systems (see below) it is practically impossible to verify what is happening or to scrutinise the basis on which companies receive and operate logging concessions. What we can say in the context of further economic growth is that natural resources are being exploited with the aim of maximising revenue in the short term, in the belief that this stage in development can be sloughed off as manufacturing produces a larger slice of GDP. For those countries which have translated the one-off bonanza of natural resources into advanced industries this belief may not be untenable (leaving aside for the moment the global consequences of ecological disturbance). But those which exploit resources without being able to develop the next generation of industries – as the Philippines did in the 1950s and 1960s[45] – may be left with only the husk of an economy. That sobering thought concentrates some minds on the advantages which cheap labour can offer as an alternative means of attracting investment and stimulating development.

LABOUR

Labour has played a vital role in the industrialisation of Asian economies. The early stages have been characterised by a reliance on cheap labour as a prime source of international competitiveness, both in attracting investment and in capturing export markets. For some countries only now beginning their industrialisation possession of an abundant supply of cheap labour is their principal, if not only, asset. Those already in the throes of industrialising want to preserve the advantages conferred by cheap labour as long as they can. As Malaysian Prime Minister Mahathir said in early 1994 in response to Western criticism of low wages: 'Once we moved into manufacturing and produced the same things they were producing, at a lower price, they seemed to want to take away the only comparative advantage that we have: this lower-cost labour. They know very well that if we lose that and we have none of the other comparative advantages, then we will not be in a position to compete.'[46]

Early stages of industrial development favour sectors in which the comparative advantage of cheap labour can best be deployed without large capital investment. Textiles and clothing are a classic illustration of this, as the World Bank's study of the East Asian miracle revealed. The shares of these sectors in manufacturing GDP in the 1980s exceeded the level predicted by the Bank's model for Hong Kong, Japan, South Korea, Singapore and Thailand.[47] (For Indonesia and Malaysia the share was less than expected, though the Bank had apparently predicted a negative share for textiles and clothing in Indonesia's GDP for 1986, which seems to confound common-sense expectations.) The NIEs are moving on from garment manufacturing in the 1990s and relocating production elsewhere in the region. The source of comparative advantage in the industry has not changed, however, and the sector is still the first handhold to be grasped in the industrialisation ascent. Combined with the workings of the garment quota system (being phased out over ten years under the GATT agreement signed in 1994) and the low capital cost of a start-up (as little as US$250 000), cheap labour has made garments one of the most mobile industries in Asia. The sector has become the leading export revenue earner for otherwise poorly developed economies such as Laos and Bangladesh (where the share of garments in total exports rose from 16 per cent in 1985–6 to over 50 per cent in 1992–3[48]) as well as the lynchpin of regional development policies in Sri Lanka. These are all countries at the lower levels of industrialisation which have little in the way of readily expoitable raw materials and are obliged to compete on the basis of cheap labour in this sector.

Companies in mobile industries such as garment and toy manufacturing or basic electronics assembly are now looking at other reservoirs of cheap labour in the region. Vietnam, where labour is available at or around US$1 a day following a cut in the minimum wage in 1992,[49] is highly appealing in this regard. After Vietnam the last untapped reservoirs are Burma, where wages in 1993 were as low as 20 kyats a day (US$0.20 at the black market exchange rate or over US$3 a day at the official rate[50]) and North Korea, where wages are 10 per cent of those in the South.[51] South Asia is also a low wage area. Sri Lankan garment workers earn 2000 Rupees (US$42) a month[52] while the authorities in Bangladesh offered Taka 1493 (US$37.6) a month to avert a general strike in mid-1993.[53]

The World Bank's analysis of the metal products, electronics and machinery (MPM) industries in East Asia tallies with that of the garment industry. This group's output was also larger than expected in the Bank's model for the 1980s. Although the Bank regards the MPM sector as capital-intensive, any study of today's Malaysian electronics industry, for example, would pinpoint the presence of relatively cheap, relatively skilled and docile labour as a key ingredient, explaining its above average growth (and also Mahathir's determination to prevent trade unions driving wages up in the industry). What was true of the Malaysian, Thai and Indonesian electronics industries in the 1980s was also true of the initial industrialisation of Taiwan and South Korea in the 1960s. Development of the Taiwanese electronics industry from its infancy was the direct result of cost-related competition between US and Japanese manufacturers of transistor radios and other consumer electronics. After General Instruments of the US became the first major electronics company to set up in Taiwan in 1964, other US and Japanese firms followed suit in search of cheap labour that was rigidly disciplined through the strict martial law then in force in Taiwan.

South Korea also drew on its comparative advantage in labour costs when building up the textiles, clothing, rubber footwear and electronics industries which spearheaded its export growth in the 1960s and 1970s. Competitiveness in these sectors, known sometimes as 'female' manufacturing industries,[54] rested on the employment of young women drawn to urban centres by the squeeze on agriculture described above. In the 1960s 30 per cent of all wage workers were women aged between 14 and 24[55] and by 1973 women accounted for nearly half the South Korean manufacturing workforce. Average manufacturing wages in the 1970s were US$40 a month, against Bank of Korea estimates of urban family needs of US$90 a month.[56] As organised trade unions have pushed wages up, South Korea and Taiwan have had to abandon this kind of super-exploitation of labour in manufacturing and move towards more capital- and knowledge-intensive industries, even if some industrialists hanker for a return to the old methods. So too have Hong Kong and Singapore, where the toy and electronics industries were also built up in the 1960s and 1970s on the basis of cheap labour. As they have done so, Chinese labour has substituted.

China's initial opening to Hong Kong and other overseas investment was premised on the natural fit between overseas capital and its reservoir of labour, made available in the controlled environment of Special Enterprise Zones (SEZs). In Shenzhen, just over the border from Hong Kong, two-year contracts offered long hours, seven days a week and pay of around Rmb500–700 (US$ 90–127 a month in 1992).[57] Yet the quest for still cheaper labour (perhaps Rmb150–200) helped to spread development beyond Shenzhen, the other SEZs and the coastal provinces into the interior of China. Hong Kong businesses, which employ as many as 3–4 million workers in China, have been able to maintain competitiveness in the kinds of cheap labour products for which Hong Kong itself was famous in the 1960s and 1970s.

While the more remote Chinese provinces continue to provide fresh reservoirs of cheap labour, there is growing pressure, of the kind referred to by Mahathir, for better wages in the more prosperous economies of the region. Indonesia, which retained a strong comparative advantage in its cost of labour into the 1990s, was forced into a series of wage rises which saw daily rates in Jakarta and the surrounding area pushed up to 3800 Rupiah (US$1.9) a day at the start of 1994.[58] This compares with an increase in the Bangkok daily minimum wage to 132 Baht (US$5.6) in 1994 (against Bt 125 in 1993[59]) or 399[60] Ringgit (US$150) a month for Malaysian workers at the better-paid end of the Asian scale.

Minimum wage legislation of this kind is not only frequently unenforced, it is often circumvented entirely by the employment of illegal immigrants or illegal child labour. Estimates of the latter vary widely, for example between 17 and 100 million in India or between 1.4 and 7 million in the Philippines.[61] Even Thailand, which is relatively more developed, may have as many as 1 million 13–14 year olds employed in agriculture, earning less than US$32 a month, as well as a rising child prostitution problem, which it shares with Taiwan, the Philippines, Sri Lanka and other countries. In Pakistan child labour is just one abuse in a range of semi-feudal practices that included bonded labour.

More important in the macro-economic picture of the region is labour migration. As with Malaysian plantations and their dependence on immigrant labour, the importation of workers who are paid less than the national average allows countries to prolong their comparative advantage in sectors they would otherwise have to cede to those behind them on the industrialisation ladder. In Singapore imported labour has played the role of 'moderating the upward pressure on wages'[62] and of retaining industries that would otherwise have left in the 1970s. In all, 23 per cent of the workforce – 300 000 people – is composed of immigrants. Immigrant workers in South Korea can expect to earn just over half of what citizens would receive and to find themselves employed in one of the '3D' jobs – dirty, dangerous and difficult – that citizens no longer want to do. Thus South Korea retains a competitive presence in sewing, leather processing, dyeing, plastics, plating and casting, industries it might otherwise have relinquished. The government even sanctioned the admission of 20 000 immigrant workers for these 3D industries and a further 15 000 for the shoe and textile industries, despite worries about a rising domestic unemployment rate and other measures to restrict the inflow of labour.[63] For companies in South Korea, therefore, the North has an enormous attraction in this respect and most corporate plans for the North have centred on the utilisation of labour in closely-controlled conditions. The Taiwanese government has been more willing to accept the departure of labour-intensive industry such as footwear and clothing, although there is still a substantial body of immigrant workers in Taiwan, earning between a half and a third of average wages. Anecdotal evidence suggests that illegal construction workers among the 300 000 Burmese in Thailand earn around Baht 80 a day and in Hong Kong construction sites are regularly turned over by police hunting for illegal immigrants. One in eight of Hong Kong's employers underpays foreign workers.[64]

Cheap labour provides revenue in other ways. Those countries which cannot attract capital, because of infrastructural or political problems, can turn instead to labour exports. The Philippines may have as many as 5 million of its citizens employed overseas[65] in a variety of roles from World Bank economists to the 100 000 maids in Hong Kong and the 650 000 construction and domestic service workers in Saudi Arabia. Bangladesh has become an aggressive exporter of cheap labour to its fellow-Muslim states in the Gulf, as well as having up to 1 million workers employed in Pakistan, and Sri Lanka has taken advantage of its high standards of spoken English to send large numbers of maids (often weeping all the way on their flights) to the Middle East. In labour camps in Siberia, 10–15 000 workers sent from North Korea log the surrounding forests while the government pockets the hard currency proceeds in a split with the Russians;[66] elsewhere in Russia as many as 200 000 Vietnamese are at work. Remittances make a vital contribution to GNP for labour exporting nations. They added 0.6 per cent to GNP growth in the Philippines in 1993, raising it to 2.3 per cent. In 1992, the effect was even more dramatic, with the domestic economy expanding just 0.1 per cent, while GNP rose 1 per cent thanks to remittances.[67] In 1985, migrant workers in the Middle East were contributing over 5 per cent to Sri Lanka's GNP and nearly 7 per cent of that in Pakistan.[68]

Besides children and immigrant labour, employment of women is also used to keep costs down, as it was in South Korea in the 1960s and 1970s. Women have comprised around 40 per cent of the labour force in Taiwan and received two thirds of men's pay.[69] In Malaysia they constitute more than 75 per cent of the electronics workforce and one third of the total workforce, while earning 74–79 per cent of male pay.[70] Women's agricultural earnings in Bangladesh have been less than half of male pay and little account is taken of unpaid female labour in agriculture anywhere in the region.[71]

The existence of a large measure of surplus labour has also helped keep the price of labour down. As we saw in relation to South Korea and Taiwan, the squeeze on agriculture in the 1960s created the mobile reserve of labour that could be drawn into industry. The changes resulting from decollectivisation are doing the same in Vietnam and China today. The pull of opportunities in the cities also draws peasants away from marginal employment in the countryside. Unemployment levels of 38 per cent in Indonesia (admitted, belatedly, by Labour Minister Abdul Latif in 1994[72]), 22 per cent for urban Vietnam,[73] and totals of perhaps 100 million in India[74] and 150 million in China indicate that there is no shortage of labour in less developed economies in Asia. Population growth rates add a million workers a year to the labour force in both Bangladesh and Vietnam, for instance.

This means, however, that a strategy of reliance on cheap labour is inherently precarious. The availability of large reservoirs of labour and the relatively low capital cost of many labour-intensive operations exposes this kind of manufacturing to constant competition and threats of relocation. Moreover, there is only a finite amount of capital that is likely to be relocated from advanced manufacturing countries and a finite amount of migrant labour that they will absorb. Labour competition of the type described by Dr. Mahathir also provokes a two-pronged backlash in the OECD countries: not just pressure for Asia to improve wages and conditions, but also pressure in Europe and North America to hold down or reduce wages and to compete more effectively with additional capital.

CAPITAL

Asian countries striving to make optimal use of their natural resources and labour endowments cannot hope to do so without capital investment. Foreign capital is particularly prized, not only as a source of job creation, but for additional benefits: assistance to local industrial development from the spin-offs of training, technology and opportunities for networks of indigenous suppliers; the stimulation of joint venture investment; the particular export-orientation of these industries, which generate foreign exchange earnings that can be used to cover essential imports; and the avoidance of debt. As technology and training percolate through the economy they can help compensate for weaknesses in domestic industry that is sometimes characterised as 'technologyless',[75] and, as the World Bank points out, export-oriented industries have to strive for best practices in order to be internationally competitive, thereby furthering the diffusion of improved techniques. Where domestic savings and aid flows are inadequate or drying up, foreign investment helps fill the resource gap.

Foreign investment in the region began under colonial auspices and its legacy is apparent in the names of Western European and US companies on stock exchanges and roadside hoardings. Many of the 'hongs' – the old trading houses in Hong Kong – or the plantation companies in Malaysia have long since been acquired by local owners. But oddities persist like the signs on the Dhaka airport road advertising 'GEC for everything electrical' (something consumers in GEC's UK base stopped thinking a long time ago), as a reminder of the substantial continued presence of OECD multinationals. These companies are also making modern investments, drawn by cost considerations and the appeal of growing Asian domestic markets. The European chemical industry has stepped up investment during the 1990s in response to just these factors.[76]

Japanese investment has been most important in volume terms and in conforming to the ideal picture of the benign effects of foreign investment. Japan has been very important as an investor in the region since the 1950s, particularly for Taiwan, Thailand, Indonesia and Malaysia. This importance was accentuated in the wake of the Plaza Accord of 1985, which triggered a sharp appreciation in the yen. As domestic costs increased, Japanese exporters shifted production to Asia to take advantage of lower costs. This underlay the successful take-off of export industries in Malaysia and Thailand in the 1980s, turning electronics almost overnight in Thailand's largest category of exports. Indonesia, too, was able to boost manufactured exports from 2 per cent of total exports in 1980 to 30 per cent in 1988. In Malaysia, 70 per cent of manufactured exports derived from foreign-owned firms in its Export Processing Zones (EPZs) by 1980.[77] Similarly, in Taiwan as much as three quarters of the exports going to the US in the late 1980s came from

US-owned plants.[78] In Singapore, Japanese investment combined with other foreign investment to account for just under 30 per cent of total investment between 1986 and 1991.[79] The phenomenal success of Singapore as a manufacturing exporter can be traced to its record of attracting investment by a variety of international corporations in search of an initially cheap and efficient manufacturing base in Asia. This has meant, however, that more than a third of GNP is produced by foreign-owned firms.[80] In 1993, Asia as a whole accounted for a fifth of Japanese overseas investment, helped by the spread of component suppliers around the region.

As costs have risen and currencies have appreciated in the NIEs, they have followed the example of Japanese companies, creating a kind of cascade in which investment that originally spilled over from Japan is now overflowing from the NIEs to the next tier of low wage economies. A 40 per cent appreciation of the New Taiwan dollar in the late 1980s pushed Taiwanese companies into a search for new locations, some of them in China, where they now have at least US$10 billion invested.[81] Under pressure from their government to refrain from over-committing themselves to mainland China, which is still regarded as the sworn foe of Taiwan's ruling Kuomintang, Taiwanese investors are also seen as highly susceptible to invitations from other parts of the region. Hong Kong companies, as we have seen, have been the biggest investors in China. The Singapore government has adopted a broader 'regionalisation' policy as part of a national strategy. For the engineering companies Sembawang and Keppel this has meant investments in the Philippines; for the government equity investments around the region; and for individuals exhortations to follow their companies into new markets and enjoy the higher relative standard of living which the Singapore dollar will bring them abroad. Besides trade and investment links to Vietnam and Burma, Singaporean companies believe the legal environment, skill base and compact size of the Sri Lankan economy make it a natural fit for their overseas operations. South Korea's large conglomerates, the *chaebols*, have adopted international strategies that reflect the requirements of particular industries for markets and cost advantages. For Hyundai, this has included a plant in Canada, while the electronics industry has invested in both Europe and Asia.

Reliance on foreign investment is now spreading across the region. India's restrictions on foreign ownership discouraged investment in the 1970s and 1980s, but these limits have now been lifted and governments in the rest of the subcontinent are at pains to stress a new, welcoming attitude to investment. The same is true in the Philippines, where the government now sees foreign investment as one of two central conditions for realising its turn of the century objectives, the other being a solution to its energy problems. The acid test of the Philippines' ability to attract foreign investment will be the facilities at the former US Navy base of Subic Bay, including ship repair yards, an airport, hotels, golf courses, pipeline facilities and accommodation, backed up by 35 000 skilled workers, all of which the head of the Subic Bay Metropolitan Authority has been touting around the world, with a special eye on Taiwan. Market-Stalinist economies have followed suit. Vietnam had approved over US$6 billion by the end of 1993[82] and up to 30 per cent of investment in China is now either foreign or directly linked to it in the form of joint ventures.[83] The effect is apparent in exports: around 10 per cent of China's total exports in 1992 came from foreign-invested firms in Guangdong province. Previous nationalist objections to foreign domination of industrial sectors and residual Communist ideological inhibitions are being jettisoned in the search for more investment of this sort.

Those Asian governments which have recently allowed foreign participation in stock markets to begin or to increase tend to interpret the resulting rises in portfolio investment as a sign that direct investment is also on the way. India and Pakistan, for instance, have seen sizeable capital inflows,[84] much of it in the form of portfolio investment. What this view of foreign investment ignores, however, is the short-term focus of much of this portfolio investment, which can be switched quickly to other emerging stock markets in search of improved capital gains. From the perspective of portfolio managers the Asian markets are interchangeable with those of Latin America or Eastern Europe.

It also raises larger questions about the mobility of foreign investment. Foreign capital can be rapidly withdrawn, especially where it has come in on terms that explicitly include repatriation without hindrance. Export processing zones (EPZs) in which such investment is concentrated are particularly prone to this as plants are relocated in search of more attractive incentives. Both Bangladesh and the Philippines have seen departures on these lines. The very mobility which has brought the garment industry to Bangladesh and Laos can just as easily remove it to an alternative location. The nightmare for planners in any of the industrialising countries is that they might see the industrial base eroded from beneath by low wage competition, while the next level of development cannot be reached with the available domestic skill, technology and capital base. The speed with which Thailand and Malaysia have become major exporters of electronics goods is testimony to the shallow nature of investment. Economists expected to see 30 000 out of Thailand's 800 000 textile jobs disappear[85] in 1994 as low wage competition began to make itself felt, at the same time as alarm about the poor standards of secondary education and consequent skill shortages draws attention to the difficulties in moving to higher technology production. Taiwanese planners are beginning to worry correspondingly about the 'hollowing' of their industrial base as more labour intensive industry switches to China.

The foreign investment debate is more important given the high levels of debt reached by some countries in the region and the tendency for more aid to be made conditional or cut off altogether. Debt has become more of a constraint for India, Indonesia, Sri Lanka and the Philippines. In Sri Lanka, debt now exceeds GDP[86] and interest payments amount to 6 per cent of GDP. The Indonesian Coordinating Minister for Economy, Finance and Development, Saleh Afiff, voiced his concern as debt crossed the US$90 billion threshold early in 1994 and tried to reassure investors that there was no prospect of a devaluation.[87] With a relatively high proportion – 40 per cent – of Indonesian debt denominated in yen, the appreciation of the Japanese currency has added to the burden. India's debt has also been rising sharply – up from US$71 billion in 1991–2 to US$77 billion in 1992–3,[88] and relatively low export volumes mean that more than a third of export revenues are consumed in servicing this debt. The Philippines has long been mired in debts accumulated during the Marcos years (1965–86), which now total over US$30 billion. Although recent debt buy-back schemes have helped to keep the debt service ratio below 20 per cent, a study by the National Economic and Development Authority and the United Nations Development Programme concluded that 'efforts to reduce the burden of debt will remain a policy issue at least in the short term'.[89] Extensive further borrowing is difficult for these countries to contemplate and investment is consequently appealing. Others, especially South Korea and Thailand, have used borrowings to fund industrialisation without incurring serious debt service problems. Rapid growth in both countries reduced debt service ratios below 10 per cent in 1993. This compares with 1987 levels of 32 per cent and 22 per cent in South Korea and Thailand respectively.[90] China's debt is also rising steeply and was predicted to total US$100 billion by the end of 1994, against US$83.5 billion at the end of 1993, when the debt service ratio was 7.7 per cent.

For poorer countries, worrying debt levels have coincided with tougher attitudes to aid. There is talk of aid allocations being cut where, as in Bangladesh, Pakistan or Sri Lanka, aid has not been spent because of 'absorption' problems that have, for example, left US$10 billion unspent of the US$45 billion that Pakistan received from 1950 to 1992.[91] Aid is also being made conditional on the fulfilment of policy prescriptions from the IMF and the World Bank. Although aid is running at record levels – Indonesia received over US$5 billion agreed at a meeting in Paris in 1993, Pakistan got pledges of US$2.5 billion for 1994/95, Vietnam was promised nearly US$2 billion in exchange for IMF guidance of the economy and over US$2 billion a year was committed to Bangladesh in 1992 and 1993 – this has been tied to market opening measures, public sector redundancies or, as has now happened in the India Development Forum,[92] multinationals being included in the aid negotiating body. The collapse of aid from the Soviet bloc has, similarly, forced Vietnam, Laos and Cambodia to turn to foreign investment. Vietnam, especially, relied on Soviet aid worth US$1–1.5 billion a year until this was abruptly terminated in 1989.

The weight attached to foreign investment is all the greater where domestic savings are small and cannot be easily drawn upon to fund investment. This is certainly true of the Philippines, where inflation and other forms of instability have discouraged savings and the IMF's stipulation that the savings ratio rise to 23.6 per cent by 1996 is unlikely to be met.

Other weaker economies in South Asia and Indochina are characterised by an inability to mobilise domestic savings effectively. The absolutely poorest countries in the region have very few surplus funds to mobilise and rudimentary financial systems which inspire little confidence. Even a country with slightly higher *per capita* income like Sri Lanka has a savings-investment shortfall estimated at 6–7 per cent of GDP,[93] which it needs to cover either with foreign aid or investment. India has had some success in boosting its savings rate from below 10 per cent in the 1950s to over 20 per cent in the 1970s and 1980s[94] and the introduction of mutual funds and other savings vehicles has helped draw more savings from beneath mattresses and into the financial system where they can be used for investment purposes. China has probably the largest such accumulation of savings secreted away – up to 1 trillion yuan worth[95] – but the danger in China's highly unstable economy is that these will be enticed out, not to be channelled into productive investment but to be gambled in financial markets, squandered in speculative schemes or squirrelled away in alternative stores of value, whether gold or foreign exchange or consumer durables. It is generally in the poorer and less stable economies of Asia that the financial system competes for savings against a variety of non-productive assets that have proven their attractiveness over time.

The HPAE have, however, achieved high levels of savings. In the case of South Korea this helped planners to dispense with foreign investment except where absolutely necessary. Although it was able to draw on US aid to the tune of US$6 billion between 1945 and 1978[96] to cover imports, the main source of funds to support 'forced' investment was domestic savings, which have been running at one of the highest rates in the world – 35 per cent in 1992.[97] Savings were sustained partly by draconian restrictions on domestic consumption which also helped ensure goods were channelled into export markets. When, in the 1970s, South Korea had to raise money externally to fund the development of heavy and chemical industries, President Park preferred to use borrowings rather than allow foreign ownership of key sectors. Singapore has also achieved very high domestic savings through the mechanism of compulsory contributions to the Central Provident Fund (CPF), which underlay the rise in Singapore's savings rate from 19 per cent in 1970 to 46 per cent in 1989.[98] The funds thus accumulated were used to build up Singapore's impressive transport and communications infrastructure and supplement investment from overseas. Malaysia has also used forced savings through the Employees' Provident Fund to ensure savings rates above 30 per cent.

However, when savings do find their way into the financial system there is a tendency for them to be drawn off into investment in the property sector, in search of speculative returns, or in loans to questionable projects. The prolonged slump in Japan in the first half of the 1990s resulted from the bursting of three 'bubbles' – stock market prices, property prices and corporate expansion – the second of which plunged Japanese banks into severe problems. Despite assurances that bankers elsewhere in Asia have learned the lesson spelt out in Tokyo and across Japan banking authorities still struggle to limit real estate lending. In Hong Kong, banks are under pressure to restrict property lending to 40 per cent of total lending, to avoid a repetition of the events surrounding the collapse of the Carrian Group in the early 1980s.[99] In Indonesia, bank regulators pushed Bank Summa into liquidation in 1992 after it was crippled by bad debts in the property sector and forced its owners, the Soeryadjaya family, to sell their controlling interest in Astra, one of Indonesia's largest companies, to foot the bill. All over China in 1993 and 1994 panic measures were taken to try to stem investment in property and redirect it to infrastructure. New private-sector banks in Taiwan have been lending heavily in the property sector, and over-investment left Ho Chi Minh City with a glut of hotels by the end of 1993 and four of the ten biggest foreign investment projects in the property sector.[100] A property crisis is regularly expected in Bangkok and, across the region, the vanity factor encourages businessmen to buy property assets early in the development of their companies.

In South Asia and the Philippines, the problems have been different. Non-productive investment such as gold or, in the Philippines, high-yielding government treasury bills, siphon off savings. Some of the largest business groups in the Philippines are in the real estate sector. In Sri Lanka, the easy profits to be made from exclusive import licences have diverted resources into acquiring these licences. These economies have also had a structural bias towards import-substituting industries, which are protected by high tariff barriers and which encourage capital imports by exempting them from the tariffs. Too much capital has ended up in internationally uncompetitive sectors which offer none of the best practice diffusion that comes from export-oriented manufacturing. Indian planning accentuated this tendency on the assumption that capital intensive industry would stimulate secondary and, eventually, consumer goods industries. But the result is that the Indian state sector absorbs half the available capital, yet produces only 27 per cent of output:[101] an unproductive use of capital paralleled in other South Asian economies. In Bangladesh and Pakistan, the same problems of inadequate capital that have held back natural resource development have also prevented the development of integrated weaving, finishing and dyeing.

With domestic investment falling short of requirements or being diverted to non-productive outlets, there is a greater concern about signs of a downward trend in foreign investment. China has been largely exempt from a trend that has been particulary noticeable in Malaysia, Thailand and Indonesia. If anything the early 1990s saw the beginnings of a sea-change in investment in China, away from the short-term, quick-return, labour-intensive investment typified by Hong Kong-owned garment or toy factories in Southern China, towards more serious, longer-term investment directed as much at servicing the Chinese domestic market as at export markets. This is certainly true of McDonnell Douglas, ICI, Pilkington Glass, Hewlett Packard and Volkswagen and other major corporations which now have a manufacturing presence in China. But it is plainly not true of the much higher proportions of foreign investment going into property – over half of that in some coastal provinces. The downturn in investment apparent in the first half of 1994[102] was partly the result of a fall in property investment and partly of curbs on some incentives given to foreign investors, though major corporations like Ford continued to invest.

For the Malaysian government, the problem in 1993 was a 66 per cent fall in foreign investment.[103] There was also a 19 per cent drop that year in approvals for foreign investment in Indonesia, although there were predictions of a rebound in investment to US$18 billion in 1994.[104] In Thailand the value of project applications to the Board of Investment dropped sharply after 1990 and foreign investment volumes in 1993 were at least 25 per cent down on 1992.[105] Japanese investment in South Korea was 80 per cent lower in 1992 than in 1988.[106] This downturn focused keen attention on the next wave of Japanese investment expected to begin as the Japanese economy recovers and as the effects of the yen's further rise against the US dollar sink in. With only 8 per cent of its manufacturing capacity located offshore (in contrast to 20 per cent of Germany's) there is arguably considerable scope for a further outflow of investment into the Asian region. Japan's Ministry of International Trade and Industry forecast in mid-1994 that the proportion of Japan's overseas investment going to Asia would rise from 16.4 per cent to 37.5 per cent in the year to March 1995.[107] Thailand, which was a leading recipient of Japanese investment in the 1980s, has been awaiting the next wave particularly anxiously. Thai commentators talk up the country's relative attractions to reassure themselves that it will materialise. They can take little comfort, however, from the Asian Development Bank, which concluded that 'the labour intensive industries of the investor countries have now largely been relocated or phased out'.[108]

The downturn in foreign investment and subsequent anxieties about further inflows betray the vulnerability of an expansion strategy in which foreign investment is encouraged to take the lead. Yet, even where investment stays in place the development of a local supplier base is sometimes not as great as expected. What is implanted is a relatively shallow industrialisation. EPZ operations frequently continue to rely on a high proportion of imports in their final output, as much as 75 per cent in some cases, particulary garments.[109] In Malaysia, a United Nations Conference on Trade and Development (UNCTAD) survey found that, 'the subsidy on electricity [in EPZs] outweighed the combined benefits from the use of local raw materials and capital equipment plus tax revenues raised'.[110] In the most extreme case, the Bataan EPZ made a negative contribution to the balance of payments of the Philippines in 1989.[111] Where local content targets have been set in more demanding and complex production, a high percentage of components continues to be imported. Pakistan's collaboration with Suzuki in small car production encountered just this stumbling block and Malaysia's Proton cars have only met their local content targets through the establishment of Japanese parts manufacturers to serve the Mitsubishi-engineered plant in Shah Alam. What can easily emerge in foreign investment-led economies is a dual track economy, with a proportion of production linked to world markets, but no meshing of this with the domestic economy. Value added is small even in that section linked to world markets, transfer-pricing by multinationals minimises any addition to the tax base and only a limited addition to purchasing power filters into the domestic economy.

FUTURE GROWTH

The negative picture we have painted of the limits to agricultural growth and to raw material exploitation clearly puts the burden of sustaining Asian growth on manufacturing. This in turn implies the need for newer and more productive combinations of capital and labour: more capital, more highly skilled labour or more productive technology. In each of these areas there are weaknesses which may compromise Asia's development.

Reference to the previous challenges which Asian economies have faced in achieving just such a transition to new and more productive industries may offset some of the pessimism. South Korea and Taiwan are again the best illustrations of successful industrial upgrading. As industries like footwear and textiles have shifted to lower cost countries, South Korea has made a successful transition to heavy and chemical industries (HCI) that include shipbuilding, iron and steel, petrochemicals, electronics, machinery and transport equipment. The share of these in exports rose from 14 per cent in 1971 to 60 per cent in 1984.[112] Taiwan, similarly, met the challenges of the 1973 oil shock and of declining competitiveness in textiles, footwear and electronics with its 'Ten Major Projects' in steel, shipbuilding, petrochemicals and infrastructure improvements. The Singapore economy was likewise repositioned during the 1980s as a provider of computer manufacturing facilities, an infrastructure hub for the region in communication and air and sea transport and a financial services centre. Hong Kong's parallel development has been reflected in a massive shift in employment from manufacturing, which now accounts for less than a quarter of employment,[113] to the service sector as it fulfills a specialised role in relation to the economy of Southern China. On the showing of the four NIEs so far there are grounds for believing that the Asian economies can make a transition to more productive, skill- and capital-intensive industries.

However, having completed one upgrading in the course of the 1970s and 1980s, the NIEs themselves now face a fresh test in repeating that achievement in the 1990s. The task is all the more demanding for requiring a greater technological input than the previous transition did. Shipbuilding or steel require substantial capital but the technology is not of a very high standard and in the case of South Korea it was available from Japan. It was not essential to have an extensive research and development (R&D) capability in order to establish many of the heavy industries built in the 1970s and 1980s. But, for Taiwan and South Korea to move beyond these to the next generation of products and industries, technology will have to be forthcoming. Taiwan is handicapped in this respect by the structure of its industry. Despite the emergence of internationally recognised companies such as Evergreen (the world's largest container company), Acer (computers) and President (foodstuffs), much of Taiwan's indigenous industrial base is composed of small and medium sized firms. Company size does not necessarily inhibit inventiveness but the commercial development and exploitation of new products does require larger sums of capital that are often beyond the reach of Taiwanese companies. The manufacture of advanced semi-conductors, for instance, requires an initial investment of around US$100 million and a substantial R&D effort. With a limited R&D capability, Taiwan is at a disadvantage in relation to its OECD competitors.[114] Despite producing an estimated 78 000 science and engineering graduates annually, research scientists are still in short supply. Postgraduate training is still concentrated overseas and, up to 1992, only 20 per cent of those who went abroad to receive science and technology training returned to Taiwan.[115] Efforts to bypass the domestic R&D blockage by, for instance, establishing a domestic truck industry and an export-oriented automobile plant foundered on the reluctance of Japanese partners to transfer technology and on bureaucratic and industry rivalry. More recent attempts to leapfrog into aerospace technology have witnessed abortive negotiations with McDonnell Douglas and with British Aerospace (which saw an opportunity to offload its loss-making regional jet business). The growing weight of the service sector in Taiwan – as in the other NIEs – inevitably means slower growth over the long term, even if the financial services industry in Hong Kong and Singapore has been a substantial source of the growth in the first half of the 1990s.

The result is that Taiwan, in common with Hong Kong and South Korea, is placing a good many of its eggs in the China basket. Taiwanese planners map out a future in which it will serve as an offshore 'regional operations centre'[116] for multinationals supplying the China market. The growth of European and Japanese-owned car plants in Taiwan is targeted at this market, as are new indigenously-owned steel and petrochemicals facilities. For Taiwanese companies China is a marketing opportunity and a cheap manufacturing base with US$10 billion already invested. For Taiwan as a whole, proximity to China offers hope of inward investment and service industry growth – so a lot rides on China's stability and prosperity.

Hong Kong is much further committed in its integration with and dependence on the Chinese economy. Estimates suggest that 80 per cent of investment in Guangdong and 60 per cent of that in China as a whole comes from Hong Kong.[117] Around 70 per cent of Hong Kong's manufacturing operations have now moved into Guangdong, with investments totalling between US$8-18 billion.[118] Chinese investment in the colony may be of comparable magnitude, at US$12-20 billion.[119] The profile of Hong Kong investment is changing: besides assembly factories in the south of China a substantial proportion is now also concentrated in property investment. Virtually all of Hong Kong's major corporations have ambitious plans to increase their asset base in China. Wharf, for instance, announced in 1993 a China strategy entitled (despairingly or otherwise) 'Do something' based on infrastructure investment that could see up to 20 per cent of the company's balance sheet committed to China over a ten-year period. Wharf believes that the central city of Wuhan will be the 'Chicago of China' and Hong Kong-based investment in general has spread its tendrils far beyond Guangdong. In doing so, Hong Kong companies have avoided the challenge of technological upgrading that their counterparts face. Whether in cheap labour-intensive manufacturing or in infrastructure projects Hong Kong capital is applying a formula already tested in the territory itself. But the price of sidestepping technological challenge is a critical dependence on China's continued prosperity.

South Korea too has seen relations blossom with China after the formal establishment of diplomatic ties in 1992. The visit of President Kim Young-Sam to Peking in early 1994 cemented a number of commercial collaborations. These business deals emphasise the extent to which South Korea sees the 'natural fit' between its technological base and China's labour supplies and domestic market as an easier option than trying to compete more aggressively in the world market. A pact signed in March 1994 could see investment by South Korea in China rise from US$1 billion in 1993 to US$4 billion by 1997 and trade increase from US$9 billion to US$28 billion.[120] China has become an increasingly important manufacturing base for electronics, textiles and food companies, offering the *chaebols* cost advantages as well as enormous market potential. China is already the largest market for automobiles from South Korea and a car plant is expected to be set up in China by 1997. Telecommunications and electronics represent further cost and sales advantages. China will provide technical skills in aerospace to help develop regional airliners, although this is a highly competitive market in which collaboration is unlikely to yield rapid commercial success.

China is all the more alluring for producers from South Korea squeezed between the lower costs of some competitors and the higher quality offered by others, especially as Japan becomes increasingly chary about transferring technology to South Korea. The number of transfer agreements between the two countries fell from 354 in 1988 to 232 in 1992,[121] exposing South Korea's R&D shortcomings all the more painfully. With a total R&D budget only slightly bigger than that of General Motors or IBM of the US, equal to around 2 per cent of GNP,[122] and a lack of co-ordination between government and commercial research it is unlikely that an ambitious plan to build new high-technology industries can succeed. Based around micro-electronics, mechatronics (computer-controlled machine tools), new materials development, optics, aircraft, fine chemicals and biotechnology the plan envisages these sectors contributing 40 per cent of the country's exports by the year 2000, against 11 per cent at the start of the 1990s.[123] The 'G7 Project' announced in April 1992 set target dates for commercial development of specific products (including an electric car by 1996).[124] To achieve these goals inadequate domestic R&D will have to be supplemented by greater technology transfer. In an era of much tighter protection of intellectual property rights and more complex technology it will be more difficult to resort to reverse engineering or simple theft of designs, as was possible in the 1950s and 1960s, and South Korea has already been in the front line of a US and EU offensive on intellectual property rights. The painful disputes over the construction of the new Seoul–Pusan high speed train link may well serve as a deterrent to companies willing to deal with South Korea. A Japanese bid for the link was rejected as offering insufficient transfer of technology. For GEC–Alsthom the winning bid was something of a Pyrrhic victory since the Anglo–French consortium will have to transfer technology that will enable its partners – Hyundai, Daewoo, and Hanjin – to compete in international markets after 2002. The service sector is unlikely to take the lead in South Korea's growth in the medium term. A liberalisation programme for the banking and finance sectors will not be completed until 1997 and in the meantime significant restrictions remain on the operation of foreign financial enterprises. Many domestic banks are still saddled with bad debt burdens and other financial institutions are waiting to offload shares which they had to buy to shore up the stock market on government instructions. For the tourist industry threats from North Korea to turn Seoul into a 'sea of fire' did little to encourage civilians to share in the 'Visit Korea Year 1994'.

For both Hong Kong and Singapore the service industries, especially financial services and tourism, but also shipping and other transport activities, have generated a great deal of value added, as well as transforming waterfront skylines. Competition between the two remains strong in virtually all areas of services, although neither can expect unimpeded growth. For Hong Kong the service sector as a whole is bound up with China's development and financial services and associated legal business are especially vulnerable to the danger of greater interference and corruption after China regains sovereignty over the territory in 1997. The tourist industry, contributing 5–7 per cent of GDP would be adversely affected by any serious disruption in China.

For other would-be financial centres in the region, from Taipei, Bangkok and Sydney to outsiders like Colombo, the 1997 deadline has created an air of expectancy. Each hopes to corner some share of a disintegrating Hong Kong financial services market but Singapore sees itself as the best alternative. It already has the only foreign exchange market to rival Hong Kong's in the region (excluding Japan) as well as highly developed money markets, commodity trading and an emerging derivatives business. A legal system following Anglo-Saxon principles and a spotlessly clean reputation burnish the image. But Singapore's financial system remains hidebound in contrast to Hong Kong's, still being policed in a manner that ensures it creates the maximum advantage to the Singapore government while minimising disruptive side effects. The sclerotic growth of the Singapore stock market in contrast to Kuala Lumpur's, after the two parted in 1990, exemplified Singapore's lack of momentum: only a decision by the government to encourage more investment of CPF funds in the market revived it in 1993, though at the risk of political repercussions. Criminal prosecution of stockbroking analysts for handling leaked offical information then reawakened concerns that a society in which information flows are so tightly controlled (Singaporeans cannot watch the innocuous *Asia Business News* broadcast from the city-state itself because of a ban on satellite dishes) cannot function as part of the global financial services network.

Singapore has also suffered the brain drain apparent in Hong Kong and Taiwan, although it has encountered no problems in replacing local staff with those recruited abroad. Past deficiencies in the local education system are being rectified, such as the excessive focus on commercial education – MBA degrees – in higher education at the expense of fundamental research. To create a technological base the government has set a target of 40 research scientists and engineers per 10 000 in the labour force for 1995. By 1992 the level had reached 39.8.[125] When, however, the government tried during the first half of the 1980s to force corporations into increasing the productivity of capital by pushing up wages the results were gravely disappointing. Unit labour costs rose 40 per cent over six years but this simply discouraged investment rather than eliciting a commitment to higher technology. By early 1986 the government had retreated to welcoming any investment, freezing wages and recognising that it could not dictate terms to multinationals.[126]

Singapore's real weakness for the future is that it has reached the limits of its development within the confines of the city-state. The government sees the economic future in the regionalisation strategy of expansion. But there will be several problems: many of the largest Singaporean corporations are 'government linked corporations' (GLCs) and unused to operating in competitive markets without the guidance of their political masters. Local capitalists in an economy dominated by the GLCs and multinationals tend to run small enterprises lacking the resources to expand their manufacturing base around the region. An attempt to give a formal framework to 'regionalisation' through high profile intra-governmental co-operation in the 'growth triangle' of Singapore, the southern Malaysian state of Johor Bahru and the Indonesian Riau Islands ended with Singapore being excluded from future triangles (Malaysia–Indonesia–Thailand and Malaysia–Indonesia–Philippines). Singaporean planners failed to conceal the fact that they saw the triangle purely as a means of bringing a large supply of cheap Indonesian labour within their orbit and thus alienated both the Malaysians, who were made to feel irrelevant, and the Indonesians, who felt they were being exploited and taken for granted by insensitive ethnic Chinese. Unlike Hong Kong, Singapore has no natural hinterland and both the triangle's failure and Singapore's expulsion from the Malaysian federation in 1965 showed how difficult it is to create one. Lee Kuan Yew's most recent intiative is to go further afield with plans for an industrial park at Suzhou near Shanghai, an enclave in which Singaporean companies will be able to draw on cheap Chinese labour, but one which has no obvious commercial connection with Singapore.

The need to move on up to the next level of technological development is most acute for the four NIEs as they watch Malaysia, Thailand and Indonesia attracting more of the investment that was earmarked for them 20 years ago. But all three are feeling similar pressures as South Asia, Indochina and the Philippines bid for the same capital and their indigenous R&D weaknesses are exposed. In Thailand, despite the technical enthusiasms of King Chulalongkorn in the early twentieth century which echoed Japan's adoption of Western innovations, a technical culture has never really emerged. R&D is less than 0.3 per cent of GDP[127] and very little of it is conducted by companies. The optimists have to seek comfort in the 'inventiveness', 'adaptability' and 'good business sense' of the Thais to substitute for it. The only significant signs of technological upgrading penetrating the corporate sector have been in the rush of companies into telecommunications in response to Thailand's shortfalls in this sector. Companies with no track record in telecommunications, such as the agribusiness giant Charoen Pokphand, have emerged overnight as the holders of major concessions. Tourism, as the ADB concludes, is 'not likely to experience the rapid growth of the late 1980s without greater progress in developing new destinations outside Bangkok and in maintaining their environmental integrity'.[128] Malaysia too has only a modest R&D resource (0.8 per cent of GDP[129]) as well as an economy heavily concentrated in electronics and textiles. It listed only 405 scientific papers in the BIDS database in 1992, as against 184 for Indonesia, 1192 for Singapore, 1358 for Hong Kong, 4528 for Taiwan, 9843 for China and 15 659 for India.[130] This has not prevented Malaysia from developing its electronics and automobile industries but it does underline the extent to which such industries have been indebted to foreign technology. Relations with Japan, Malaysia's chief supplier of technology in the 1980s, have not always been cordial on this point. Prime Minister Mahathir's policy of 'Look East' (that is, towards Japan) was discredited when it became apparent that the first Proton Saga cars would be effectively prevented from competing in overseas markets with the Mitsubishi Lancer from which they were derived.[131] Thanks to Mahathir's commitment and high protective tariffs, the Proton Saga and its successor, the Wira, have survived and Malaysia is developing a 600cc car in collaboration with Daihatsu of Japan. Projects of dubious commercial sense have only survived because of the Prime Minister's determination to commit public funds. Although – like Proton – these projects are sold to the private sector once profitable, Mahathir has to overcome the short-term preferences of most Malaysian industrialists in building up these assets. The next test of that resolve is in the aircraft industry. Malaysia has a tie-up with the German aerospace firm Dornier and acquired a small Australian aircraft manufacturer in 1993. If Mahathir remains Prime Minister long enough Malaysia can probably attain an aircraft manufacturing capability. But the future of these advanced industries rests on a shaky combination of political will and protective tariff barriers. In the meantime, what one analyst describes as 'copycat growth' can allow Malaysia to raise its *per capita* income to US$7000: beyond that increments get progressively more difficult.

The danger, as demonstrated in Indonesia, is that advanced industries remain little more than a series of expensive prestige undertakings. The Indonesian aerospace industry is the brainchild of the Science and Technology Minister B. J. Habibie, who has also championed the creation of a shipbuilding and ship repair industry. Both are regarded sceptically inside and outside Indonesia. As *The Economist* reported, one of Habibie's cabinet colleagues calls them 'bonsai industries', for 'they need obsessive attention and they never grow'.[132] The IPTN aerospace plant, which has been in operation since the late 1970s, has not evolved beyond assembly operations and continues to enjoy the luxury of large subsidies that reflect Habibie's political influence with President Suharto. The shipbuilding and ship repair industries have had to rely on the Indonesian navy as a captive customer.

The white heat of Habibie's technological revolution has not fused with the rest of the Indonesian economy and it is doubtful whether such enterprises can be transferred profitably to the private sector. But so long as Habibie has the President's ear these industries will continue to enjoy official support.

Besides the question marks over the technological base in Indonesia, Malaysia and Thailand, economic growth is also starting to run up against the constraints imposed by the skill limitations of the workforce. As wage rates rise in Penang, the centre of Malaysia's electronics industry, workers need to upgrade their skills or see jobs disappear over the border to lower-paying Southern Thailand. Between 1991 and 2000 Malaysia is expected to face shortages of nearly 10 000 locally trained engineers and nearly 20 000 engineering assistants.[133] The focus of education is partly to blame. Too many graduates have qualification in the liberal arts or business administration rather than a training in science or engineering. The use of the education system for the political objective of assisting the Malay *bumiputras* (literally 'sons of the soil') also denies opportunities to some talented ethnic Chinese. Large numbers of Malaysians are trained overseas to remedy the deficiencies but not all of them are guaranteed to return home. For Indonesia the constraints at technician level have been less of a problem as lower wages (relative to Malaysia) have meant that there has been less need to substitute capital for labour and find the more qualified workers to operate more complex machinery. Indonesia has a technocratic élite – the so-called 'Harvard mafia' which has managed the economy – many of whom have finished their education overseas, but there is little between them and the US$2 a day production workers. Filling the gap to facilitate technological upgrading will not be easy. In Thailand, educational problems are severe at secondary level where an enrolment rate of 29 per cent is insufficient to sustain growth at 7 per cent. 'Shortages of engineers and scientists are very real,' the Thailand Development Research Institute reported in 1990, and the domestic supply has improved little since. Wage rises caused by these shortages are likely to erode competitiveness and, as the Institute concluded: 'with rapid structural changes and the need for Thailand to upgrade the technological and skill base of all its productive sectors, human resources may become the key constraint to sustained growth.'[134]

One constraint affecting nearly all the economies in the region – with the exception of Singapore and possibly Hong Kong – is infrastructure. A combination of decay and neglect has left both the successful and the unsuccessful economies with very little of what Dr Hafeez Pasha, director of the Applied Economic Research Institute in Karachi describes as 'slack'[135] in their infrastructure provision. Growth rates of 7 or 8 per cent in the successful economies have not been matched with an expansion of power and transport services. Malaysia is a case in point, where 'investment sentiments are not very encouraging against the backdrop of an acute labour shortage and infrastructure bottlenecks.'[136] In the unsuccessful, if growth were to reach targets of, for instance, 10 per cent a year in Pakistan or the Philippines, similar problems would soon appear.

Although construction plans are being implemented across the region, it is unlikely that enough of the big projects involved can be completed in time to prevent infrastructure becoming a major medium-term constraint on growth. In all, as much as US$2.5 trillion may be needed between 1992 and the year 2000, a sum beyond the means of domestic investors, especially in the poorer countries where very little has been added to infrastructure in the past 40 or 50 years or where war has destroyed parts of it.

Constraints are already appearing, whether in the form of the US$2–6 billion a year that Thailand loses for traffic problems,[137] or the 1 per cent of GDP consumed in Jakarta every year in boiling water to make it potable,[138] or the lost production resulting from power cuts in Vietnam, Pakistan, India or energy-rich Malaysia. New Indonesian factories had difficulty obtaining electricity supply in 1992, so that nuclear power generation is now being discussed there and in Thailand. China's energy shortfall is already of the order of 20–30 per cent above supply[139] and in the country as a whole de-mand is growing twice as fast as the domestic industry can construct capacity.

China's rail transport system is also overstrained, so much so that the volume of freight being carried fell in 1993. Economies at different stages of development – South Korea, Thailand, Pakistan, Sri Lanka, Burma and Cambodia all badly need to improve transport facilities. And new constraints appear all the time. When the energy crisis eased in Manila, the city's trans-port difficulties soon replaced it as a constraint on growth while, in rapidly-growing Cebu City, a water shortage threatened to frustrate development. Water shortages have also hit Thailand and an irrigation crisis endangers agriculture in the Pakistan province of Sindh.

The economies of South Asia, Indochina, Burma, North Korea and the Philippines are also afflicted by inadequate education and training at the lower end of their skill ladder and by the brain drain at the top. Sri Lanka has lost much of its Tamil intelligentsia following anti-Tamil riots in 1983 and as a result of the continuing civil war while many educated Burmese are in exile. Pakistan has seen a drift of economists to international institu-tions and skilled professionals from the Philippines find it more rewarding to work as domestic servants in Hong Kong or seek work in the OECD. The result is that only one in 25 of those teaching physics in Philippines schools has a qualification in the subject,[140] while just about every doctor graduat-ing from the élite University of the Philippines plans a career overseas. In-dia is a large enough economy to sustain some losses of technically qualified workers, even of computer programmers migrating to the Western US, and the skill situation is not yet a problem.

Criticism of India's use of its R&D base centres instead on the disproportionate resources devoted to pure science, to prestige projects like rocket technology and to the sizeable defence R&D effort, which includes development of nuclear weapons. The perceived need to match the Indian nuclear capability has also diverted Pakistan's more limited R&D effort into this dead end, while the industrial base remains tied to a handful of product areas and US$350 million a year is paid out in royalties for using overseas technology.[141] North Korea, notoriously, has also been striving to acquire nuclear weapons technology at the expense of a shrinking economy. The Philippines Congress has only allocated a small sum to R&D – P2.8 billion – while there is little indigenous R&D capability at all in Indochina, Sri Lanka or Burma.

The hopes for industrial upgrading and future growth in these economies do not rest on product innovation. Rather it is a matter of attracting more labour-intensive manufacturing with proven technology. In this context, less dramatic but no less debilitating to long-term prospects is the effect of denuding Bangladesh of virtually its entire English-speaking working class to fill vacancies around the region while many students pursue subjects that are not likely to lead to domestic employment.[142] Long-term development in a world dominated by foreign capital depends on relatively skilled as well as cheap labour. Education alone is no longer enough to secure investment, as Sri Lanka is finding. Despite its having one of the highest literacy rates in the region, prospective investors in electronics, for instance, are deterred by the absence of a pool of experienced workers to draw on when establishing a factory. High rates of literacy in the Philippines have similarly been insufficent in themselves to secure investment. Much lower literacy rates of 35 per cent in Bangladesh, 52 per cent in India and 56 per cent in Laos,[143] or the 2 per cent secondary school enrolment rate and 70 per cent illiteracy rate in Pakistan put people in these countries at an even greater disadvantage. Governments and companies alike attack the cost of labour in the hope that driving wages down further and removing trade union rights can compensate for poorly developed skills. Or they can follow the example of President Ramos and retreat into saying that 'optimism and confidence are our most important weapons.'[144] They may be the weapons with which the Philippines is most liberally supplied, but they are not the most effective. The search for effective weapons has led governments to adopt a variety of policy instruments to which we turn in the following chapter.

2 Economic Policy

The 'Asian model' of economic policy is sometimes popularised as a pat, uniform set of formulas with which to chart a steady growth path. There is no such thing in economic policy. What the World Bank describes as the pragmatism of the East Asian economies has meant that policy reponses have varied considerably. 'Contest-based competitions', for instance, figure in the Bank's discussion of the *East Asian Economic Miracle*. These procedures, through which bureaucrats allocated credit and incentives to firms which performed well in export markets, in fact only existed in their pure form in South Korea, Japan and Taiwan. Hong Kong's 'positive non-intervention'[1] has been at odds with considerable intervention in Malaysia or South Korea. When we include the rest of Asia it is soon apparent that any talk of an Asian model is highly inappropriate. Different governments have plucked different policy instruments from their tool-chests at different times, in the quest for combinations of productive factors to maximise growth from the endowments described in Chapter 1. What is worrying for those governments now is that instruments which could be relied upon in the past are no longer so serviceable, that some have always been flawed and that new instruments have alarming unintended consequences.

PLANNING

As *The East Asia Miracle* goes some way towards conceding,[2] planning tools have been employed effectively by several East Asian economies in the post-war period. Planning enjoyed its Asian heyday in the post-war and post-independence periods, when it was applied to reconstruction and basic industrialisation. Even Pakistan, where economic growth has generally been fitful, implemented two highly successful plans in the 1950s, which were then taken by South Korea as a model for its planning exercise after 1960. The 1950s also saw India grow steadily at 3.8 per cent under a planned regimen[3] and China achieve an average 8.9 per cent rise in national income under its first Five Year Plan, from 1953 to 1957.[4] The biggest successes for planning were South Korea and Taiwan. Explicitly copying Japanese development, President Park Chung-Hee created an Economic Planning Board, introduced five-year plans in 1962, set targets for individual firms and oversaw the inclusion of heavy and chemical industries in planning from 1972 onwards. Equity, social development and innovation also became objectives of

49

the planning process after 1972.[5] The success of planning in South Korea was, of course, in the context of cheap labour, an undervalued exchange rate and easy access to international markets. Taiwan enjoyed the same favourable international environment and utilised the same control of labour as foundations for its success. Its planning, which began with the first Four Year Plan in 1953, was not as strong as in South Korea. It served to reinforce a commitment to an export-oriented economy from the late 1950s onwards, in which a greatly undervalued currency was of critical importance. The planning mechanism was also used to implement the recommendation of US management consultants for the establishment of new industries to sustain export growth in the 1970s.[6]

Since the 1970s, however, planning has begun to encounter problems. In North Korea it emphasised the same kind of heavy industrial growth as that achieved by the Soviet Union in the 1930s. Just as in the Soviet Union, the productivity gains from this kind of planning have been exhausted and it cannot arrest the shrinkage of an economy increasingly starved of imports. Crisis management and efforts to boost production regardless of input availability have replaced any rational planning. In Burma the 1952 Eight Year Plan was abandoned after just three years.[7] A grandiose Twenty Year Plan was adopted in 1972 and its serious implementation began in 1974.[8] Within this framework government figures state that the second and third Four Year Plans yielded significant average annual growth rates from the mid-1970s to the early 1980s (4.8 per cent and 6.7 per cent respectively). But in the second half of the 1980s imports had to be reduced and state enterprises found it increasingly difficult to meet targets. As political upheaval engulfed the country, even official indicators registered a severe drop in activity. Long-term planning was formally abandoned at the end of the 1980s in favour of annual plans, which are formulated 'without any coherent notion of both the macro policies and the industrial priorities required in the future'.[9]

In Pakistan after the 1950s, planning met growing obstruction from landowners and the civil service and was undermined by the departure of key staff. By the time the Eighth Plan was being formulated in the mid-1990s, planning was little more than an indicative 'wish list', largely disregarded by policymakers.[10] The same is true of the Philippines, where planning agencies have lacked political clout, a cycle of boom and bust has wrecked any consistency in policy and low tax revenues have prevented governments supporting planning with their own resources. Planning has been scaled back to a weak, indicative form elsewhere in the region. In Indonesia, President Sukarno unveiled a plan in 1961 that had the hallmark of his rhetorical flourishes: it comprised eight books, 17 chapters and 1945 paragraphs, corresponding to Indonesia's declaration of independence on 17 August 1945.[11] Since then hyperbole has been replaced by the five-year Repelita plans, now into their sixth cycle, which stress food production and infrastructure devel-

opment within an indicative framework. Similar indicative planning is practised in Thailand and, at a broad level, in Malaysia's twenty-year Outline
Perspective Plan.

Planning is also being watered down in South Asia and in the market-
Stalinist economies where there is considerable ambiguity about its future.
The State Planning Commission in Nepal and the State Planning Committee
in Vietnam both have an undecided future in a predominantly free-market
environment. The period of Vietnam's first National Plan after reunification,
launched in 1976, was one of dismally poor industrial growth, leading to a
drastic overhaul in the 'triple plan' system of 1981 and a Second National
Plan from 1981 to 1985,[12] since when ambiguity has set in as a result of
Vietnam's *doi moi* policies. The Plan for 1991–5 sets indicative targets in
key sectors but resources to support them are very limited. China, likewise,
resides in a halfway house as far as planning is concerned. After the success
of the 1950s, planning disappeared beneath the chaos of the Great Leap
Forward and the Cultural Revolution. In the former, 30 to 40 million people
died, in the latter perhaps another 4 million[13] and, amid the starvation and
executions, the economy collapsed. Although the formalities of planning survive,
market mechanisms and dynamics have largely overwhelmed them. This left
the State Planning Commissioner, Chen Jinhua, mouthing little more than
bemused platitudes about reining in the economy in his speech at China's
nominal parliament, the National People's Congress (NPC), in 1994. India's
stance is less ambiguous, with the distinctive Nehruvian model of state socialism and state-controlled growth categorically ditched since the 1991 elections[14]
in favour of indicative planning. In Bangladesh and Sri Lanka, planning has
been jettisoned almost completely and replaced with short-term policy prescriptions dictated by the IMF, World Bank and Asian Development Bank.

The more successful economies have grown to the extent that planning
tools devised in the 1960s are no longer appropriate for managing a much
larger and more complex system. In Taiwan, for instance, planners failed to
prevent investment by companies in mainland China while the planning body,
the finance ministry and central bank do not agree on priorities. Doubts also
abound about the government's ability to fund and implement its infrastructure programme, originally costed at US$300 billion and now scaled back to
US$200 billion. This was part of an ambitious six-year National Develop-
ment Plan intended to reassert the leadership over the economy which the
government exercised in the era of the 'Ten Major Projects' in the 1970s.
However, in mid-1994 it had to concede the opening of the construction
sector to foreign companies to help raise funds for the schemes. In Thailand, the inadequacy of 'cylindrical' policymaking bodies, each of which
has successfully managed a single area of macro-economic policy, has been
revealed by their collective incapacity in the face of Bangkok traffic jams,
water shortages, infrastructure deficiencies and other issues which cut across

these divisions. Road-building in the 1960s was often tied to military needs and today often incompatible urban transport plans are overshadowed by the insistence of corrupt politicians on taking their cut from infrastructure projects and by the desire of developers to maximise returns from tax breaks and property developments. Negotiations on one project ended in failure after 17 years. South Korea's planners in the once dominant EPB are fighting a rearguard action to retain control of the economy in face of demands for greater freedom from the *chaebols*, which now believe they can compete better without the direction of the EPB. There has even been the threat of merging the EPB with the Ministry of Finance[16] to forge a single instrument for regulating the economy as a whole.

Infrastructure in the region illustrates the problems which result from inadequate planning. In economies that have been growing rapidly, the need for improvements to infrastructure should have been recognised and anticipated, as they have been in Singapore and Hong Kong. Elsewhere, however, they have been neglected or delayed and only now are belated efforts being made to improve facilities. South Korean planning has become so immersed in the questions of corporate and industrial strategy that bigger infrastructure problems have been left unattended. In Taiwan, the KMT's preoccupation with the recovery of mainland China meant that it neglected Taiwan's infrastructure until the late 1980s. Even then its efforts were hamstrung by corruption and by a political desire to curry favour internationally, resulting in the sharing out of contracts on the mass transit railway to a mixture of foreign firms with predictable delays and confusion.[17]

Incoherence in Malaysia has resulted in the conflicting aims of encouraging the spread of car ownership to assist the development of the automobile industry, while also needing to ease Kuala Lumpur's rapidly escalating traffic problems. Indonesian planners have been unable to check the growth of Jakarta as the centre of industry and business and to prevent the resulting congestion. For China the counterpart of the surging growth of the 1990s has been a belated adoption of hugely ambitious infrastructure plans that far exceed the capacity of the domestic economy or the implementing bodies. To install 10–15 million phone lines a year, double port capacity, triple the electrified rail network and ensure that power generation keeps pace with growth during the rest of the century is unrealistic.[18] Where growth has been less rapid, the inattention to infrastructure has been even greater: no power stations were built in the Philippines during the Cory Aquino administration, and no railways in Pakistan after 1947.

FOREIGN INVESTMENT

National governments in Asia have responded to the shortfalls in infrastructure by placing a greater emphasis on foreign direct investment (FDI). 'Build–operate–transfer' schemes and their derivatives have been floated in a number of Asian countries specifically to draw long-term investment into infrastructure. These projects allow the developer to collect the revenue for a set period – often 20 or 30 years – before handing it over to the government concerned. Seeking investment in this way reinforces the weight accorded to foreign capital as a factor in growth and as the basis of manufacturing expansion.

Such is the perceived significance of foreign investment that it has become one of the most important influences on economic policymaking. A subordinate position in the world economy compels governments to seek capital on its own terms. Whether prostrated by debt and economic failure like the Philippines or anxious about the deterrent effect of rising labour costs like Malaysia, they have no alternative but to enhance the attractiveness of investment if they wish to remain part of that system. Many governments in the region are now caught in a cycle of competitive tax-cutting that seeks to lure investors away from rival locations in the region or further afield. In reality, it is doubtful whether competing incentives significantly affect the overall level of investment, whatever their effect on the distribution of investment. Competing incentives rapidly neutralise one another and, in any case, are often outweighed by broader economic and political risk assessments. No amount of inducements will matter if commercial considerations relating to production, distribution and sale of goods are not met. Moreover, the taste for incentives is never satisfied and foreign investors will negotiate hard for further concessions once they know a project is badly needed.

Infrastructure projects are a case in point, particularly with the ADB withdrawing from lending at the urging of the US to make way for commercially-funded projects. One of the major private investors in the sector has been Hong Kong's Gordon Wu, whose Hopewell Holdings has built power stations in China and the Philippines. Hopewell's Philippine subsidiary earned a 34 per cent return in 1991[19] from power station refurbishment and installation and President Ramos' 'fast track' programme of power station construction held out equally lucrative profit opportunities. Wu's search for similar margins in China was cooled by Prime Minister Li Peng's reported aim of limiting the return on infrastructure projects to 12 per cent. Hopewell is looking instead at Indonesia, where initial returns from private sector power projects were 23 per cent.[20]

Wu knows perfectly well how widely his expertise is sought and how much competition there is for capital in the region. By the year 2000 Vietnam wants US$4 billion a year[21] and Pakistan hopes to have attracted US$10 billion[22] while President Ramos of the Philippines breaks into eulogies describing 'the forerunners of globalization – the courageous men and women of transnational or multinational companies. Not knowing any better, governments initially did not look kindly at them. But not any more. They are now the much-sought-after catalysts of economic change for development'.[23] The change in attitude detected by Ramos has inspired these and other quantitative targets for investment and pitched Asian governments into an intensifying competition for foreign investment. Ramos himself introduced measures in mid-1994 to allow foreign investors 100 per cent ownership in all but a handful of sectors,[24] having earlier allowed in more foreign banks for the first time in 45 years.[25]

The principal sweeteners for investors are tax cuts and changes to requirements for local ownership and other conditions imposed on investors. Where foreign investment has a longer-established presence, as in Singapore or Malaysia, conditions have been accommodating for some time. As the World Bank noted, as early as 1967 Singapore's incentives were 'more generous on average'[26] than those of other developing countries. To improve on these as competitors emerged, new categories of activity and corresponding incentives have been invented, covering currency trading, research and development and headquarters functions. In Malaysia, local ownership requirements have had to be specially relaxed in the electronics sector and the National Development Policy, which replaced the New Economic Policy in 1990, has avoided setting a target for the date by which 30 per cent of companies should be owned by *bumiputras*. A downward spiral of tax-cutting has also taken hold. The 1993 budget cut profits tax from 34 per cent to 32 per cent in 1994 and promised a further reduction to 30 per cent in 1995.[27] The budget also increased allowances and exemptions to stimulate investment in particular sectors, such as oil exploration and R&D, all in the context of falling FDI, greater competition in the region and efforts by the Trade and Industry Minister Rafidah Aziz to drum up investment from ASEAN partners. Thailand's Board of Investment has stepped up its incentives as part of the same competition.

Countries with a less accommodating track record have had to follow suit. Indonesia witnessed a dramatic turnaround in policy after the fall of President Sukarno, who had nationalised first Dutch and then other foreign investments in a confrontation with former colonial powers. Almost immediately after Suharto displaced Sukarno in 1965, he declared Indonesia once again open to foreign investment and guaranteed it against nationalisation for 30 years. Large-scale foreign investment was particularly noticeable in the 1980s. During the 1990s Indonesia has had to entice further investment with additional sweeteners. In mid-1994 a string of sectors including the media, transport, telecommunications and nuclear power were all opened to for-

eigners.[28] Vietnam has also undergone an apostasy as far as foreign investment is concerned: having been an economic client of the Soviet Union, the
Vietnamese Communist Party revised labour statutes in 1990 to make hiring
and firing of workers easier and now publishes *The Blazing Flame of Reform* which sets out in some detail the attractions for foreign investors, among
which are that 'Firstly, it is a big and cheap labour market' where 'the
labour price. . . may be lower than 35 US dollars a month'.[29] in the future.
There have been efforts to extract a price from investors, as in the insistence on a high capital base of US$15 million for foreign banks setting up in
Vietnam after 1990.[30] But this rearguard action has been overwhelmed by
legislation which provides for 100 per cent foreign ownership, and gives
guarantees against nationalisation and for the transfer of income, profits and
capital out of Vietnam. EPZs are under construction as the Vietnamese authorities compete directly for investment in labour-intensive industries and local
investment licensing bodies are to be swept aside. Laos has echoed the Vietnamese example by allowing 100 per cent ownership and a flat 20 per cent
tax rate for foreign investors,[31] while in the shattered Cambodian economy a
new foreign investment code (offering a string of tax exemptions) became
the top priority for the government in 1994.[32]

India has witnessed a similar transformation in government attitudes to
foreign investment. After decades of foreigners being limited to minority
stakes, the Rao Government has allowed majority foreign ownership in all
but a handful of sectors. The telecommunications and roadbuilding sectors
have been opened to foreign investors. India has by no means become as
accommodating as some other Asian economies, but the symbolic battle of
allowing foreign companies to re-enter the market with their own brand names
– best exemplified by Coca-Cola – has seen a defeat for opponents of foreign
capital. Their appetite whetted, investors are now pressing for reform of the
Industrial Disputes Act, which requires businessmen to obtain consent for
major layoffs or closures, and have lobbied Rao for more concessions on
intellectual property rights and the transfer of capital out of India.[33] Even
the Government of West Bengal, which is run by the Communist Party of
India (Marxist), has been forced to join the competition for investment capital
by offering a series of tax incentives to encourage infrastructure investment.[34]

With concessions being made to investors in India the smaller states of
the subcontinent have had no choice but to follow suit. Bankers in Sri Lanka
enthuse about the country's relative advantages over India, including the
fact that 100 per cent foreign ownership is permitted. Such was President
Premadasa's desire to court investment that at one stage the whole island
was declared to be an export processing zone. Pakistan has devised a new
energy policy that gives a bigger slice of production to foreign investors
and corporate tax rates are to fall steadily up to 1998–9.[35] Nepal staged a
conference in late 1992 to declare itself open to foreign investment. Seven-

year tax holidays and 100 per cent ownership were made available, along with over 80 projects for joint ventures.[36] Bangladesh's Board of Investment meanwhile runs a series of magazine advertisements describing 'the lowest cost production base on the globe' complete with 'generous tax holidays', 'relaxed foreign exchange controls' and 'unlimited equity participation with no approvals necessary'. Other incentives and programmes are on offer 'all designed to make it easy for foreign investors to take advantage of opportunities for business growth and profit.'

North Korea and Burma have been more circumspect. Since first formulating rules for foreign investment in 1984, North Korea has slowly been pushed into further concessions as it has become more dependent on FDI after the collapse of Soviet aid. 1992 saw a new law permitting wholly foreign-owned enterprises, tax incentives and some rights to remit profits.[37] By the end of 1993 foreign companies had also been permitted to lease land.[38] The Burmese military government regards foreign investment in similar terms. A new law was enacted at the end of 1988, extending the range of industries open to foreign investment, removing the risk of nationalisation implicit in the previous law, passed in 1959, and granting various tax incentives.[39]

Amid this competition for investment resources, it is all too easy for policymakers to lose sight of their development priorities. By handing the initiative to foreign investors and paring back their own tax and development spending, governments risk substituting short-term export-oriented investment for spending on infrastructure, training, education or other long-term priorities. Allowing foreign companies to tap local capital markets diverts limited domestic savings into serving the priorities set by those companies. Surrendering control over more and more sectors makes an economy inherently more difficult to plan and control and inherently more volatile. This becomes even more noticeable when the demands of foreign investors extend to the public sector. Ceding ownership and control of public sector assets undermines one of the key mechanisms which governments have used to regulate virtually every economy in the region.

PUBLIC OWNERSHIP

Planning has been implemented in many Asian countries through ties between the state and particular enterprises. These can take a variety of forms. In some the state owns outright a substantial portion of industry and banking, either as formally nationalised enterprises which can operate under the direct instructions of controlling ministries or through controlling shareholdings in outwardly independent commercial organisations. The clearest form of this has been in the market-Stalinist economies, where sectoral ministries have been responsible for the control of industrial enterprises. Other forms of control have been used elsewhere in the region. In Taiwan, the ruling Kuomintang (KMT) exercised control of a substantial portion of the economy through government-owned enterprises and banks. When planning began in the 1950s the state controlled over 50 per cent of output through these enterprises.[40] This share has since fallen to 20 per cent,[41] though the state remains dominant in shipbuilding, steel, power, petroleum refining, tobacco and alcohol. Besides state enterprises the KMT itself has interests worth up to NT$400 billion (US$10 billion) in various companies,[42] although these were not, until recently, run in a particularly commercial fashion. Only in the 1990s has the state begun selling off holdings in heavy industry and allowed private-sector banks to break the state banking monopoly. State banks have been used, as in South Korea, to direct funds to favoured strategic enterprises. Smaller companies have received little of the available credit, forcing them to seek capital in the more expensive unofficial 'kerb' market.[43]

Singapore, which abandoned formal planning after an experiment between 1960 and 1964,[44] also relied on state ownership of leading corporations – utilities, Singapore Airlines, technology companies and shipyards as well as banks – to steer the domestic economy. These government-linked corporations account for 18 per cent of of employment[45] and 23 per cent of the assets of Singapore's 500 largest firms. Partial privatisation of telecommunications, the airline and eventually other utilities will leave the government retaining a controlling interest. Very little in the way of a locally-owned private sector has emerged beneath the giants of the public sector and the multinationals.

In Thailand, however, nominal planning has been the counterpart both of limited ownership or control of companies and of sometimes contradictory control of government departmental budgets. Similarly, in Indonesia, the state exerts limited direct control over enterprises and the state sector is weighted towards unprofitable high technology enterprises and heavy industry, particularly steel and petrochemicals tied to the state oil company Pertamina. The state also controls just under half of the banking sector's assets.[46] In Malaysia, too, the public sector has taken responsibility for natural resource exploitation and the development of heavy industry as well as transport and utilities. Government ownership of the largest banks – Maybank and Bank Bumiputera – has reinforced control of the economy, though allocation of funds from these institutions has often been used to assist favoured interests.

In South Asia, public ownership has been more widespread. In Sri Lanka it was extended to major banks and tea estates under Mrs Sirimavo Bandaranaike's Sri Lanka Freedom Party (SLFP) government, from 1970 to 1977, and the government also acquired a mixed portfolio of assets in industry and the service sector. The 'commanding heights'[47] of Pakistan's banking and industry were nationalised by Prime Minister Zulfikar Ali Bhutto in the

1970s as part of an election pledge to dispossess the '22 families' which he accused of controlling the economy. This set a precedent for state intervention in Pakistan's industrial and financial activity, which is implemented today more through contracts, bank lending and taxation policy. Nationalisation occured partly by default in Bangladesh after independence from Pakistan, when property was abandoned by its former Pakistani owners. The Awami League government in the early 1970s then took major industries into public ownership and set ceilings on private sector expansion. Extensive public ownership also developed in India as directly owned state enterprises grew steadily. Between 1960–1 and 1990–1, their share of industrial output rose from 11 per cent to over 50 per cent.[48] Leading banks were nationalised in 1971 as a populist gesture by then Prime Minister, Mrs Indira Gandhi, and 40 per cent of lending has been to politically favoured sectors.[49] Strategic enterprises like railways, airlines, coal, oil and gas and telecommunications have also been held by the central government, while state governments have been responsible for electricity distribution.

PRIVATISATION

Under pressure from foreign investors and the international agencies, public sector assets are being put up for sale across the region. Portfolio investors are anxious to secure a share of the profitable enterprises in the more dynamic economies, while direct investors are more interested in acquiring and rationalising those in the less dynamic.

Where outright sales of assets have been forced through, the hand of the Bretton Woods sisters can frequently be detected: the IMF and the World Bank have given governments in most of the economically powerless states of the region no alternative but to reduce the scale of their public sector as a condition for continued financial assistance. The meeting of donors to Bangladesh in April 1993, for instance, ordered the sale of half of some 42 industrial units and textile mills by June 1994 and set accompanying targets for public sector job losses.[50] In all, Prime Minister Khaleda Zia said she would cut 110 000 jobs, bowing to calls from the Asian Development Bank and other donors.[51] Privatisation is, in reality, an integral part of the drive to incorporate economies like Bangladesh into the international and regional system of competition based on cheap labour. By undermining state sector employment, in which workers have been able to resist more effectively the pressure to compete primarily on wages, the international agencies and compliant governments are priming the weaker economies of South Asia for labour-seeking investment.

To date, however, other governments in South Asia and the Philippines have sold chiefly the more profitable enterprises.[52] They have shied away from the harsher aspects of privatisation, entailing a full-blooded confrontation with politically important sections of the working class. The Pakistani government displayed an urgency in transferring assets into the private sector when Nawaz Sharif's administration undertook what was billed as the 'world's fastest privatisation programme',[53] the speed of which did not conceal the fact that assets were being sold to his associates. Bigger state assets in telecommunications, water, energy and banking, around which formidable economic and political interests are grouped, were meanwhile held back from being sold off. The Sri Lankan government disposed of a mixture of industrial undertakings and service sector companies in what President Premadasa termed his 'people-isation' programme but it hesitated to privatise the tea estates whose workers were an important vote-bank for Premadasa.

Indian privatisation has been designed to give the outward form without changing fundamentally the relationship between enterprises and the state. Minority shares have, for instance, been sold to government-controlled unit trusts. As a result there has been no wholesale restructuring of its state-owned enterprises. Bank workers have strongly resisted any attempts at rationalisation and have gained the support of the Prime Minister, P. V. Narasimha Rao, who together with his finance minister, Manmohan Singh, were able to defend public sector jobs against IMF demands thanks to the improvement in India's international reserves between their taking office in mid-1991 and mid-1994. This enabled them to resist pressure to accelerate the reduction of the budget deficit by cutting state assistance to industry, although such pressure continues to be applied through the Aid India Consortium.

In the more successful economies and those in which state enterprises have played less of a role in development, privatisation tends to be limited to the sale of minority stakes, often in utilities, as in Taiwan, Singapore, South Korea and Thailand. In Hong Kong, there is very little for the state to sell. In Malaysia, 77 enterprises were wholly or partially privatised in the ten years up to 1994. The 1990 privatisation masterplan envisaged the sale of 250 enterprises over the course of the decade of the 1990s, including major units like the rail network, postal service and car manufacturer, Proton.[54] This would mean the transfer of 13 per cent of the public sector workforce into the private sector. A subsequent statement by Finance Minister Anwar Ibrahim that up to 1200 federal and state enterprises were to be sold reflects the fact that, beside high profile sales of major assets, the Malaysian government has quietly been divesting gambling and toll collection operations to favoured businessmen.[55] Foreign investors have benefited from the former, local cronies from the latter.

THE RISE OF THE PRIVATE SECTOR

Reformers in the market-Stalinist economies and in South Asia hope that an influx of investment and development of the private sector will allow them to leave the state sector to atrophy quietly, thereby sidestepping the question of dismantling it. Expansion of the private sector so far has had a dramatic effort in transforming the growth performance of the market-Stalinist economies. When reform began in China in the late 1970s the non-state (private and co-operative) sectors accounted for around 20 per cent of output. By 1993 they produced more than half.[56] Part of this change has come from the influx of foreign capital and the remarkable growth of coastal areas, part from the growth of rural industries as agricultural purchasing power rose, and part from the permeation of spending power and business opportunities through the entire country. China's policies have succeeded in achieving a fillip to growth in the 1980s and early 1990s without the government having to retrench the state sector too sharply though at the cost of growing enterprise indebtedness.[57] The same is true of Vietnam, where private sector firms have grown alongside state enterprises which compete or co-operate with them. The state sector meanwhile continues to receive subsidies and up to 95 per cent of credit.[58] In some instances it has reoriented production to more profitable lines, but formal privatision has been resisted in Vietnam as much as in India. Even so, with state enterprises now producing only one third of output,[59] the private sector is clearly at the leading edge of Vietnamese growth.

In Laos changes have gone further than in Vietnam, with the sale of the state brewery and other assets to the private sector. The privately-owned garment sector has grown and Thai investors have begun producing consumer goods. If growth is sustained it will be led by the private sector. In Cambodia virtually any state property, from factories and plantations to hospitals was put on the market in a cut and run approach to privatisation ahead of the elections organised by the UN in 1993. Much of the private investment during the period of the United Nations Transitional Authority for Cambodia (UNTAC) was related to the temporary expansion of purchasing power generated by UNTAC's 20 000 personnel. Cambodia's task for the foreseeable future is one of basic economic reconstruction in which industry will play a relatively minor role. The resettlement of refugees and the rehabilitation of agriculture and infrastructure will be assisted by international aid: if industry does begin to emerge it will be in the private sector.

The two economies in which the state has conceded least to the private sector are Burma and North Korea. Burma has encouraged foreign investment in some sectors, but indigenous private enterprises have been confined to small-scale operations. As of 1989–90 enterprises with fewer than ten workers were overwhelmingly private, those with more than 100 almost exclusively in the public sector.[60] Nevertheless, the private sector did produce 55 per cent of industrial output by value and, in the search for measures to reinvigorate the economy after the crisis year of 1988, the State Law and Order Restoration Council (SLORC) sought to encourage further private sector growth as well as foreign investment. These, SLORC hopes, will continue to drive the economy. In North Korea scope for private sector activity remains heavily circumscribed, with foreign investment sealed off in remote enclaves and very little by way of an indigenous private sector. Some of the leaders of North Korea now appear to believe that this investment, however tightly controlled, is essential, although decisions in this regard will hinge on the final outcome of leadership manoeuvrings following Kim Il Sung's death.

The result of these kinds of changes in China is that it is caught half-way between a market and a command economy, foreshadowing problems of a similar nature which can be expected in Vietnam. While Chinese policymakers have been congratulating themselves on avoiding the catastrophic drop in production which has hit the former Soviet Union, the problems they have accumulated are just as disastrous. They are trying to control a hybrid monster of an economy with policies and institutions which are neither fully understood nor in full working order. The scale of China's economic problems has increased in proportion to the responsibility given to one man – the so-called 'economic tsar' Zhu Rhongji – to solve them.[61] There are good grounds for believing Zhu has been chosen as a scapegoat, having been appointed as China's senior vice premier charged with economic policy, and then as central bank governor in mid-1993. His attempt to rein in the economy in mid-1993 was short-lived and ineffective and the magnitude of each crisis is growing as economic expansion continues at levels which are outpacing the institutional capacity for economic management. Official predictions of a 9 per cent growth rate in 1994 looked likely to be exceeded, especially after growth hit 11.6 per cent in the first half of the year.

Short-term adjustments to structural problems do not address the underlying weaknesses. Tackling economic problems will require a readiness to run the risks of political confrontation, something the weak and fractious leadership in Peking is reluctant to do. Inflation, which peaked at 18.5 per cent in 1988 and was a contributory factor in the Tiananmen Square protests of 1989, was stifled in the subsequent squeeze on the economy, only to make its cyclical reappearance in 1993 at a level – 14.5 per cent[62] – in excess of that in most other Asian economies. With the deregulation of prices nearly complete, this upsurge in prices reflected structural imbalances in demand and supply. Yet rather than try to address these, the government resorted to the reimposition of price controls on basic commodities early in 1994: despite this, inflation was still running at 22 per cent in mid-1994. Likewise, to respond to the re-emergence of China's trade deficit in 1993 for the first time since 1989 with import controls (car imports were banned in the second half of the year) suggests a less than fundamental approach. Moving towards convertibility with a currency reform at the start of 1994 merely complicated the situation. None of the institutional weaknesses which allow China's demand excesses have yet been seriously addressed.

Over-investment, which has been another cause of inflation and 'overheating' in the economy, has been met with measures banning certain kinds of investment, such as golf courses and horse-racing tracks.[63] Efforts have also been made to limit capital spending to projects already under way. Yet selective bans on investment, even if enforceable, hardly seem to go to the root of the problem. Lending by Chinese non-bank financial institutions (NBFIs), and even the total number of these institutions, has grown far beyond the People's Bank of China's knowledge, let alone its regulatory reach. State bank lending, much of it to loss-making state enterprises, had proved uncontrollable as inter-enterprise debts mushroomed and the so-called specialist banks have been equally unreceptive to calls for restraint. After six months of trying to restrain lending in 1993, Zhu admitted that inflation and the money supply were both above target. His attempt to call in all unauthorised lending by state banks ended humiliatingly, despite an extension of the deadline, with only a fraction successfully recovered. Neither Zhu nor any other Chinese leader had the economic tools or the political support to make an austerity campaign tell. The budget deficit has ballooned spectacularly, forcing the government to make its largest ever domestic bond issue – worth US$11.5 billion[64] – to cover the shortfall. Covering the deficit with bonds is another temporary expedient: the underlying cause is a combination of ineffective tax collection and rising debt at state enterprises.

As a liberalised economy becomes more unstable, so individuals seek to protect themselves. Large-scale capital flight reflects the growing belief that China's economic growth will not last. Money is being sent out to safe havens to guard against economic collapse and a day of reckoning for profiteering officials. Unlicensed stock exchanges spring up here and there across China as market operators look to tap the savings of the millions of Chinese desperate not to see their assets further eroded by inflation. Others pitch investors straight into the bewildering uncertainties of futures and foreign exchange markets. Financial markets are also used as a means of short-term enrichment for China's new 'entrepreneurs'. Companies raise funds and use them, not for their expressed purpose of investing in additional capacity, but to enlarge their speculative resources. Enterprise zones appear as freewheeling officials look to cash in on the investment boom: over 1000 were closed between August and September 1993 alone.[65] This froth of speculative activity will continue as long as real economic policymaking remains paralysed by political disagreements at the very top. So long as Deng Xiaoping's dying droplets of speech can be used to bolster the line that 'growth is healthy', the free-for-all will continue. And even if a consensus could be formed on curbing growth the Communist Party lacks the will or the means to enforce it. In that respect reform is unstoppable, but where the private sector will lead China is far from certain.

STATE-BUSINESS RELATIONSHIPS

Outside the market-Stalinist economies, the private sector has a much longer pedigree. But it has relied heavily on various forms of assistance from the state. The state grants privileges to selected enterprises, encourages a particular structure of industry or simply creates channels for private business to voice concerns to government (a development which the World Bank characterises as 'proto-democratic' rather than proto-corporatist). The Hong Kong government has been the least interventionist in this regard, though 'positive non-intervention' can work to the direct advantage of banks and industry. Allowing banks to operate a cartel on interest rates – the Interest Rate Agreement which has been preserved for 30 years – enabled them to make an extra HK$5 billion (US$640 million) in profits in 1991.[66] The government also bailed out banks and deposit taking companies in the 1980s and has assisted industry with good infrastructure and export promotion efforts.

In contrast, South Korea has had the strongest nexus between private industry and the state. As one observer put it: 'In the 1970s and 1980s government was the wife of business in the West; here it was the husband; now it is becoming androgynous'.[67] The policies of Park Chung-Hee's administration were the archetype of this relationship, with everything from personal exhortations by the President to financial incentives and penalties applied to companies to encourage them to export more, remain competitive and hold wages down.[68] The existence of an industrial structure dominated by *chaebols* was central to the functioning of the relationship. Big companies which proved their ability to compete in new areas of business were needed to absorb the large sums of capital to continue growing and competing internationally. Failure was punished by the withdrawal of state funds. The relationship also funnelled money back into the social and political organisations run by Park and his successors Chun Doo-Hwan (President from 1980 to 1988) and Roh Tae-Woo (President from 1988 to 1993).[69]

Only in the 1990s has it come seriously into question, as *chaebols* seek greater freedom from political control and from providing donations. The campaign for the Presidency mounted by Chung Ju-Yung, the founder of Hyundai, in 1992 embodied capital's desire to free itself from the tutelage of the state, but the use of the state apparatus in investigations of Hyundai and the prosecution of Chung himself in connection with campaign contributions showed that the government and the bureaucracy were not yet ready to concede this. Prosecution of the boss of Daewoo, Kim Woo-choong, on corruption charges was also interpreted as a political warning shot to someone who had considered contesting the presidential election in 1992. The directive to all the *chaebols* to concentrate on just three areas of production, for all that it is likely to be circumvented, is another indication of how government continues to oversee the private sector.

The state/business relationship in Taiwan has been highly supportive. US aid in the 1950s and 1960s was channelled into building up large private sector enterprises shielded behind protective barriers.[70] Low cost inputs from state enterprises – especially China Petroleum Corporation – underpinned the development of large petrochemicals companies. The concern of the ruling KMT has been to ensure that a considerable part of this assistance has gone to its political allies within business, the so-called 'mainlander' enterprises, owned by those who fled with the KMT to Taiwan in 1949. The KMT has also favoured the large Taiwanese landowning families which were given shares in major enterprises in return for landholdings seized after 1949.

In Indonesia, the growth of selected private companies has been encouraged by the allocation of monopolies and licences that have covered foodstuffs, timber, trade and manufacturing. Substantial conglomerates have emerged, most of them Chinese-owned and best exemplified by the Salim Group, which now controls up to 5 per cent of GNP.[71] More recently indigenous *pribumi* groups (i.e. companies owned by Indonesians of non-Chinese descent), especially these centred on President Suharto's children, have joined the ranks of major corporations. They have been helped by assistance from the state and state-owned banks, creating corporations which profit from concessions, rather than growing on the basis of rational organisation or national need.

The use of licences and monopolies to encourage the private sector to engage in industrial growth has been most prominent in South Asia. This system supposedly gave governments greater control over the economy – if only through the ability to revoke licences – though in reality it became a means of guaranteeing profits for small cliques of industrialists and importers. During the 1950s and 1960s India guaranteed protection to industrialists who began manufacturing import substitutes in specified product categories. This produced a sprawling patchwork of privately owned plants, very few of which were capable of competing internationally. Where companies proved unprofitable, they were acquired by the state under the Sick Industries Companies Act that created an equally haphazard structure of public ownership. The dismantling of what became known as the 'licence raj' only began in earnest in 1991, as domestic industry was delicensed, more foreign competition allowed and planning formally scaled back. The pattern of corporate growth in Sri Lanka has been similar to that in India, with four rambling conglomerates owning interests in a mixture of sectors and a heavy weighting to trade and services in the structure of GDP, reflecting the attractions of import licences as a source of profits.

DYSFUNCTIONAL CRONYISM

For all the various ways in which the state has supported economic growth through the corporate sector, there are also abundant counter-examples of dysfunctional cronyism, which have either wasted resources or imposed high opportunity costs on these economies: elements of the state have been captured by its clients for individual or corporate gain rather than national development. In South Korea, which was held up by the World Bank as a model of civil service impartiality and insulated technocratic decision-making, Kim Young-Sam's anti-corruption drive has forced officials into declarations of their assets which have profoundly shocked ordinary people.[72] The revelations made it clear that bribery extended far beyond the judiciary and other sections of the state in which it was widely acknowledged to be prevalent. The corollary of bribery has been corporate negligence in construction projects.[73] Corruption scandals have become the order of the day in Taiwan, where the opposition Democratic Progressive Party (DPP) has a 'bottomless well'[74] of murky relationships and history to draw on to discredit the government. Suspicion of the grounds on which past contracts were awarded is taking its toll on the economy as the government is paralysed by intensive scrutiny of any commercial arrangements it enters into, such as that mooted with British Aerospace. In Thailand politicians controlling sectoral ministries have traditionally used them in classic pork barrel fashion, which has had the cumulatively adverse effect of building infrastructure for maximum political advantage rather than economic benefit. Thailand's public purchasing policies have also been dictated by the pecuniary considerations of ministers and officials, resulting in armed forces with incompatible, obsolete or ineffective equipment and a Thai Airways fleet that is a maintenance nightmare because of the huge assortment of aeroplane and engine types bought to net backhanders from different manufacturers.

Nevertheless individual payments to secure contracts probably do not have as debilitating an effect on an economy in the long term as do monopolies and licences which build in a permanent diversion of revenues into private pockets. This kind of cronyism reached its zenith during the later Marcos years in the Philippines, from 1975 onwards, when monopsonies and monopolies were created in key commodities, such as coconuts and sugar, for the personal benefit of Marcos's cronies, while state-owned banks guaranteed payments by crony corporations which were never honoured. Seven years after Marcos's flight the chronic debt problems of the Philippines'

Central Bank[75] could still be traced to the guaranteed lending of that period and national interest rates were kept damagingly high so that the Bank could continue to meet its obligations. Up to US$6 billion may have been borrowed in fraudulent, corrupt or incompetently administered loans.[76] Little has changed in the business world since the overthrow of Marcos. Powerful interests have been able to protect themselves through Congress and the courts, while Eduardo 'Danding' Cojuangco, the coconut king of the Marcos era, nearly succeeded in becoming president in 1992. Only the fear among a section of the ruling class that Cojuangco would line his pockets too liberally at their expense led them to switch their influential support to Fidel Ramos. The characteristic history of cartels in the Philippines has left it with comparatively few of the smaller companies that have contributed to rapid growth in, for instance, Taiwan.

Indonesia's cronyism does not always go by that name, though the pattern is broadly similar to that of the Philippines in the Marcos era. State banks underwrite favoured individuals close to the President, as was shown on a list of their bad debts – totalling over US$3 billion – circulated in Jakarta in 1993.[77] The list was a roll-call of well-connected groups, some of them so cash-rich that their failure to pay interest on their debts could only have been a measure of their contempt for the state banks. Despite efforts by the World Bank to force these banks to act more commercially and periodic hard-talking from Bank Indonesia, the central bank's revamped management still included at least one member who could 'turn the spigots on'[78] to lend to favoured groups. Early in 1994 one state bank turned up a single bad loan of US$430 million.[79] This led to the conviction and 17 year prison sentence for businessman Eddie Tansil, which did suggest that some of the worst abuses of the state banking system are being checked.

In any large project it has become normal to make payments or give stakes to the groups associated with President Suharto's children. These are principally Bambang's Bimantara, Tutut's Citra Lamtoro Gung and Tommy's Humpuss, although the president's other three children also have an array of corporate interests. More damaging to the economy in the long term are the monopolies and concessions held by the President's family and its associates. Tommy Suharto's stewardship of the monopoly in cloves (the distinctive ingredient in Indonesian *kretek* cigarettes) helped push the third largest manufacturer into a financial crisis and seriously frightened foreign investors.[80] Tommy's brother Bambang's orange trading monopoly in West Kalimantan is widely resented by farmers, 12 000 of whom have been ruined by it. Longer-running monopolies have resulted in flour prices 30 per cent higher than in neighbouring countries and a string of industrial input costs above world market prices. Polythene, for example, is 17 per cent above international prices. Removing these distortions could, one estimate suggests, add 3 per cent to growth rates.[81] Yet, in each round of the progressive liberalisation being urged on Indonesia as the price of its record levels of foreign aid, reform proposals are scaled down or new monopolies – often connected to sales and purchases by state corporations – are invented to compensate for the loss of the old ones.

Malaysia likewise has such a rich raw material base that the damaging effects of corporate and financial mismanagement are overshadowed by rapid growth. The furore provoked by British press criticism of the Pergau dam project which, it is calculated, will increase electricity charges to Malaysian consumers by £100 million,[82] was small beer in comparison to the foreign exchange losses of the central bank, Bank Negara, in 1992 and 1993, totalling M$9.3 billion (US$3.5 billion) and M$5.7 billion respectively.[83] Only after the second of these was made public did its governor resign. Government funds also had to be used to bail out Bank Bumiputra, after its subsidiary Bumiputra Malaysia Finance, became embroiled in ruinous property lending in Hong Kong in the early 1980s. Another US$250 million was wasted in an ill-fated attempt to corner the world tin market.[84] The money squandered in these ventures could have been far better employed in domestic investment, but in the context of 7 or 8 per cent growth lame excuses by ministers and officials are more easily swallowed. Even where funds are put into domestic projects like the North–South Highway, the contract was given to a company controlled by the ruling party and the final cost was nearly double the original estimate.

In the adversarial political climate of South Asia misuse of resources more quickly becomes the subject of public controversy, although this does not always prevent damage being done. The structure of licences and monopolies allowed selected groups to earn excess profits for many years and state-owned banks have been major lenders to favoured clients, among whom a 'defaulters' culture' has taken hold. The exposure of their names on lists circulated by finance ministers in Pakistan and Bangladesh has done little to shake their composure. The problems continue to accumulate in Sri Lanka where the late President Premadasa's instructions for banks to lend to his pet garment factory projects have generated fresh bad debt problems. Journalists and academics in Colombo expected that Premadasa's death in 1993 would mark a return to the political allocation of funds to preferred businesses at ministerial level – via the 51 per cent holding which has been retained in public sector banks – in place of the concentration of patronage exclusively in the president's hands. Among the parallels between Premadasa and Marcos was the favouritism towards cronies which was behind an abortive Air Lanka deal with Airbus Industrie for a fleet replacement programme costing US$700 million.

Links between the Indian state and business for private advantage have grown apace since corporate political donations were outlawed in 1970. Since then, these contributions have continued illicitly in exchange for lucrative contracts or commissions in state-related business, or loans from state-owned banks. The need for cash payments also encouraged the growth of India's black economy, placing more resources beyond the reach of the tax authorities. In Pakistan, state contracts and economic patronage have become the chief political prize for ruling parties, elected or not, to be withdrawn from opponents and handed to supporters. The shipbreaking industry was destroyed by tariff changes in the 1980s, to the great advantage of the private sector foundries. One of the main beneficiaries was Ittefaq Industries, the company controlled by Nawaz Sharif, then Chief Minister of Punjab. When his rival, Benazir Bhutto, became Prime Minister in 1989 tax changes affecting sugar and cement penalised Ittefaq, as did obstruction by Pakistan Railways.[85] When he succeeded her, Sharif then prosecuted Bhutto's husband, Asif Zardari, for corruption in government deals. Three years later, Benazir returned to power and motorway contracts were scaled back to withdraw government support from companies that had backed Sharif. This unedifying spectacle could only have damaging consequences for Pakistan's long-term development and for those workers whose jobs disappear when industries are discriminated against.

WORKERS' RIGHTS

As well as subsidising and supporting enterprises, the state provides a kind of negative assistance to business in the negligent enforcement of worker protection and the denial of trade union rights. Thailand is one of the most notorious examples, with a miserable history of industrial accidents and infringements of building safety rules as well as periodic denials of trade union rights. Minimum wage legislation is enforced for perhaps 30–40 per cent of plants, while factory inspectors are required to give notice of their visits.[86] The daily tally of industrial accidents in South Korea runs at six deaths and 82 people disabled[87] and some occupations have a frightful attrition rate (for example, there were 264 deaths or disappearances in deep-sea fishing between 1988 and 1990[88]). China's PLA-run factories are immune from serious inspection, while the proliferation of unlicensed industrial development in the coastal areas has alarming implications for workers' safety. In India, only 6 per cent of women are employed in workplaces protected by labour laws.[89]

Complicity in abuses reflects a wider resistance by many Asian governments to demands for trade union rights. A variety of measures have been used to prevent workers pressing for better pay and conditions and endangering competitiveness based on low wages. One approach has been, of course, to assist companies in repression and even to use them, as in South Korea, as a cat's paw for the state: the EPB used its control of credit to companies to encourage them to enforce wage rise limits[90] and there was a deterioration in the rights of trade unions during the 1970s. President Park introduced a more authoritarian constitution to counter the threat from growing concentrations of workers as industry expanded. Two decades later the trade unions still face a government that resists wider, more effective unionisation, whether of white-collar or blue-collar workers, and uses its police force quite unambiguously in support of management against factory occupations and demands for greater industrial democracy.[91] Labour laws introduced before the political democracy changes of 1988 continue to be enforced. Businessmen from South Korea carry their habits with them when investing elsewhere in the region: a delegation visiting Pakistan demanded changes in the labour law as a condition of opening factories.[92]

Another measure has been the pre-emptive establishment of a tame and all-embracing union federation covering certain industries or all workers. Hence, in Indonesia, the fight for recognition by the unofficial Indonesian Workers Welfare Union (SBSI), which groups workers outside the officially-run All-Indonesia Workers Union (SPSI), while in China all attempts to set up independent unions outside the framework of state unions have been harshly squashed.[93] In Malaysia, workers in the electronics industry have been denied the right to organise a national union and have had to settle for in-house unions. Alternatively, unions are banned outright, as in the EPZs in Bangladesh at present, in Taiwan until 1987, or in the Thai public sector after military rule replaced civilian government in 1991. Even where unions are permitted the right to strike may be denied, as in China under the constitution of 1982 and the draft labour law published in 1994 and as it was in Indonesia before 1990.[94]

When it comes to political reforms, trade union rights are seldom considered in the emerging bourgeois democracies of the region. They do not feature in Governor Patten's plans for more democracy in Hong Kong, where employers retain the right to sack workers for striking and unionisation remains confined to 17 or 18 per cent of the workforce. Nor are there minimum wage provisions.[95] Divisions within the trade union movement itself have weakened its bargaining power in Hong Kong and the Philippines, while in Singapore the incorporation of the National Trade Union Congress (NTUC) within the state is virtually total. The NTUC's role is principally to control the workforce, not to argue with government or employers on its behalf. As the World Bank noted in explaining how the Singapore government was able to reduce employers' contributions to the CPF: 'Such a move meant a reduction in workers' earnings by 12 per cent and would have been difficult to implement without the support of the NTUC'.[96]

Only in South Asia, especially India and Bangladesh, are there vociferous and lively trade union movements. Because publicly owned enterprises account for such a large proportion of the formal or 'organised' sector,[97] unions tend to be concentrated in the public sector, where they are engaged in defensive struggles against the retrenchment of jobs. In the private sector – Bangladeshi garment factories or Indian carpet factories – union protection is negligible or non-existent and workers' rights are unenforced by the state. In India, for instance, the maximum fine imposed for the illegal employment of child labour was, up to 1992, Rs100 (around US$3).[98]

EXPORT ORIENTATION

Governments have also sought to use an 'export orientation' to assist companies. As *The East Asian Miracle* points out, export-oriented economies have achieved higher rates of growth thanks in part to large foreign market opportunities and the quicker diffusion of advanced production techniques. Exporting more has been a good way of accelerating growth rates that are otherwise constrained, as, for example, India's has been for much of the post-war period, by the rate of growth of domestic demand. However, the gains from an export orientation cannot be assured over the medium to long term. One reason for this is that aggressive undervaluing of exchange rates is no longer so easy as it was in the 1960s and 1970s. The World Bank's analysis discounts the importance of undervalued exchange rates in helping to secure export growth during that period. But for both South Korea and Taiwan markedly undervalued exchange rates were of great importance in enhancing the competitiveness of their exports. From 1960 to 1985 the New Taiwan dollar was pegged to the US dollar, which was worth around NT$40. Given the sizeable accumulation in Taiwan's trade surplus with the US over this period the 1985 level allowed Taiwanese goods to enter the US at far lower prices than would have been set by market exchange rates. (The New Taiwan dollar has subsequently appreciated by nearly 40 per cent, to US$1:NT$25). South Korea abandoned overvalued exchange rates in 1964, when the won was devalued by 100 per cent, and has since used devaluation as a means of retaining a competitive edge for exports, devaluing by 20 per cent in 1974 and by another 20 per cent in 1980. The business community continues to press for devaluation as a way of restoring cost advantages lost as a result of wage increases. Thailand has been flexible in its exchange rate policy. It was able to peg the baht to the US dollar during the 1960s and 1970s and thereby support its rising exports. When the floating US dollar started to cause problems in the 1980s the Bank of Thailand switched to valuing the baht against a basket of currencies. By manipulating the composition of the basket as exchange rates moved the Bank was able to achieve an effective 30 per cent depreciation of the baht between 1983 and 1991.[99] The Malaysian authorities have had problems trying to prevent the appreciation of the Malaysian ringgit, forcing them to print money and thereby stoke inflation.[100] Competitive devaluations have also become a staple policy elsewhere in the region: Filipino economists estimated in late 1993 that to recover competitiveness the peso would need to be devalued by 30 per cent, 40 per cent and 76 per cent respectively against the baht, the Chinese renminbi and the Indonesian rupiah, taking into account the two 'maxi' Indonesian devaluations in 1983 and 1986.[101] Nor has South Asia been exempt from this trend: India devalued sharply in 1991, while Pakistan and Sri Lanka have been devaluing fairly steadily since the 1980s.

As a policy tool, devaluations can provoke competitive retaliation. Although devaluation may be 'aimed' at export markets in the OECD and, in that sense, have relatively little effect on other Asian economies the competitive effect is to displace exports from these other economies and risk provoking retaliation. Second, tolerance of undervalued currencies in the markets of developed countries is shrinking: it was partly US pressure over the mounting bilateral trade deficit between the US and Taiwan which forced the upward revaluation of the New Taiwan dollar in 1985. The US applied similar pressure to South Korea in 1987 and 1988 as the bilateral deficit rose to nearly US\$10 billion.[102] Penetrating the huge US market with underpriced goods in the 1960s was one thing; as US problems multiplied in the 1980s and the political importance of Asian client states shrank in an era of superpower rapprochement and subsequent Soviet collapse, cheap imports became a potent political rallying call in the US. Despite all the international approval of export-oriented policies, US administrations are no longer sympathetic to undervalued exchange rates. And where the US has trod in trade relations with Asia, the European Union (EU) is never slow to follow.

Asian commodity producing economies also face a problem with the elasticity of demand in response to price cuts resulting from a devaluation. It may mean more rupees or pesos for each dollar the exporter earns but it does not necessarily translate into more tea or cotton or sugar being sold. India's experience of the 1966 devaluation was that the policy did not generate the expected boost to exports: only as the economy has diversified away from commodity exports has the effectiveness of the policy improved. The recovery in Indian exports since the 1991 devaluations can be attributed to the broader and more price-sensitive composition of Indian exports. For Sri Lanka, where tea, rubber and coconut accounted for nearly 30 per cent of exports between 1988 and 1992, and quotas impose limits on garment exports, another 47 per cent of the total, devaluation remains of questionable merit. Hopes of a tea cartel with India are unlikely to lead to firm agreement on pricing. The IMF's structural adjustment programmes accompanying devaluation and loan packages have actually done little to restructure the Sri Lankan economy in such a way that there are export industries that can benefit from a more competitive exchange rate. Pakistan, likewise, continues to depend on cotton and cotton-related products to generate 60 per cent of export earnings.[103] Devaluation has had only limited effects, and exports in fact fell in 1993. The Philippines meanwhile remains gripped by structural problems which produce a regularly recurring cycle of balance of payments crisis, devaluation, inflation, slowdown, government borrowing, recovery and then another balance of payments crisis. The perennial problem which is not addressed is that the Philippines imports too much and makes too little: it is, according to one central bank official, 'a developing country with the tastes of a developed country'[104] with a high import dependence ratio in many export industries.

Besides exchange rates, debates on industrial policy, the forms of state support to industry and the role of foreign investment all influence export performance. This can also be assisted by measures to restrict domestic consumption and force producers into export markets, a tactic employed in South Korea and in Vietnam. However, potentially the most important constraint on an export-oriented policy is the emerging protectionism of the OECD economies. Despite the completion of the GATT Uruguay Round and the creation of the World Trade Organisation (WTO), the risk of anti-dumping cases and bilateral trade actions has not been removed. Labour standards will be on the agenda of the WTO from the start. US Trade Representatives have seized upon 'managed trade' as a means of forcing Japan to reduce its trade surplus with the US and one of its effects has been to encourage the relocation of Japanese investment to Asia. In just the same way exporters from Taiwan and Hong Kong have shifted factories to China, from which they now sell to the US while pointing to a shrinking bilateral trade surplus as proof of their responsiveness to US concerns. Managed trade does not, therefore, solve problems so much as spread them. It can only be a matter of time before the managed trade principle is applied more widely in Asia, pushing ripples of investment further into the region. US moves to redefine garments by the location where they are 'assembled' rather than cut will accentuate this.[105] Tariff barriers protecting Asian markets have already become the target of IMF-inspired reforms and foreign firms and banks are seeking to reduce other barriers to entering the Chinese and Taiwanese markets as the price for admission to the GATT and the WTO. Overall, the EU has sought to obtain for its members the same privileges accorded to the US, while also seeking to restrict access to its domestic market, where Asian competition is defined as unfair. Most quantitative EU trade restrictions are directed at Asian producers.[106] Tougher access to these developed markets has been a factor pushing more Asian economies into closer relations with China, as we saw in Chapter 1. Muslim states in Asia have also been looking to the Gulf as a potential market and the successor states of the former Soviet Union provide other openings. But none of these markets has the same rich consumer stratum as the OECD. Whatever new outlets are tested none will make export-orientation so easy a means of accelerating growth. The long-term key to sustained and secure growth for Asian economies must be in the satisfaction of needs in the domestic market. But that will require a much more even distribution of income than that which growth has generated so far.

3 Dividing the Spoils

When President Ramos declared a 'National Day to Overcome Extreme Poverty' in October 1993, the magnitude of the task confronting him was hard to gauge. Depending on the sources used (which include two different government estimates), the Philippines has 40.7 per cent, 50 per cent, 59 per cent or 70 per cent of its population living in poverty, and 21 per cent in 'absolute poverty'.[1] Ramos' own Philippines 2000! programme puts the figure at 50 per cent and specifies a characteristically optimistic target of 30 per cent by 1998. The Philippines cannot hope to meet this target except by fiddling the figures and adopting criteria for poverty closer to the World Bank's standards for 'absolute poverty'. The only consolation is that the percentage of people in poverty is not rising steeply, as it did during the later Marcos years, which saw an emphatic reversal in poverty reduction. In 1972 49 per cent of families were in poverty; by 1985 the proportion had increased to 59 per cent.[2]

Estimates of poverty vary considerably partly because definitions use different measures: relative or absolute incomes, calorific intake or a 'minimum acceptable standard of living for the society' in question.[3] Such definitions are clearly prone to fluctuations, as when a movement in the price of rice supposedly takes 10 million people out of poverty in Bangladesh[4] in what is obviously an all too easily reversible change that takes no account of other indicators of impoverishment. The multiplicity of estimates also allows favourable constructions to be placed on the smaller figures, particularly the World Bank's figure for the numbers in 'absolute' poverty. These indicate that only 2 per cent of the Malaysian population and 10 per cent of the Chinese population remain below an internationally drawn poverty line.[5] The World Bank singles out Indonesia for having the best record in reducing poverty between 1970 and 1990, when the percentage of people living in poverty was brought down from 60 to just 15. The Bank does however concede that 30–40 per cent of Indonesians are still 'poor' or 'near-poor'.[6] Improvements in South Asia have been less dramatic and, according to the World Bank, substantial proportions of the population remain in poverty in India (25 per cent), Bangladesh (49 per cent), and Pakistan (31 per cent).[7] The United Nations Economic and Social Commission for Asia and the Pacific (UNESCAP) estimates that 27 per cent of people in Sri Lanka and 40 per cent of those in Nepal live in poverty. In South East Asia, Thailand has also been a relative laggard, with virtually no reduction in the percentage of the population in absolute poverty between 1980 and 1990 (17 and 16 per cent respectively[8]), reflecting the highly skewed pattern of growth which keeps large numbers of rural families in poverty, especially in the North East.

The East Asian Miracle uses the ratio of the income share of the richest fifth of the population to that of the poorest fifth to argue that there has been a 'positive association between growth and low inequality in the HPAEs'.[9] The World Bank does, however, add two qualifications, one noting the recent increase in inequality in South Korea and the other the 'relatively minor' reductions in poverty in Thailand. It could have added evidence of a widening gap between the richest and poorest fifths of the population in Taiwan.[10] But the big problem with using the richest and poorest fifths of the population as indicators is that they conceal the gross inequality between the top 1 per cent who own huge sections of the indigenous industrial and financial base in several Asian economies and the remainder of the populations. Only when the income of that 1 per cent is spread amongst the other 19 per cent who make up the top fifth do the figures appear respectable by the standards of developing countries.

The personal wealth and income reflected in such facts as that Chung Ju-Yung and three of his sons were four of South Korea's five largest tax-payers,[11] or that 80 per cent of wealth in India is held by 80 families,[12] or that a single privately owned company accounts for 5 per cent of Indonesian GDP,[13] or that Thailand's Sophonpanich family control the fifth largest bank in the region (Bangkok Bank) betray the true underlying inequalities. Crude top and bottom fifth figures also neglect the effects of taxation which, we shall argue, tend to be regressive, and take no account either of Asia's vast black economy,[14] whether in drugs or money-lending or smuggling, or of corrupt payments, the profits of which flow disproportionately into the hands of the rich.

Land ownership is also a powerful source of income inequalities. The expulsion of Japanese landlords from South Korea and Taiwan at the end of the Second World War allowed a redistribution of land to small farmers, but in the Philippines the victorious Douglas MacArthur spared his rich friends the indignities of dispossession inflicted on their Japanese counterparts, despite their wartime record of collaboration. A series of cosmetic land reform programmes have meant that large landowners have retained their wealth. The same is true in Pakistan, in large parts of India where the momentum for land reform was spent early on in the post-independence period,[15] and in Bangladesh where 'successive governments have done virtually nothing to promote a more egalitarian distribution of landownership'.[16] Sri Lanka's income distribution is among the worst in Asia on the ratio of richest and poorest fifths, which is nearly 12:1.[17]

GROWTH AND INEQUALITY

The World Bank's belief that growth leads to the reduction of inequality is painfully naive at some points. *The East Asian Miracle* quotes President Suharto's endorsement of a research report stressing shared growth as evidence that his advocacy of 'economic democracy'[18] means a commitment to redistribution of the benefits of growth. The stark facts of Suharto's favouritism and the monopolies enjoyed by his cronies make a mockery of his official pronouncements on 'economic democracy'. Equally naive is the Bank's view that the Singaporean leadership pursued equity goals through 'effective consultation arrangements between labour, government, and business'[19] when, as we have seen, the functioning of the NTUC was to ensure that the working class accepted the burden of adjustments in wage policy. A formal commitment to greater social and economic equality has also featured in the national plans of South Korea, Malaysia, Indonesia, Thailand and India and in the constitution of the Philippines at one time or another. Yet the reality is that the growth path adopted first by the HPAE and now being urged on the nations of South Asia and the market–Stalinist economies is inherently incapable of delivering equality. There may be temporary redistributions to achieve specific social and political goals, such as measures to reallocate income back to farmers in South Korea in the 1970s. But neither these nor the initial post-war land reform have created lasting structural mechanisms for re-distribution. The more the industrial economy grows in South Korea and Taiwan, the less is the influence of that one-off redistribution from land reform which may have been the single most important factor explaining subsequent equality.[20] As the World Bank itself admits, leaders in South Korea did not have a 'synchronized' view of growth and distribution. The worsening of equity and the persistence of poverty in Thailand are similarly identified by the Thailand Development Research Institute as 'consequences of market-based industrialisation and the failure of institutions – both public and private – to counteract some of the negative consequences of rapid economic growth'.[21]

In Malaysia, there have been the gestures of the New Economic Policy (NEP),[22] to redistribute income to the *bumiputra* community, although as Malaysian critic Chandra Muzaffar points out, 'Most of the government's energies as far as the NEP is concerned have been directed towards the incubation of Malay contractors, wholesalers, importers, executives and professionals'.[23] Between 1957 and 1990 the ethnic Malay proportion of the four middle class occupational categories rose from 22 to 48 per cent.[24] The NEP has also been used to sanction the emergence of Malay tycoons as an embodiment of the success of the Malay community and a way of bolstering its 'ego' (leading cynics to diagnose the 'Ali Baba syndrome' of Malay frontmen for Chinese-controlled businesses). Even at the formal level the

NEP failed to reach its target of 30 per cent of equity ownership in Bumiputra hands: the level of Malay ownership was 20 per cent in 1990. Bodies set up to channel benefits from financial dealings to ordinary citizens, such as the Malays' *Majlis Amanah Rakyat* or the ethnic Indians' Maika Holdings, have themselves become embroiled in scandals and accusations of misallocation of funds.[25] The benefits to ordinary Malays, beyond the psychological reassurance of having a government that claims to be on their side, are, therefore, questionable. The end result of the whole process has been that, even by the doubtful quintiles standards, Malaysia has the most unequal income distribution among the World Bank's eight HPAE. The income share for the richest fifth is more than 15 times greater than that of the poorest fifth.

Besides its faith in Suharto's good intentions and its acceptance of the NEP at face value, the Bank believes Taiwan's leaders saw a need for shared growth to avoid a repeat of three of the reasons for its defeat on the mainland: the KMT was too identified with landlords, it allowed unions to 'run out of control'[26] and government was beholden to vested interests. Disposing of Japanese landlords after 1945 was easy enough and made a contribution to greater equality. But the government's calculated repression of unions and its support for private and state-owned enterprises had quite the opposite effects. In Hong Kong, there has meanwhile been no improvement in the distribution of household income since 1971,[27] although reductions in average household size have had some positive effects. Changes in the employment structure connected to Hong Kong's transformation into an 'advanced' service sector economy have not meant improvements in income distribution. As the World Bank notes, an enlarged influx of unskilled workers from China in the 1970s and 1980s 'lowered the income share of the poorest quintile, thus contributing to greater inequality'.[28] Many of the service sector jobs created have been in low-paying trade or hotel work and the income gap between salary-earners and wage-earners increased during the 1980s as real salaries rose 65 per cent between 1985 and 1991 while real wages rose just 14 per cent from 1982 to 1991.[29]

Throughout the region, income distribution is adversely affected by a combination of active 'reform' policies and inaction in response to their consequences. Policies to stimulate growth by cutting taxes and subsidies, limiting welfare spending and privatising the state sector hit the poor hardest; so do neglect of the environmental consequences of growth, regional imbalances and the inequalities between and within rural and urban areas. There are no structural mechanisms to ensure that growth is, as the World Bank puts it, 'shared'. In the market Stalinist economies, greater inequality has even become a condition of growth, with the Vietnamese government increasing maximum income differentials from 1:3.5 to 1:13[30] and pay in Chinese state enterprises being tied increasingly to profitability. Any mechanisms that did exist to redistribute growth are being dismantled. Inflation in China – especially in the cities – continues to erode the living standards of those without assets or access to foreign exchange. Fudging of statistics elsewhere conceals the impact of inflation on the poor who are least able to protect themselves against it, and affects figures in economies as disparate as Sri Lanka, Singapore and China.[31]

TAXATION AND SUBSIDIES

We have already seen how the competition for foreign investment to spur growth rates has helped to lock Asian governments into a spiral of competitive corporate tax cuts. Pursuit of growth on the terms dictated by foreign and domestic capital distorts the tax system into one that works against the poor. As tax reliefs and tax cuts flow to corporations and their owners, either indirect taxes must rise or government expenditure has to be cut if governments are to satisfy the IMF/World Bank orthodoxy of reducing budget deficits.

Tax reliefs and exemptions are used, like all tax avoidance mechanisms, most effectively by the wealthy and powerful. Profits accumulated legitimately or otherwise in China, for instance, leave the country as part of the capital flight and then re-enter under the guise of 'foreign' capital, thus qualifying for tax exemptions. Flaws in the tax system have aggravated the chronic problem of revenue shortfall facing the Chinese government: deductions against tax for interest on loans have been maximised by huge overborrowing, revenues are siphoned off into subsidiaries or false claims are made for tax refunds. The most egregious examples of manipulation of the tax system for corporate and individual gain are from the Philippines, where the central government has chronic difficulties in increasing revenues to reduce the budget deficit. Exemptions were worth P25 billion in 1992 – equivalent to one third of the budget deficit.[32] Any attempt to extend taxation is greeted with an indignant outcry from affected interests, intensive lobbying and, usually, a blockage in the legislature. Lucio Tan, one of the richest men in the Philippines, has turned tax avoidance into a fine art with his tobacco businesses.[33] Likewise, a proposal to introduce a tax on soft drinks in 1992 was typical of the kind of measure that favours some specific interests at the expense of others: similarly, rival beer producers offered alternative taxation proposals for the brewing industry that would be to their own particular advantage. In all, only 53 per cent of personal income tax and 65 per cent of corporate tax is collected.[34]

Pakistan's taxation system has paralleled that of the Philippines in being used for sectional advantage. To tighten a system 'riddled with concessions and exemptions'[35] the caretaker administration of Mooen Qureshi selected some 23 'intervention points' in mid-1993 (such as importation or payment of interest), at which to try to collect more tax and reduce evasion and corruption. Pakistan also offers one of the worst examples of the superficial taxation of the rich at a personal level. As the Qureshi government revealed in a list of tax payments by prominent figures, the former Prime Minister Nawaz Sharif and his brother paid just US$150 between them in the 1992–93 tax year despite being members of one of the wealthiest business families in the country.[36] In all, barely 1 per cent of Pakistan's 110 million people pay tax, and redistributive measures, such as the wealth tax, can be brushed aside. Inspectors can be easily bought off, or the land register on which wealth assessments are based is tampered with and the scheme is unlikely to raise more than a few hundred million rupees.[37] In the Punjab, the Pakistani province where agriculture is most developed, income derived from it goes untaxed.

Efforts to extend taxation have been smothered elsewhere. Taiwan's popular Finance Minister, Wang Chien-Shien, was brought down on the land tax question in late 1992. In India, only 7 million of the 850 million population pay income tax despite the emergence of a widely heralded Indian 'middle class' supposedly numbering between 100 and 350 million.[38] Property and capital gains also go untaxed in much of Asia, sometimes as a result of foreign investors' pressure for tax-free capital gains in stock market transactions. Enormous gains from the rapid rise in Asia's stock markets during the 1990s have, therefore, accentuated existing inequalities in wealth by benefiting the small percentage of the population who own shares. The World Bank was even moved to criticise South Korea on these grounds and to accuse the government of an over-reliance on indirect taxes.

For the poor, tax rates rise steadily as reform policies and lower direct taxes translate into indirect taxes increase. China introduced a standard VAT at 17 per cent early in 1994, two years after Thailand, while both Pakistan and India also increased indirect taxes in their 1994–95 budgets. Direct taxes in Bangladesh have traditionally raised a below-average proportion of revenues and had little redistributive effect.[39] Corporate income tax yielded a diminishing share of government revenues in Sri Lanka from 1982-92, while the share of general sales turnover tax and licence revenue increased.[40] As pressure continues for further cuts in direct taxes, the indirect tax burden on the poor can be expected to continue growing.

Reform policies further erode the position of the poor by reducing subsidies, particularly in South Asia and the market Stalinist economies. The vulnerable governments of the region, under pressure from international agencies and donors to reduce budget deficits and implement thoroughgoing market reforms, are forced to cut subsidies on utility prices, staple foods and fertilisers, all of which hit the poor hardest. In less vulnerable South Korea, subsidies are still allocated to politically sensitive farmers, but Indian fertiliser subsidies have been the subject of steady pressure from international agencies since 1991. Pakistan was forced to concede gas and other utility price rises as a condition for IMF support; and critics claim that Sri Lanka has seen water tax imposed and fertiliser subsidies cut at the instigation of the World Bank.[41] The growing privatisation of infrastructure also increases the number of utilities which are charged at commercial rates to satisfy investors' demands for returns. Where, as in India, unexpectedly good economic performance has reduced dependence on the IMF, the urgency of subsidy cuts has diminished. But the trend is clear: Vietnam has had to cut subsidised provision of housing and health care to workers, though it has substituted pay rises.[42] China, too, has phased out nearly all price controls as part of its integration in the world economy.

WELFARE SERVICES

The Vietnamese example is illustrative of a broader attack on the provision of government social services in an ideological climate in which social spending is seen as a wasteful hindrance to growth. Tax cuts, spending on defence and infrastructure and measures to reduce budget deficits all eat away at such provision, scant as it is. The welfare state has been bitterly resisted by politicians and businessmen who share the *Far Eastern Economic Review*'s belief that 'Not least of Asia's comparative advantages is our lack of welfare states'.[43] Many people in Asia are consequently forced to rely on their children for welfare in later life, a state of affairs which indicates how little social progress has accompanied spectacular economic growth. In Singapore, one of the richest countries in Asia, a bill has been introduced by a nominated MP, Walter Woon, to give parents the right to sue their children for maintenance. With government support the bill was expected to become law.[44] Evidently Singaporean policymakers do not subscribe to the 'shared growth' dictum to the extent of sharing growth with all old people, regardless of whether they have children or not.

For the poor in Indochina and the Indian sub-continent, what limited provision does exist is meanwhile being scaled down or rationed out through market pricing. There have been honourable exceptions and there are dedicated professionals struggling to relieve ignorance and ill-health. Sri Lanka's record of rural welfare provision and development has been a major factor in preventing the kind of urban drift that has affected so many other Asian countries and compounded social problems by adding those of intractable urban poverty.[45] Bangladesh too has had a good record of improving rural health provision, especially immunisation, and has operated a drug policy that has been a model for other developing countries.

India, on the other hand, spent less in 1992–93 on education, health and welfare than on fertiliser subsidies.[46] Housing provision generally in Asia's

poorer countries, especially in the emerging mega-cities, is one of the worst
black spots of the region. Half the people of the Philippines lack adequate
shelter, food and clothing.[47] Half of those living in Dhaka[48] and Bombay[49]
do so in 'informal' housing or plain slums and a total of 600 million people
in South Asia are without access to safe water or sanitation.[50] Even where
urban redevelopment does occur the result can simply be to clear the poor
away from land earmarked for profitable redevelopment and to offer them
expensive new flats that are too far from employment sources in the informal sector of petty trading and casual labour.[51] In Jakarta the poor creep
back into the last few untenanted crevices of the city, lining its festering
canals with ramshackle structures that are a cruel parody of traditional
fishermen's houses.

Health care is also under threat in the market-Stalinist systems. Commercialisation is driving more Vietnamese people to rely on traditional medi-
cines[52] and the availability of better rewards in urban areas means that more
doctors in China prefer to work in the cities. A variety of pilot schemes,
rural health care proposals and plans to arrange for social insurance funded
jointly by the individual, state and enterprise were advanced after 1991, but
the existence of these guidelines has not yet secured welfare benefits for
many Chinese. As state systems are dismantled these societies will become
more like Pakistan[53] or the Philippines,[54] where half the population is likely
to live and die without ever consulting a doctor. Malnutrition in Burma already
ranks higher than Ethiopia. Rather than being concentrated in certain areas,
it is endemic, with one child tending to be affected in each family of six or
seven. TB treatment at US$24 with World Health Organisation assistance or
at four times that cost without it is prohibitively expensive.[55] Vietnam is
close behind Burma and Bangladesh in the percentage of children who are
underweight and stunted.[56]

In China state employees accustomed to a cradle-to-grave welfare system,
the 'iron rice bowl' of subsidised housing, health care and pensions, see it
cracking as state firms are pressured to reduce costs and help relieve the
growing state budget deficit. Workers' resistance and the authorities' squeam-
ishness about enforcing bankruptcies of chronically indebted enterprises have
kept the system in being, although employees taken on after 1986 have had
less security of tenure in their employment rights and have had to contribute to their pensions.[57] As employment and unemployment have both grown
outside the state sector large numbers of workers have been excluded from
these workplace-based benefits. Those in private enterprises in particular
have been left to seek health insurance, pension arrangements and housing
by themselves. In the same way the decollectivisation of agriculture has
ended collective social security funding and thrown peasants in China and
Vietnam alike into a lottery in which rich villages have been able to fund
services while poor ones cannot.

At the other end of Asia's socio-economic scale Singapore and Hong Kong have been praised by the World Bank for furthering equality through enlightened public housing policies. But, ignoring for a moment the motives of political control which helped formulate these extensive housebuilding programmes,[58] their contribution to greater equality is being undermined. In Hong Kong, prices of residential property rose 28 per cent in 1993 alone and handed an enormous windfall gain to the 43 per cent of people who own property.[59] Those in government-owned flats do not share in such gains, while Hong Kong's so-called 'sandwich class', too rich for subsidised government housing, too poor to buy, is left gasping. While Housing Development Board (HDB) apartments have contributed to a home ownership figure of over 90 per cent in Singapore,[60] a combination of housing charges, utility bills, Central Provident Fund contributions, education costs and taxes imposed by the People's Action Party government (known colloquially as the 'Pay And Pay' government) leaves them disgruntled. Even the showpiece CPF now stands revealed as an unprofitable self-help scheme rather than a social insurance programme. After years of paying interest on CPF savings below the rate of inflation the government now adjudges the compulsory minimum, the pool of savings on which workers are expected to draw in their retirement, to be inadequate. The government's response has been to allow a larger proportion of CPF accounts to be gambled on the stock market, to raise the retirement age, to increase the minimum sum that must be held in accounts on retirement and to endorse 'reverse mortgages' that will enable the elderly to draw cash by selling their flats while remaining in residence. By the time many Singaporeans die their assets will have been entirely consumed – a state of affairs the burghers of Zürich might not recognise immediately as consonant with the 'Swiss' standard of living which Prime Minister Goh has decreed as his objective. Welfare provision still leaves important gaps in other relatively affluent Asian economies. Pension provision only became an issue in Taiwan after the opposition Democratic Progressive Party (DPP) put it on the electoral agenda in 1993,[61] forcing the KMT to come up with its own proposals.

In South Korea housing remains a problem in urban areas: in the late 1980s there were 40 per cent more households than houses as housing supply continued to lag behind the growth of cities.[62] In 1991 less than 2 per cent of the elderly received social security,[63] and health spending was less than 2 per cent of GDP[64] while today the disabled are still left to depend on selling chewing gum or begging on subway trains in circumstances very little different to those of Vietnamese orphans selling postcards to tourists. The Malaysian government set aside M$900 million (US$350 million) as a fund for cheap housing,[65] as plantation companies made half-hearted gestures to improve housing for their workers. Despite an increase in the number of hospitals in Malaysia, the number of people per doctor (2656) still compares unfavourably with Pakistan (2111), India (2272) and the Philippines (1016) and is below the average (2850) for lower middle income countries as defined by the ADB.[66] Health spending is less than the allocation for defence under the Sixth Plan and the over-concentration of medical facilities in urban areas[67] has resulted in unequal provision across the country as a whole. The government sees commercialisation and privatisation as the way forward for all social services to avoid a rising burden on public spending.

RURAL AND URBAN INEQUALITY

The trends in health care are an illustration of a worsening overall rural/urban income divide on which is overlaid a growing inequality among both rural and urban dwellers. At the macro level, the effects of urban economic growth have largely overwhelmed the various palliative measures which have been used to counteract distortions in income distribution. From a rough parity with urban household incomes in 1975 farm incomes in South Korea fell to 89 per cent in 1986.[68] Farmers continue to desert the land, particularly as rural debt accumulates rapidly. In Taiwan incomes have fallen to 66 per cent of urban levels[69] and the majority of rural households earn only a fraction of their income from farm work. As well as increasing non-farm income, some rural households are subsidised by family members living in the cities. This effect is particularly noticeable in Thailand, where conditions of employment allow workers from rural areas to earn relatively higher urban incomes for periods of a few months. This kind of temporary migration is also becoming a feature of Vietnam. It does, however, become more difficult as jobs require higher skill levels and as employment becomes more regular and formalised. Family ties are bound to decay over generations and cross-subsidisation will not provide any long-term alleviation of rural insufficiencies. For the moment income from migrant workers abroad also provides a valuable additional source of income for rural households in the major labour-exporting countries. In the Philippines as much as 20 per cent of the population is now dependent in some way on this remittance income.[70]

Some new opportunities for generating income do arise through the expansion of towns and associated industrial growth in rural areas. This helped create a class of richer peasant households in China, before economic reforms reversed the improvement in rural/urban income ratios. (From 1:2.5 in 1978 they improved to 1:1.7 in 1985 before deteriorating to 1:2.3 in 1992, or even 1:4 if urban subsidies and rural *ad hoc* levies are taken into account.[71]) In Thailand there are signs of growth in Chiang Mai, Khorat and other upcountry towns, offering the prospect of reducing Bangkok's 50 per cent share of national income. But widespread industrial development outside major cities is still the exception rather than the norm in Asia and most efforts to redress the divide have taken the form of measures to alleviate rural poverty, as in Malaysia and Sri Lanka. Malaysian schemes have been small scale, like the *Amanah Ikhtiar Malaysia*[72] or have been of diminishing effectiveness like the Federal Land Development Authority.[73] The Sri Lankan Janasaviya programme has focused on the creation of income-generating activities for the poor, although its staggered implementation has meant that the programme will take a long time to reach all intended beneficiaries. In Bangladesh, the Grameen Bank, a pioneering micro-credit lending institution, supplies the tiny sums, averaging US$75, which are needed to establish small-scale rural enterprises. The bank now reaches 1.4 million borrowers, of whom 92 per cent are women, but to guarantee repayments it depends on a degree of social cohesion amongst its clients that takes time to instill.[74] Grameen Bank is often highlighted in Asia because official rural credit provision programmes have failed and, with a few exceptions like Bank Rakyat Indonesia, commercial banks have considered it uneconomic to lend to small borrowers in rural areas.

While schemes of this nature mature slowly agricultural change is transforming the structure of the rural economy in ways that are often inimical to better income distribution, both in relation to the urban sector and within the rural sector. The strategic acceptance of the relative decline of agriculture in Malaysia has meant a deterioration in income relative to the urban sector. In other cases the limits of agricultural growth – whether from decollectivisation or the wider application of the Green Revolution discussed in Chapter 1 – mean that increases in the relative income shares of rural areas have been reversed as these gains subside. In the 30 years after 1961 India saw the rural percentage of its population fall just 8 per cent, from 81 per cent to 73 per cent; the share of GNP produced by this section of the population meanwhile fell from 45 per cent to 30 per cent.[75] In the absence of further large gains in productivity across the region, the rural share in income can be expected to continue falling faster than the rural share of the population. The process is driven as much by urban growth as it is by the limits of agricultural productivity. Rapid industrial growth, for example in Thailand, Indonesia and Malaysia, has helped to create greater income disparities. These are affecting countries at an early stage of industrialisation as the construction industry in Hanoi, for instance, brings in farmers from uneconomic plots in the Red River delta or the carpet industry in Nepal draws more workers from precarious agriculture to the Kathmandu Valley.

Even where productivity gains are made in rural areas the benefits are not evenly shared. The mechanisation of agriculture in the Philippines, for instance, has meant the displacement of tenants and the creation of a rural proletariat. In place of sharecropping relationships, in which a bumper harvest or sustained rises in productivity would mean additional income for tenants, agricultural workers paid a fixed rate do not share in the gains or the good years. Surplus rural labour drifts into an equally ill-paid rural service sector.[76] Likewise, combine harvesting in Malaysia cut paddy wage labour by 44 per cent and reduced the opportunities for small scale tenancy, or, as in Thailand, land rights are not recognised and peasants are forcibly turned into wage labourers.[77] The greater crop intensity possible with new agricultural methods can sometimes mean more work for the rural proletariat but has to be balanced against the disappearance of paternalistic relationships which could help tide peasants through difficult times.[78] For those peasants who seek to share in the gains of the Green Revolution as small producers, costly inputs and limited access to capital will all too often result in indebtedness when a crop eventually fails or market conditions turn adverse. Poor farmers – who need cash quickly – are unable to wait for better prices before selling their crop. Larger-scale farmers are typically better able to utilise new technology and methods, and to obtain cheaper inputs, accentuating income differentials within agriculture. Lastly, population growth in rural areas can mean falling *per capita* income where, as in Bangladesh, the land frontier cannot be extended or, where, as in the Punjab, gains from the Green Revolution have come to an end but the population keeps growing. Birth control methods are often slower to reach rural areas and the traditions of needing additional labour both for present needs and to provide for the old age of parents encourages population growth.

Urbanisation and labour-intensive industrialisation do, of course, create opportunities, particularly for women workers. Without relatively well paid jobs, it would be impossible to cross-subsidise poorer relations in the countryside out of surplus income. Women who remain single in the cities can also avoid the double burden of wage labour and household labour which prevails in rural areas. But, at the same time as more people are able to join the formal urban sector, economic development destroys informal sector employment and pushes people into the urban underclass. The process is vividly illustrated in Lea Jellinek's study of Jakarta, *The Wheel of Fortune*, which shows how occupations like petty street trading, the driving of *becaks* (pedal-powered rickshaws) and cottage industries were obliterated in the city centre from the mid-1970s onwards[79] by a combination of regulation and increasing consumer sophistication. The availability of piped water, for instance, undercuts sales of drinking water while at the same time subsidising the better off. The same processes can be seen at work today in, for instance, Hanoi and Karachi. Formal employment also tends to mean a greater insistence on educational experience, often to the detriment of the poor.

The emergence of an urban underclass in poverty is the counterpart of rural proletarianisation. In all, perhaps 50 per cent of Indonesia's urban population live in poverty,[80] just as 50 per cent of Dhaka and Bombay residents live in slums. Urban drift accentuates the problem, bringing millions of young people into Asia's cities. It is apparent in the numbers of street children – anything from 75 000 in Manila to over a million nationally in the Philippines[81] – and in the rise in prostitution. Officially, prostitution under the age of 18 is banned in Thailand and the total number working in the sex industry is 150 000: in reality there may be as many as 800 000 children[82] among a total of 2.5 million prostitutes. That figure includes up to 20 000 Burmese and the kidnapping of young women from neighbouring Laos and Southern China is becoming increasingly common in order to satisfy the demand of Thailand's sex industry. With the number of HIV infections in Thailand growing at 400–600 daily,[83] the risks to health in prostitution are considerable. According to UNICEF, India has the largest number of child prostitutes in the region, and Taiwan, Sri Lanka and the Philippines also have significant numbers.[84] The sex industry in South Korea has long been supported by the presence of US military bases.

Women among the migrants drawn to Canton in Southern China by the search for work – over a million annually at the Chinese New Year holiday – have to choose between factory work or prostitution or returning home. They are among the estimated 150 million former peasants roaming China in search of employment[85] and drifting into crime and casual labour. While official unemployment in China in 1994 was 2.6 per cent, actual urban unemployment may be nearer 20 per cent.[86] Hundreds of thousands of demobilised soldiers contribute to a similar stratum in Vietnam, where urban unemployment runs as high as 22 per cent and state enterprises have already shed 800 000 jobs.[87] Economic reform policies in market-Stalinist and South Asian economies which cut subsidies from state enterprises precipitate more people into this urban underclass.

REGIONAL DISTRIBUTION

The lure which draws non-Cantonese speakers to gamble on the labour market in Guangdong province every year is the chance of higher earnings in one of the most economically buoyant parts of China. In common with other rapidly-growing countries in Asia, China has seen its regional distribution of income badly skewed towards certain areas. In 1991 seven of the 10 most prosperous provinces – those with *per capita* incomes above US$300 – were on China's east coast and two of the other three (Heilongjiang and Jilin) were North-Eastern provinces. Guangdong and neighbouring Fujian, facing Taiwan, were two of the four fastest-growing between 1985 and 1991.[88] Such growth is the natural consequence of the Chinese policy of encouraging development first in the coastal Special Enterprise Zones. It leads to classic symptoms of distorted development: bottlenecks, infrastructure shortfalls, and conspicuous consumption while basic needs go unsatisfied elsewhere in the country.

In the absence of tax or other redistributive mechanisms regional income distribution in Asia has got seriously out of kilter. Malaysia's federal structure is sometimes commended for encouraging a more even spread of development across the country as state authorities compete for projects. Penang, for instance, has drawn in the electronics industry with a combination of incentives and other support to industry. To sceptics, however, the dispersal of investment simply represents different deals struck with Malaysia's sultans. They point out that the uneven distribution of natural resources has resulted in varying experiences of growth. Moreover, the federal government has used its powers to hamper development in those states ruled by the opposition – Kelantan in the North and, until early 1994, Sabah in the East[89] – to remind voters of the risks in rejecting governments aligned with the dominant United Malay National Organisation (UMNO). It is also accused by critics – especially in Sabah – of giving state governments too small of a share of national resource royalties.

In India state governments have enjoyed considerable autonomy, albeit with growing interference from politicians in New Delhi concerned about its effects on the distribution of power at the centre. Autonomy in the economic sphere has increased as the centre has scaled back its commitment to planning and abandoned, for instance, subsidies to coal transportation that ensured the same price throughout India. In the absence of intervention economic growth has tended to concentrate in particular cities and states. Bangalore has prospered as the centre of a strong Indian software industry; Burnpur and other steelmaking cities are struggling; garment manufacture and an enormous film industry both thrive in Bombay; automobile plants in Madras boost production but are threatened by power and water shortages. India can be broadly divided broadly into 'high speed' and 'low speed' regions.[90] The high speed regions include Punjab and Haryana, where the gains from the Green Revolution have been greatest, industrial Gujarat and Maharashtra, and parts of the Southern states of Tamil Nadu and Karnataka. The low speed regions comprise most of Uttar Pradesh, Bihar, West Bengal, Orissa and Madhya Pradesh. In Pakistan the distinctions are between, on the one hand, the Punjab, where agriculture has underlain prosperity and Lahore has a rising industrial base, together with the commercial city of Karachi and the recently more prosperous North West Frontier Province, and, on the other hand, the backward rural areas of Sindh and Baluchistan. Interference by the federal government has been chiefly at the political level to secure pliant provincial administrations. The main economic grievance is held by Baluchis, who resent the exploitation of the province's gas resources, the purchase price of which was held down for a long time to provide a cheap source of energy to consumers nationally. Wider political issues arising out of uneven economic development in South Asia are considered in Chapter 7.

In other parts of Asia regional economic differences exist within a unitary political framework. Dissatisfaction is manifest in claims of discrimination against particular regions. Every President of South Korea since 1961 has come from the North Kyongsang region, a fact widely resented in the South-Western Cholla provinces. For many years Cholla was the stronghold of the opposition leader Kim Dae-Jung and many of its people believe that it has been singled out for economic neglect and political repression, notably in the Kwangju massacre in 1980. When regional income figures were belatedly released in the early 1990s they showed the area to be doing relatively badly. Although President Roh Tae-Woo's administration planned to upgrade infrastructure in the West to assist the Cholla provinces[91] the opening of the South Korean rice market to foreign imports will have a particularly sharp impact in the region and the sense of discrimination will persist.

Thailand is notable for having more than 50 per cent of GNP produced in one city, Bangkok. There have been efforts to refocus growth on the Eastern seaboard around the port of Laem Chabang through a programme costing US$1 billion, though this area has effectively become an extension of Bangkok. Tax incentives have been used to spread development further beyond the capital and have met with some success as industry relocates in search of cheaper labour and minimum wages that are 20 per cent lower. The North East, where monthly income is less than a third of Bangkok levels, remains the poorest region. Efforts to provide it with industries processing raw materials from Southern China and Laos have not yet produced decisive results. Progress towards greater equality of income among regions is very much in the balance, depending in large measure on the fate of the Chuan Leekpai government, which came into office in 1992 and made it a priority.[92] The Philippines has a similar distortion of industry and economic activity towards Metro Manila but the fastest growth is in the provinces. The patchiness of this prosperity will be accentuated by the greater tax and spending powers recently allotted to provincial governors. Cebu is growing at twice the national average; Mindanao contains such pockets of progress as the cities of General Santos and Cagayan D'Oro; and the government's 'master plan' for tourism also looks to encourage development at selected sites outside the capital. As these pockets develop poorer provinces will be left further behind. This pattern of selective growth is also apparent in Burma, where Mandalay is at the heart of a prosperity based on smuggling. In Vietnam Ho Chi Minh City has taken the lion's share of foreign investment – 40 per cent – and produces a third of the national industrial output. In the North 16 million peasants in the Red River delta each produce on average only 46 per cent of the rice grown by their counterparts in the fertile Mekong delta in the south[93] while Central Vietnam has missed out on increasing inward investment.[94]

In Indonesia it is not so much a single province as an island that has prospered most. Java has attracted 65 per cent of all investment into Indonesia. Jakarta and Surabaya in East Java are the two largest industrial cities, while the outlying fringes of what is sometimes regarded as a Javanese empire have seen less development. In Aceh, at the northern tip of Sumatra, resentment stemming from disputes over natural gas revenues fuels an active separatist movement. In Irian Jaya (West Papua), at the other end of the archipelago, more than three-quarters of the province's sub-districts have over half their population living in poverty. For the Eastern provinces as a whole this applies to over 40 per cent of sub-districts.[95] Manufacturing there accounts for just 5.6 per cent of GDP, against over 20 per cent nationally. In Sulawesi real incomes are 65 per cent of those in Java and the elaborate Javanese bureaucratic machine superimposed on the provinces is little but a wasteful encumbrance.[96] As foreign investment drives Java's economy forward the remoter provinces see their relative positions further eroded.

THE ENVIRONMENT

The environmental consequences of growth highlight powerfully the ways in which the poor are exposed to an unfair burden of its costs. They are least able to protect themselves against air or water pollution. Two million people in Hong Kong are affected by air pollution;[97] in Seoul the sulphur dioxide level is five times that in Taipei,[98] one of the most polluted cities in Asia where the large number of scooter riders suffer daily doses of airborne pollution. The less developed countries have big pollution problems too: in the Philippines police make spasmodic attempts to deal with 'smoke belchers' - overcrowded decrepit buses – while dustcarts are emblazoned with a slogan typical of the gesture politics of the Philippines, declaring them to be part of the 'Presidential Task Force on the Environment'. The owners of 'Jeepneys' – the gaudy converted vehicles that provide much of the public transport in the Philippines – are seldom able to afford new engines or good quality petrol, while the upsurge in motorised transport in South Asia is bringing more vehicles propelled by heavily-polluting two-stroke engines on to the roads. In Thailand, airborne lead shaves four points off the average IQ of children by the age of seven.[99] Unsafe water is commonplace, especially in the new mega-cities. Karachi already has 30 per cent less water than it needs with a population of 11 million. By 2002 that population will have reached 19 million.[100] The Orangi Pilot Project, which has brought drains and social services to parts of a district of Karachi inhabited by a million people, is justly renowned in Pakistan and beyond, not least because it is so unusual.[101] In Taipei the problem is not so much the water as the buildings: since 1992 more and more have turned out to have been built with irradiated steel, poisoning workers who have spent a lifetime buying their apartments.[102]

The environmental consequences of growth extend far beyond dangerously polluted cities. Industrial damage to the environment is being addressed in Taiwan, but the measures are frequently circumvented by illegal dumping of waste, sometimes through secret pipe networks, while blackmailers use the regulations to extort money from companies which fear exposure of their practices. In factories, occupational diseases are born more heavily by production workers, just as it is agricultural workers who suffer the damaging effects of exposure to pesticides.[103] As enforcement gradually restrains heavy polluters in the more developed economies the effect is simply to transfer the problem to neighbouring countries with less stringent regulations. China is a favourite destination, with lax environmental rules and an easy-going attitude to the health and safety of workers. OECD countries also take advantage of the weaker Asian economies and see them as an easy dumping ground for environmental waste.

The poor are also the chief victims – and seldom the beneficiaries – of the huge energy projects being devised to provide the power to sustain future growth. In Malaysia, India and China hydroelectric schemes involve the flooding of vast expanses of the country. The Three Gorges dam project in China could lead to the displacement of up to 1.6 million people, whom the Chinese authorities may then resettle in Tibet as a neat way of continuing the suffocation of Tibetan culture by the transfer of large number of ethnic Han Chinese. Prompted by disquiet about the project nearly a third of the delegates to China's rubber-stamp national parliament, the National People's Congress, were emboldened to vote against it or abstain when it came up for a vote in 1992. But with Prime Minister Li Peng backing the project it is likely to be pushed through if he and his supporters remain a force in the leadership. India's equally controversial Sardar Sarovar dam in the Narmada valley also continues to enjoy high-level support from Prime Minister Narasimha Rao, despite opposition from his own environment ministry. The World Bank, growing increasingly jittery about the project, began insisting on environmental and resettlement conditions in exchange for the last US$170 million of the US$450 million to be lent towards the cost of the dam.[104] Rather than give a full account of how it intends to resettle 250 000 displaced people, the Indian government rejected the World Bank's conditions. If the dam is completed, rich farmers in Gujarat are most likely to benefit from the irrigation schemes associated with it. Since independence in India 30 million people have been displaced by development schemes.[105] Rural environmental damage thereby adds to the drift towards the cities and, in turn, to greater urban pollution problems.

The effects of pollution are also felt in the fishing industry, as industrial and mining wastes, fertilisers and pesticides wash into rivers and coastal waters. As inshore fish stocks dwindle, poorer fishermen without the capital to purchase engines for their boats or to set up in fishpond production are left with a shrinking source of income. The aquaculture boom across the region presents a further threat, displacing fishermen, destroying spawning grounds and poisoning the soil of neighbouring fields, whether in Taiwan, Malaysia or the Philippines. Six or seven million people in the Philippines have depended on fishing for their livelihood, but production is becoming increasingly capital intensive, thereby marginalising the smaller producers. Export-oriented aquaculture also deprives local consumers of a cheap source of protein.

Environmental despoilation in the quest to extract more resources often tends to mean intrusion on the land and rights of indigenous peoples. Prime Minister Mahathir of Malaysia has been strident and acerbic in defending development in Sarawak, arguing that once given the chance of education and a better living standard, people such as the Penans have no desire to return to a 'primitive' life. Even this stark choice is, however, denied to such people in Malaysia and elsewhere. Logging companies are concerned with profits, not the welfare of indigenous peoples. Local politicians are more anxious to share those profits than to protect rights: Sarawak environment minister James Wong controls one of the state's biggest timber companies[106] and two of the sons of chief minister Abdul Taib Mahmud are leading shareholders in the company planning to build a dam on the Rejang River that will displace 8000 people and flood an area larger than Singapore. Meanwhile, up to 80 per cent of Malaysia's *orang asli*, its aboriginal inhabitants, live below the poverty line[107] and are often unable to prove the existence of land titles in face of developers.

The story is a familiar one across the region: increasing marginalisation, loss of rights, cultural obliteration and high levels of poverty. The aboriginals of Taiwan, known as 'mountain people', have seen their land exploited and sold to developers and their culture suppressed (except as a tourist attraction), while education and health care are neglected and they have few prospects of employment outside the most dangerous occupations.[108] The tribal minorities of India have suffered equally badly from both the social control typified in the vasectomy campaigns of the 1970s and economic marginalisation resulting from the loss of land and forest, so much so that there are now demands in central India for a separate tribal state – Jharkhand – in which their rights would be respected.[109] The Igorot, the Bagobo and other peoples among a total of 80 cultural minorities in the Philippines fight a constant battle against encroachment by loggers, as well as having to contend with destructive mining.[110] The same forms of oppression have characterised the market-Stalinist economies: the Vietnamese government has invested little in the provision of services to its 8 million citizens who belong to ethnic minorities in the mountains; the long record of ethnic insurgency in Burma has turned minority areas into war zones in which little state-sponsored development has been possible, if it was ever intended.[111]

WEALTH AND LEGITIMACY

In the absence of redistributive mechanisms growth creates a pattern of consumption in which the wants of the rich are satisfied ahead of the needs of
the poor. This textbook criticism of capitalism is powerfully illustrated in
contemporary Asia. The counterpart of inadequate housing, sanitation or hospital
care is the burgeoning of luxury imports and the rapid growth of leisure
facilities tailored to the rich.

Sales of luxury automobiles are expanding, with Rolls-Royce selling record
numbers of cars in China, while Mercedes is assembling its cars in the Philippines and India to satisfy local demand. Casinos have become an indicator
of the surplus cash of the rich. In Malaysia gambling absorbs up to US$3
billion a year (the highest level in ASEAN[112]); the first casino in the Philippines has opened at Subic Bay;[113] and in Macau the government's revenues from gambling rose by 35 per cent in 1992 as mainland Chinese headed
for the territory's eight casinos.[114] Only one casino exists in South Asia, at
Kathmandu's Soaltee Oberoi hotel, where rich Indians no longer able to
visit their former playground in Kashmir come to drink Johnny Walker Black
Label whisky and play the tables.

Golf courses are meanwhile carved out of jungles, farmland and parks
alike across the region. Membership fees serve to exclude almost all locals
– at the Song Be course near Ho Chi Minh City, for example, where they
amount to between 25 000 and 30 000 US dollars, only 1 per cent of the
members are Vietnamese.[115] Such fees can also provide a convenient way of
passing bribes to government officials or company officers, who can sell
membership on through vibrant secondary markets. In China membership
can be bought for around HK$250 000 (US$35 000), in Thailand for up to
US$40 000.[116] On the Eastern seaboard of Thailand inadequate basic infra-
structure hampers industrial and economic development, but 35 golf courses
are nevertheless under construction. Indonesia and Malaysia are building
with the same urgency.

In Singapore government policy has contrived to turn even a standard
motor car into a luxury item by allowing a free market in the Certificates of
Entitlement which are required before residents can buy cars. After the stock
market boom of 1993 the price of CoEs on large cars rose to S$70 000
(US$42 000).[117] When combined with the cost of a basic vehicle the CoE
puts the cost of a car at a minimum of S$90 000, nearly four times annual
per capita income. Although Prime Minister Goh Chok Tong talks of creating a 'Swiss' standard of living, in reality what Singaporeans experience is
a Swiss cost of living, dragged up by indirect taxation and the purchasing
power of the rich.

Inequalities of wealth and income have long existed in Asian societies,
irrespective of the form and duration of colonial rule. For all its iniquities

colonial rule did seek to justify inequality by reference to the 'development' or *mission civilisatrice* that it was bringing. In the Indian subcontinent, Indochina, Indonesia and Malaysia colonial rulers also preserved monarchies and hereditary privileges to help legitimate social and economic inequality. Many of the privileges were attached to land ownership, with attendant obligations (however superficial). The inequality in the new Asia of the 1980s and 1990s is less encrusted with traditional justifications, inherited rights or spurious notions of racial superiority. It is also much more visible, in the cars, the apartment blocks and the luxury hotels in the heart of cities, cheek by jowl with the urban poor. It rests much more on the legitimacy of the market, the supposition that wealth is attainable by dint of hard work, inventiveness and a slice of luck. Such notions are plausible while growth continues to deliver evidence of social mobility: graduation from the insecurities of the informal sector to the security of regular employment; from manual labour to middle class status and income and on towards the privileges enjoyed by expatriates and the internationally mobile rich. As growth falters and social mobility begins to be choked off, however, the legitimacy of the 'new wealth' could be undermined more quickly than that of a traditional society.

In the market-Stalinist societies inequality has been growing more rapidly as more resources are allocated through the market. By 1988 inequality in China was reportedly greater than it had been in Taiwan in 1978.[118] Bureaucrats profit from obtaining market prices for the resources over which they exercise residual controls, yet they do so while depending on the shrunken legitimacy of the Communist party. Its formal commitment to social and economic equality is visibly at odds with a reform process in which cadres' offspring are the biggest individual beneficiaries. In the late 1980s Deng Xiaoping's son Deng Pufang controlled the largest of the 'attaché-case companies', trading companies parasitically feeding off the dual price system.[119] Four of Deng Xiaoping's children or their spouses had interests in 14 companies in Hong Kong.[120] Other children of senior political and military figures – the so-called 'princelings' – have participated in money-making activities, many of them from berths in CITIC (China International Trust and Investment Corporation). Peking connections are used to overawe local officials in land transfers. Other lower-level officials have been caught up in the burgeoning number of financial scams perpetrated at the expense of anxious savers. More than 100 were implicated in swindling savers out of 1 billion yuan in a junk bond racket run by the Great Wall Machinery and Electronics High Technology Industrial Corporation.[121]

Unlike much of the corruption which has existed for centuries in China, this kind has become short-termist, at both higher and lower levels. It is no longer a case of officials increasing their income on a permanent basis by demanding additional payments to facilitate the operation of a system – something which is accepted, albeit grudgingly, by people who recognise it as a necessary evil to be endured to get things done. Rather it is the maximisation of income by officials who know that neither discrepancies between market and state-controlled prices nor their influence and connections in the productive sector will last. Illegal charges for selling railway tickets, changing residence, handling luggage or even renting desks in schools, or rural grievances including confiscations, refusal of permissions, unfair pricing and withholding of payments are not about facilitating matters, but are sheer profiteering which makes people's lives harder. Ordinary people become the victims in Vietnam in the same way, as officials look to profit from the short-term opportunities of economic transition. Jobs, hospital treatment, education, visas and licences are all subject to bribes, and abuses are worst at the lowest level where local Communist Party bosses wield the greatest power.

The growing presence of foreign investment throughout the region adds to inequality, by dividing Asian societies sharply into sections with or without contacts with the world economy. Although working conditions in Export Processing Zones and other foreign-owned factories are often harsh the regularity of employment they offer is preferable to the unpredictability of making a living in the informal sector. Added to this is the ability, particularly in the market-Stalinist economies, to extract other benefits from access to foreign exchange – especially in the tourist industry – or to acquire skills. Such benefits are, however, often cornered by officials or ex-officials, who trade their knowledge of market-Stalinist systems for jobs as consultants or managers of enterprises established or purchased by foreign investors. In Cambodia, officials profited hugely from the influx of UN personnel, whether by renting villas or conniving at the theft of vehicles. The opportunities opened by foreign involvement in Asian economies are welcomed in the same way as other avenues for social mobility. Where, however, these opportunities are unfairly distributed there is the potential for dissatisfaction.

One of the earliest forms of foreign interaction with many of the economies of the region was the growth of networks of Chinese traders from the sixteenth century onwards. These communities have often been the object of violent struggles over the distribution of income. During colonial times the Spanish and Dutch authorities encouraged massacres of the Chinese in Manila and Batavia (now Jakarta) as they grew envious of richer members of the community.[122] In the post-war period governments in South East Asia have had to perform a balancing act with regard to Chinese capitalists. Ties between government and capital mean that contracts, assets and monopolies flow to favoured individuals and companies, whether ethnically Chinese or from a Malay, Thai, Filipino or other background. These governments are also aware that cronyism, regardless of its ethnic dimension, can be a focus for opposition, as it became under Marcos. In Indonesia references to 'conglomerates' have become a proxy for direct criticism of the Suharto family and its ties to favoured entrepreneurs.

In these circumstances restrictions on Chinese businesses become a convenient way of deflecting criticism from the existence of state-business relations *per se*. Orchestrated ethnic conflict and its equally orchestrated resolution is intended to substitute for the emergence of class conflict. Such restrictions are often nominal and easily circumvented, or are left unenforced once a gesture has been made. Thus discrimination barred the Chinese from certain sectors of economic activity in the Philippines – especially retailing, in which they were supposed to have innate and unfair advantages – though it did not prevent the rise of successful Chinese-owned businesses. More recently President Ramos coaxed six prominent Filipino-Chinese into supporting a campaign for greater social responsibility by business, a token concession which it was easier to extract from businessmen aware that an ethnic card could be played against their wealth. In Indonesia Suharto became conscious of concern at his role in nurturing ethnic Chinese businesses and, in 1990, made the gesture of telling 31 leading Chinese businessmen to divest 25 per cent of their equity holdings to co-operatives.[123] This alarmed some Chinese but temporarily placated critics. In reality, given his reliance on Chinese capital, Suharto is loath to risk provoking a serious capital flight and the measure has gone largely unenforced. To offset Chinese wealth visible *pribumi* capitalists are being built up as countervailing examples of prosperity, though many are linked to the Suharto family. Malaysia's NEP, similarly, has used the existence of wealthy Chinese individuals to justify buttressing ethnic Malay entrepreneurs in the same way, while UMNO uses anti-Chinese propaganda to bolster its electoral following. In short, concessions by Chinese capitalists are required as the price for the continuation of capitalism. Only in Thailand, where the assimilation of the Chinese into commercial and banking circles and the population at large has been the most successful, are ethnic Chinese interests largely immune from this kind of pressure.

CONTESTED INEQUALITY

This kind of manoeuvring shows that the social consequences of unfair income distribution are not lost on political leaders. As Indonesian Science and Technology Minister B. J. Habibie noted early in 1994: 'If you have only economic growth and ignore the fair distribution of opportunities and income, you will create internal stress'.[124] Allowing for the heavily encrypted nature of any remark by an Indonesian politician at the centre of the country's subterranean power struggles, Habibie's remark is incontrovertible.

The stress which he predicts will take several forms. Inequalities are not accepted as a necessary condition for and byproduct of economic growth, but are at the heart of rising economic and political conflict. The commonest nexus for this conflict is in the struggles for higher wages, better working conditions and the defence of jobs. Whether or not articulated in the framework of wider social objectives, this kind of struggle is about the distribution of income. So, too, are some of the regional conflicts which we will examine in more detail in Chapters 4 to 7. Demands for an end to corrupt practices – especially those which operate at the direct expense of workers and peasants – are part of the same contest.

The pattern of these conflicts is far from uniform across Asia. South Korea, one of the most economically developed countries in the region, has seen some of the most savage battles between trade unions and the employers and government, while at the other end of the Asian development scale the resistance to job losses in the public sector in South Asia has been just as determined. Struggles can accumulate steadily over a number of years or break out suddenly in response to arbitrary actions on the part of government or employers.

The industrial disputes in South Korea between 1987 and 1989 were the culmination of a long build-up of demands during years of repression and rapid industrial growth. Strike action spread quickly among the *chaebols* and white collar workers in education, health, banking and other sectors, all of them in defiance of the legal requirement for 'cooling-off' periods. The duration of strikes increased during the period and demands broadened from questions of wages and union recognition to questions of industrial democracy and profit-sharing.[125] Although disputes have not been so widespread during the 1990s South Korean unions do still confront the *chaebols* in large scale strike action, as at Hyundai in the middle of 1993 and 1994, and issues of industrial democracy continue to feature.[126] The organisation of workers outside the government-funded Federation of Korean Trade Unions is growing in the search for effective means of pressing demands.[127]

The structure of industry in South Korea has contributed to this pattern of action. A small number of major companies operating plants with big workforces create the right conditions for mass organisation and mobilisation. In Taiwan, in contrast, the concentration of small and medium-sized firms is less conducive to union organisation, especially since unions are officially banned in workplaces employing fewer than 30 people.[128] Unionisation in Hong Kong, as we saw in Chapter 2, is limited by the lack of legal protection afforded to strikers and has also been retarded by the similarly small scale of many manufacturing establishments. Organisation in the growing service sector is always difficult. In Singapore the grip of the official NTUC has been powerful enough to ensure that no independent trade union emerges. Struggle over income shares in Singapore has been best reflected in the decay of support for the People's Action Party. Its share of the vote has fallen towards 50 per cent as disenchantment with its economic policies gradually affects more and more voters.

Indonesia's experience of industrial struggle over wages is following South Korea's more closely than that of the other NIEs. The unofficial SBSI founded in 1992, which now has 250 000 members, has been far more active than the official SPSI in leading demands for better wages. It was seeking an Rp 7000 (US$3.5) daily minimum wage against the official level, in early 1994, of 3100–3800 Rupiah (the rate varies across the country). This demand was one of the factors which brought workers onto the streets of Medan in Sumatra in the most serious recent outbreak of economic unrest in Indonesia. The death of prominent labour activists, in Sumatra and Java, has been another radicalising factor. Workers were also emboldened by the threat that the US would withdraw GSP trade privileges from Indonesia on the grounds of its poor labour record. Aware of the sensitivity the government would need to show in the handling of protests, trade unionists pushed hard in 1994 for improved wages and conditions, with the number of strikes rising sharply early in the year. Given favourable circumstances of this sort, Indonesian workers are clearly ready to engage in struggle for a better share of growing national income.

There is potential for conflict on similar lines in Thailand further in the future. At present unionisation levels are low and many workers who migrate only temporarily to urban centres do not become a permanent part of the workforce committed to a long-term struggle to improve wages and conditions. Given, however, considerable evidence of wages below minimum levels and the threat of redundancies in industries like textiles, the issues exist around which to organise. In Malaysia, meanwhile, the battle is still for the basic legal right to organise independent unions.

Conflict has been more in evidence in foreign-owned factories in China and Vietnam. Despite better pay, labour discipline often tends to be harsher and an awareness of the profitability of foreign-owned enterprises has led workers to push for higher wages and improved conditions.[129] Over 70 per cent of foreign-funded or controlled enterprises in Guangdong, for instance, abused workers' rights or violated the law[130] and over a thousand disputes affected the mostly foreign-owned firms in the Shenzhen Special Enterprise Zone over a two year period in 1992–94.[131] More than 12 000 disputes were recorded in China in 1993, against a little over 8000 in 1992,[132] and the authorities were forced to promise an investigation of foreign-owned firms to counter charges of exploitation, as even the tame state-controlled All China Federation of Trade Unions complained of foreign employers openly exploiting workers. Legislation was also introduced in 1994 to make unions mandatory in foreign-invested enterprises and to encourage unionisation in township enterprises. Such unions would be part of the official movement and designed to head off the emergence of independent unions,[133] albeit this is a minor trend as yet.[134] The same thinking partly explains new legislation to outlaw child labour and set locally-determined minimum wages.[135]

The upsurge in industrial struggles has been one element in a wider conflict over distribution in China. The search for 'scapegoats of frustration'[136] among urban dwellers often leads to identification of the wrong targets: 'private households', workers in profitable collective enterprises and peasants. While these groups arouse resentment, the insecurities of their income and work conditions and the conditions of peasants not in contact with the urban areas (that is, those without a surplus to sell) make their actual situation on average far less enviable than it appears. The various members of what Anita Chan has called the 'new moneyed élite' have been the real winners in China's economic growth – the '10 000 dollar households', owners of 'private enterprises', lessee-managers of state and collective enterprises, and officials and their offspring benefiting from arbitraging between the regulated and the market economy. The last of these categories is becoming the target of more resentment as their parasite role in the economy becomes increasingly clear. This was particularly apparent in the peasant unrest which shook China in 1993, coming to a head in June that year when more than 10 000 peasants stormed offices in Renshou County, Sichuan. Protests focusing on the taxes, levies and fees charged by local bureaucrats affected more than a dozen provinces.[137] Arbitrary imposts have added to the dissatisfaction of seeing incomes decline relative to those in the cities. Corruption itself was also one of the main issues in the Tiananmen Square protests of 1989, heightened by the effects of inflation on urban incomes.

The Chinese leadership is clearly fearful of triggering further large scale unrest by forcing reductions in subsidies to state enterprises to the point of causing large numbers of bankruptcies, for fear that workers in state enterprises will join with those in foreign-owned companies. In Vietnam, similarly, privatisation has been delayed because of workers' determination to resist the loss of jobs and income that this would entail. A willingness to defend jobs is also apparent in the public sector in South Asia, and even in a more developed economy like Taiwan. The transfer of resources to the private sector which the international lending agencies are urging will not be a completely straightforward affair. Similarly-inspired measures to increase oil prices in the Philippines were defeated after a mass mobilisation early in 1994, and Indian farmers have been resisting subsidy cuts in the same spirit.

4 Veiled Authoritarianism: Indonesia, Malaysia and Singapore

Malaysia, Singapore and Indonesia all claim to be democracies on the grounds that they hold periodic elections. Yet democracy as operated in Malaysia, for example, has been described variously as 'cutaneous'[1] or 'controlled',[2] creating a 'spectator culture',[3] while Sukarno's term 'Guided Democracy' might be applied to all three. As used by Sukarno, it meant personal, dictatorial rule scarcely masked by any formalities: Suharto, Mahathir and Lee Kuan Yew have dressed up just the same dictatorial behaviour with a more elaborate fig leaf.

Singapore is the most economically developed of the three and Indonesia the least, yet none has seen any significant improvement in political freedoms as prosperity has increased. Rather, the political system has grown more repressive in each country as economic growth has given rise to the kind of stresses described in Chapter 3. To be paid this kind of compliment by an official from North Korea might make some governments blanch: 'There is good order, discipline and observation of laws there. There is very little social disruption . . . That's why we would like to take Singapore as a model'.[4] Not so in Singapore, where Senior Minister and former Prime Minister Lee Kuan Yew has been quick to commend his recipe of repressive politics and reliance on foreign capital to Asian governments seeking to industrialise.

In Lee's view no opposition party should be allowed a chance of taking control of the state in case it reverses the policies of the People's Action Party (PAP) and puts prosperity at risk by frightening foreign investors. The PAP came to power in 1959 in a period of considerable instability. Ethnic violence had broken out in the 1950s and 1960s and the Communist Party was active in the trade union movement. Expulsion from the Malaysian Federation in 1965, after just two years in it, and the announcement of the closure of the British base soon afterwards made Singapore look very exposed. On the grounds that economic development could not proceed in conditions of political conflict and disorder, Lee Kuan Yew had locked up most of his Communist opponents in the 1963 'Operation Cold Store'.[5] In this he was following the helpful tradition of jailing trade union opponents set by the British. Since then the vision of a slide back into ethnic violence and economic destabilisation has been constantly invoked to justify the continuation and even intensification of repression while the PAP has been highly successful in securing continued re-election. At the 1991 general election it won 77 of the 81 seats, having held every seat from 1968 to 1981.

Despite what Garry Rodan terms the 'high degree of relative political autonomy enjoyed by the PAP',[6] the state has become increasingly tied to the needs of foreign capital. Domestic capitalists were too dependent on the departing colonial regime to be an effective influence in the early years of the republic and the PAP's strategy has been reliant on foreign capital to develop the economy since the 1960s. As wage rates have risen, the government has emphasised its control of labour and the provision of infrastructure. facilities as a lure to investors. To guarantee these, democracy has been pared back to the formalities of parliamentary elections. The parameters of political debate have been systematically narrowed to ensure that they do not extend beyond refinements to the efficiency with which the state serves the needs of capital.

In the same year that Singapore departed from the Malaysian federation, Indonesia witnessed the bloody events of the 'Year of Living Dangerously': the murder of six generals, Suharto's seizure of power from Sukarno in. a counter-coup and the massacres which convulsed the archipelago as the military hunted down its opponents under the guise of an anti-Communist purge. The events of 1965–66 were a reassertion of the military's claim to a place as an integral part of the regime, something it first secured through its continuation of the struggle for independence after the surrender of civilian leaders to the Dutch in 1948, but which it had seen eroded as Sukarno came to depend more on the Communist Party and its mass base. Although their influence has fluctuated since 1965, officers of the armed forces (ABRI) still occupy 9500 civilian posts,[7] including provincial governorships, 100 seats in the legislature and seven seats in the 1993 cabinet under a system known as *dwi-fungsi*, or dual function. Indonesia is not a military state in which the interests of ABRI are dominant. Rather, ABRI is part of a shifting pattern of influence along with the bureaucracy (which controls state industry) and foreign and domestic capital. Alliances between elements of the bureaucracy and favoured fractions of capital (see Chapter 2) have divided the domestic bourgeoisie, while foreign capital has been more successful in bringing its influence to bear since the 1980s. While competition between these groups is reflected in pressure on the state and on Suharto himself, the resulting factionalism also has its echoes in the enlisting of broader support from students, workers and peasants (or their outright manipulation). Except in this canalised fashion, however, the Indonesian political system seeks to exclude popular demands and to ensure that they do not intrude on the distribution of power and wealth. The label 'democratic' cannot be applied to it, any more than Suharto can legitimately label his opponents as 'Communists'.

Malaysia allows a larger democratic space, in which opposition parties have been able to win power at state level and there is a parliamentary opposition, which won 53 of the 180 seats at the October 1990 election. The *Barisan Nasional* (BN – National Front) government is dominated by the United Malays National Organisation (UMNO), led by Prime Minister Mahathir. Besides UMNO, it includes as junior partners the Malaysian Chinese Association (MCA) and the Malaysian Indian Congress (MIC) which provide the BN with votes from the minority Chinese and Indian populations. In the first decade after independence the Alliance (as the BN was then known) preserved the capitalist colonial economy bequeathed by the British, in which foreign and Chinese-owned capital were most prominent. The political alliance with the MCA reflected the compromise between Malay landed interests in UMNO and Chinese capitalists. Following the 1969 ethnic violence and the introduction of the New Economic Policy, the influence of Chinese capital has been reduced, while a new Malay entrepreneurial class has been created, bound closely to the state by its dependence on contracts and privileges. Older-established foreign companies were bought out during the 1970s in a process which the World Bank characterises as 'velvet nationalisation'.[8] More recently, however, Malaysia's renewed dependence on foreign investment has affected domestic politics, particularly in relation to resisting unionisation. As in Singapore, political leaders have sought to restrict the parameters of political activity to prevent any encroachment on the interests of capital at large or of specific favoured corporations.

ELECTIONS AND LEGISLATURES

In all three countries the emergence of an effective opposition is impeded. Campaigning at elections is heavily circumscribed and, in the few cases where opposition candidates do win elections, their ability to use parliament as an effective platform for criticising government actions has also been curtailed.

Restrictions on campaigning have been progressively tightened, with *ad hoc* measures inserted to prevent the use of particular opposition tactics. Thus car rallies were banned in the Indonesian general elections in 1992, along with the use of posters of political leaders (a measure prompted by the Indonesian Democratic Party [PDI] using pictures of Sukarno in the 1987 campaign[9]). Parties were urged to campaign via the state-owned media, rather than open air rallies – though this encouragement failed to prevent the holding of mass meetings by the PDI. Restrictions on meetings are much tougher in Singapore, where a gathering of more than five people requires permission from the authorities. Speeches were even abandoned at one Workers' Party annual dinner for fear of official intervention. In Malaysia restrictions have whittled away the time allowed for campaigning from two months in 1969 to just 10 days in 1990.[10] Chandra Muzaffar charges that opposition rallies 'have effectively been banned since 1978',[11] although Malaysia is different from Singapore and Indonesia in that independent opposition parties are able both to win federal seats and form state governments, as the *Parti Islam* (PAS) has done in Kelantan. Mahathir also promised to relax the ban on open air meetings before the elections in 1995.

The three parties allowed in Indonesia are formally required to subscribe to the state ideology of *Pancasila*, formulated in 1945 by Sukarno. Its five principles are belief in one God; just and civilised humanitarianism; a united Indonesia; democracy guided by wisdom, through consultation and representation; and social justice for all the Indonesian people.[12] These principles can be interpreted in a very elastic manner, although the insistence on regular courses in *Pancasila* for state employees and the existence of a youth wing indicate that it does constitute an ideological bulwark for the state. While *Pancasila* theoretically sets the ideological limits for political campaigning, the direct control which the Indonesian state exercises over the funding and functioning of the three parties is much more important in practice. With its origins in the 1960s[13] and now described as a 'functional group', Golkar commands by far the largest share of the votes cast in Indonesia's elections every five years. Its share in the 1992 elections was 68 per cent, down from 73 per cent in 1987. It is not a party so much as the state masquerading as one: a vote for Golkar is a vote for the bureaucracy. (The best international parallel for this entwining of party and state is probably Mexico's Institutional Revolutionary Party.) The PDI was set up in 1973 as a conduit for nationalism, a powerful force during Sukarno's Presidency and one which Suharto wanted to see kept in check. Its internal disorganisation and the extensive intervention in its affairs by the Home Minister in mid-1993 emphasised the extent to which it is dependent on the state, although the eventual election of Sukarno's daughter Megawati Sukarnoputri as chairman has given it a popular leader who could once again exploit the nationalist issue more than Suharto or ABRI might want. The PDI has been winning more support among first time voters and those in Java and took 15 per cent of the vote in 1992, up from 11 per cent in 1987. The last of the three parties is the United Development Party (PPP), also established in 1973, to ensure that a safe channel existed for Muslims seeking a party political outlet. All three parties campaign only at election time and none has yet gone significantly beyond the function allotted to it in preserving Suharto's 'New Order'.

Voting is compulsory in both Indonesia and Singapore. Whether this enhances the legitimacy of either régime is doubtful. When Indonesian students were put on trial in 1994 for urging abstention on the grounds that the electoral exercise was pointless, the government's action merely served to provide a focus for opposition. Although numbered ballot papers and compulsory voting provide the Singaporean authorities with a means of monitoring political behaviour this is becoming less effective as a deterrent, evidenced by the falling PAP vote. In the general election of 1991 the PAP's share fell to 59.3 per cent as against 75.5 per cent in 1980. To make its point more effectively the government has told Housing Development Board (HDB) residents in areas which return non-PAP MPs that they will be given lower priority in repairs and other HDB services.[14] When Singaporeans voted to elect their president for the first time in 1993, only 59 per cent supported the PAP candidate, Ong Teng Cheong, even though his superiority had been acknowledged by his opponent, former Auditor General Chua Kim Yeow.

Other forms of manipulation are used to obstruct the opposition. UMNO uses the long-established methods of gerrymandering to give a greater weight to the rural constituencies in which it has stronger support.[15] Extensive patronage networks in these rural areas operate to preserve UMNO's support among the villages. Government funds channelled through village headmen go to party supporters.[16] By-elections have been deemed unnecessary if they fall within the two years preceding a general election, thereby avoiding the risk of opposition challenges. In Indonesia civil servants vote at their place of work to discourage support for the PDI or PPP. They also receive – where appropriate – personal payments direct from Suharto in appreciation of their political loyalty.[17] In Singapore the rules governing the qualifications of candidates for the elected Presidency require three years' experience as a Cabinet minister, Chief Justice, Speaker of Parliament, chairman of a public service commission, Auditor General, permanent secretary in the civil service, or chairman or chief executive of a public company valued at S$100 million or more.[18] Not surprisingly, J. B. Jeyaretnam, the leader of the opposition Workers' Party, was disqualified from standing. These rules, along with the powers given to the new Presidency, have become another way of safeguarding financial stability against what Lee terms the 'freak result' of an election victory by any party other than the PAP. A subsequent suggestion by the Prime Minister, Goh Chok Tong, that a government panel should vet all opposition candidates was, however, shot down as excessive even by Singaporean standards. This did not discourage Lee Kuan Yew from suggesting that citizens between the ages of 35 and 60 be given two votes to weight the electoral system against the young and the old who would want to increase social spending.[19]

Restrictions on opposition campaigning are echoed in the legislatures. Indonesia's is irrelevant for political purposes, characterised by Michael Vatikiotis as 'filleted'[20] and able to do little except approve legislation. The only legislation ever introduced has come from government ministries. Only when it wishes to give the impression of responding to popular demands, as when abolishing a controversial state lottery which had offended Muslim pressure groups, does the Suharto government use parliament to initiate policy.

The legislature was, however, used by ABRI factions to send a message to Suharto about the limits of cronyism when it made the running in pursuing the issue of bad debts at the state-owned bank, Bapindo.

In Kuala Lumpur the location of the Parliament building on the fringe of the city centre symbolises the increasing insulation of Parliament from popular control. This is reflected in procedural changes: the ending of daily question time in the 1970s; the virtual abandonment of select committees and private members' bills; the restriction of the length of sittings to just five days; the allocation of less time to the opposition; the decline in attendance by ministers; and the suspension of the opposition leader Lim Kit Siang for the first time.[21] Parliament is now used chiefly as a convenience for the government – passing the budget, or amending the constitution – not as a forum for the scrutiny of its actions. Its function has become broadly similar in Singapore, where Lee Kuan Yew used parliament as a testing-ground for his younger ministers and as a stage on which to ridicule the opposition. Tinkering with constituencies and the creation of a category of nominated MPs have been designed to allow in just enough opposition and independent MPs to give the government the whipping boy of opposition it needs and enough intelligent questions to ensure that ministers are kept on their toes. It is Lee personally who continues to make and unmake ministerial careers: the various generations of interchangeable, identikit PAP politicians are answerable ultimately to him, not to Parliament.

UNACCOUNTABLE GOVERNMENT

While parliamentary scrutiny has atrophied, other means of rendering government accountable have been subverted. The press in all three countries has been muzzled, allowed to criticise only when the government wishes to discredit an opponent or to indulge in some token liberalisation. The independence of the judiciary has been undermined and the courts are used to punish opponents in just the way that Parliament and the press are used to discredit them. Scrutinising or challenging the executive is made still more difficult by secrecy laws and the Internal Security Acts in Malaysia and Singapore.

A mixture of ownership, censorship, licensing, harassment and bans stifles the press and intellectual life generally. A complicated deal in Malaysia in 1993[22] put supporters of Finance Minister Anwar Ibrahim in control of the New Straits Times Press group, comprising the country's leading English and Malay newspapers. This provided him with valuable support later that year in his fight for the Deputy Presidency of UMNO against the incumbent Deputy Prime Minister Ghafar Baba and will help to ensure a favourable press for the government in future. *The New Straits Times* already serves as a government mouthpiece, with the editor being made privy to the Prime

Minister's thinking.[23] When necessary the media are allowed to savage the government's opponents, as when Mahathir clashed with Malaysia's sultans over his attempt to reduce their immunity form prosecution. Off the leash for once, the press revelled in exposing the business practices of the families of the nine rulers who serve as constitutional figureheads for the states of peninsular Malaysia. The use of the press to criticise similar practices within the government and beyond the government's needs is not so easy. Both the *Star* and the *Sun* have lost their bite as critical, investigative papers. The Malay language press has traditionally been more tightly controlled to prevent the seepage of stories of corruption, which may appear in the English press circulating in Kuala Lumpur, into more politically sensitive UMNO strongholds in the rural areas. Selected parts of the English language media have also come under formal and informal pressure. The circulation of the *Rocket*, the journal of the opposition Democratic Action Party (DAP), was first restricted to party members and then seriously disrupted, according to party members, by pressure on printers to refuse to handle it.

The Indonesian government encourages self-censorship by the press and informally lays down a list of taboo subjects, such as political debate over the Presidential family's business dealings or separatism, which is extended as contingencies arise. The result is elaborately coded language in the press which allows an informed intelligentsia to draw inferences about political debates within the Presidential circle and between the bureaucracy and the army. Touching on sensitive issues of a religious or political nature means punishment. One publication lost its licence after publishing a popularity poll which ranked the prophet Mohammad eleventh, behind Suharto and other public figures. Another was accused of publishing news which could cause social unrest or upset diplomats in Jakarta. The attempt to ban three weekly publications – including the respected *Tempo* current affairs journal and the popular tabloid *DeTik* – was prompted by their commenting on the cost of a naval purchase by B. J. Habibie. It was another sign of the increasing factionalism between ABRI and Habibie. In reversing Suharto's year-long policy of greater openness, it also demonstrated that this policy was a matter of form rather than substance – what the President termed 'responsible openness'. Following the *Tempo* ban, reporting of demonstrations in East Timor earned several newspapers an oral warning. Two of the President's close associates also offered to buy *Tempo* and revive it, though obviously with their own factional interests at heart. The wider cultural arena is also tightly policed: the work of Pramoedya, one of Indonesia's leading novelists, is outlawed on the grounds that it is not only anti-imperialist but also questions tradition and oppressive national culture[24] (otherwise known as spreading Communist ideology) and cultural control even extends to the political vetting of the shadow puppeteers in the *wayang* theatre.

In Singapore private sales of satellite receivers are banned and any foreign press criticism of domestic affairs provokes a savage response. The domestic press is cowed through annual licences and reserve powers to ban publications and arrest journalists suspected of subversion or threatening internal security. The Malaysian government is similarly belligerent and satellite dishes, to be permitted after 1996, will be restricted to receiving signals from a satellite carrying domestic programmes. Any serious foreign newspaper or magazine commenting on Asian economics and politics in a critical fashion has been banned or had its circulation restricted in Singapore at some point. Increasingly, both governments have sought to stifle criticism of régimes considered friendly, as well as of their own domestic affairs. In Singapore's case these include China, in Malaysia's it means apologies to Indonesia when footage of the Dili massacre in East Timor was shown on Malaysian state television (RTM) and the editing of BBC footage of the unrest in Medan provided to RTM.

The judicial system has received similar treatment to the press. In Indonesia many laws have not been changed since the days of the Dutch, whose concern was with firm administrative control rather than presenting avenues by which their rule could be challenged. Presidential decrees are often used in place of legislation in a system in which the constitution places 'All power and responsibility (for the conduct of state government) in the hands of the President'.[25] The courts are used to punish political dissent, or occasionally to reprimand over-zealous members of the security forces.

The Anglo-Saxon legal traditions inherited by Singapore and Malaysia required a more determined assault by the governments to eliminate judicial independence. Singapore's continuing acceptance of the Privy Council in London as the final court of appeal was used by Jeyaretnam in 1988 to overturn his conviction for implying that the executive had interfered with the administration of justice. Although a constitutional anachronism, the link did provide one of the very few ways in which to challenge the state in the absence of an independent legal system and an effective international court of human rights. This avenue has now been closed with the removal of all such rights of appeal. The Singapore courts themselves are used aggressively against political opponents and critics at all levels. Jeyaretnam was humiliated and jailed, and other opposition candidates have been harassed.[26] In addition to the courts, the state is used against opponents: a by-election candidate for the opposition Singapore Democratic Party was dismissed from his lectureship at the National University in 1993 for a minor financial irregularity and has subsequently been hounded.[27] In any event, the provisions of the Internal Security Act (see below) enable the government to bypass virtually any legal restraints on its treatment of political opponents.

Malaysia disposed of judicial independence decisively only after a head-on confrontation between Mahathir and Tun Saleh Abas, the Lord President and head of the judiciary, who was dismissed in 1988. Five other Supreme Court judges were suspended (of whom three were reinstated) and the legal profession at large remains estranged from the government. Mahathir's actions had their immediate roots in the use of the courts both against UMNO as a party organisation and against the government in its award of contracts. In the first instance a group of UMNO dissidents headed by the former Finance Minister Tengku Razaleigh brought a case seeking to invalidate the 1987 party election in which Razaleigh lost the UMNO Presidency to Mahathir. When the courts proved less than obliging to Mahathir, he acted to remove Tun Salleh. The year before opposition leader Lim Kit Siang had embarrassed the government by trying to prevent United Engineers Malaysia (UEM), a company then owned by UMNO, from entering the contract it had been awarded by the government to build the North–South Highway at a cost of M$3.4 billion.[28] To avoid repetition of these kinds of cases, the courts have been further circumvented since the late 1980s and a more compliant Lord President has been found to endorse preventive detention and recommend the ending of jury trial for murder. The courts continue to be used against opponents: Joseph Pairin Kittingan, the Chief Minister of the state of Sabah, was on trial for two years over the award of a construction contract worth M$1.4 million[29] – a tiny fraction of the sums flowing to well-connected interests in Kuala Lumpur. Mahathir has also used a retrospective constitutional amendment to avoid a potentially inconvenient court judgement: pure expediency was behind the 1993 amendment which allows a state assemblyman to serve as a federal minister without having to resign his seat. This was to prevent an awkward by-election and enable an UMNO politician from Sabah to hold federal office. It followed a more sweeping constitutional amendment, in 1988, which provided that the High Courts should have 'only such jurisdiction and power as Parliament may law provide'.[30] A further amendment was put through in 1994, with just four days notice, to establish a code of ethics for the judiciary. Judges face dismissal for deviating from the principles set out in the code although, at the time the amendment was introduced, the code had not been laid down.

All three governments have also stifled political activity among students with specific legislation or general harassment. Lee's government expelled critical foreign university lecturers (labelling them as 'mendicant' or 'beatnik' professors[31]) and, in the 1960s and 1970s, specified that students required a 'clean' personal and family background (unsullied by Communist affiliations). In Indonesia the student movement took a leading part in the anti-Japanese 'Malari' riots in 1974 as well as in sporadic protests in the 1980s. While some political factions in the government and ABRI continue to see a use for student protests as an adjunct to their own manoeuvring they have all sought to ensure that such protest is within controlled parameters. A 'normalisation' policy was introduced in 1978, banning demonstrations and restricting freedom of debate on campuses. The government's confidence in its ability to control student activity grew almost unbounded. In 1989, during a visit by the Japanese Prime Minister Toshiki Kaifu, the Defence Minister Benny Murdani replied to the Japanese Ambassador's concern over a repetition of the Malari riots with the assurance that: 'We don't expect any anti-Japanese protests at all. But of course, if your Prime Minister wishes, we can organise student demonstrations in front of the guest house where he will be staying'.[32] Malaysia's Universities and University Colleges Act (UUCA) of 1971 was a forerunner of Indonesia's normalisation policy, prompted partly by students actively supporting peasant demonstrators coming to Kuala Lumpur from Kedah. Students are now banned from openly sympathising with political parties or contact with outside bodies while debates require permission.[33] Reorganisations of examination and teaching methods have made it more difficult for students to organise their time in unsupervised fashion. The former student leader and now Deputy Prime Minister Anwar Ibrahim has indicated that he supports retention of the UUCA, presumably a precaution in case students criticise the money politics characteristic of his 'New Malay' generation of UMNO politicians.

Another practice which the Malaysian government has carried from the colonial past is the obsessive protection of secrecy. The Malaysian Official Secrets Act, like its British counterpart, is used to exclude a mass of government documents and decision-making from public scrutiny. The Act was stiffened in the mid-1980s, giving ministers and officials the power to declare any document or material an 'official secret'.[34] The close interrelationship of business and government in Malaysia is thereby protected from investigation by the media, opposition politicians or anyone else. The financial interests of cabinet members do not have to be declared to Parliament: instead they are revealed to the Prime Minister. Knowledge of this kind is then used very selectively to keep factions and individuals under control within UMNO and the other parties in the *Barisan Nasional*. When there is a falling out, as when the mayor of Kuala Lumpur became the victim of political manoeuvrings and was dismissed in 1992, details of questionable dealings rapidly emerge.

DEINSTITUTIONALISED POLITICS

The term 'deinstitutionalisation' was applied to the politics of the Philippines by William Overholt[35] to describe the later Marcos years, in which all traditional institutions were abandoned or undermined and replaced with dictatorial rule. Although not as advanced as in the Philippines a similar process has occurred in Malaysia, Singapore and Indonesia. The results have been a mixture of indifference to the formal political process, diversion of protest into ostensibly non-political channels, demands for regional autonomy, separatism and factionalism.

Indifference to politics is most marked among students and the emerging middle class. Its concomitant is a materialism that feeds off the economic growth of the past decade. Among the Malaysian middle class, white collar employment and ownership of apartments and Proton cars have compensated for the denial of political rights. So long as growth is maintained and their living standards continue to rise absolutely the BN can be confident of retaining the support of this urban middle class. Comprising as much as one third of the population,[36] it provides a solid class base to complement the rural support which UMNO has drawn from village patronage networks. So long as the Malay middle class continues to benefit from the opportunities created by economic growth and rural Malays are placated with carefully channelled handouts, Harold Crouch's judgement on the changing class structure in which 'The small groups of middle class reformers calling for further liberalisation and democratisation were therefore easily isolated'[37] will remain valid.

In Indonesia a large proportion of the middle class are members of the bureaucracy; others are employees of conglomerates that benefit from close ties to the government or of foreign joint venture enterprises aligned with the government. Their economic interests are bound up with the preservation of the New Order and as Richard Robison concludes 'the available work suggests that the vast bulk of the Indonesian middle classes is depoliticised and materialist and remains driven by the political ideals of authoritarianism and nationalism rather than any democratic vision'.[38] In Singapore, too, the middle class is reluctant to switch support from the PAP without being sure that an alternative government can deliver a similar experience of economic growth. In each case, the legitimacy of these governments in the eyes of the middle class has come to rest heavily on the growth bargain; the ideological foundations of legitimacy have decayed.

The routinely regurgitated 'Communist threat' looks particularly threadbare to youth in all these countries. A generation in Indonesia has grown up inheriting more memories of the brutality of anti-Communist purges than of the Communist militancy that preceded them. The absurd charges of Marxist conspiracy brought against Christians in Singapore and Malaysia ring equally hollow. Repeated denunciations of the corrupting influence of the West merely draw more attention to the drugs and music that appeal to young people. In Indonesia the PDI drew the biggest crowds to its election rallies by playing rock music. Its growing hold on the votes of working class youth is not necessarily indicative of widespread demands for changes, or of class consciousness, so much as a reflection of an indifference to the dull, worthy image which Suharto and Golkar promote. The alienation of Jakarta's middle class youth more often takes the form of apolitical materialism.

Student leaders complain of narrow personal preoccupations, lost idealism and a 'lack [of] attention to public concern'[39] among the student population. Similar youth disaffection in Singapore and Malaysia has prompted the authorities to take a hard line on drugs, Western music, 'loafing' and, in Malaysia, public displays of affection. As elsewhere in Asia, young people appear to ageing leaders to be alarmingly indifferent to governments' insistence on tight labour discipline and political conformity. As yet indifference is still some way from disenchantment and cynicism but the young seem more likely to head in that direction rather than towards positive support for UMNO, the PAP or Golkar.

Positive support is flowing instead into religious organisations. Both the Christian churches and Islamic organisations have been attracting new members in Indonesia, especially, as formal political deinstitutionalisation and economic inequality drive people to seek some other way of improving their well-being. In some cases – as among Jakarta slum dwellers trying to fight eviction – religious bodies are the only structures through which people have a tradition of organising and any collective identity.[40] Religious vessels fill with the wider discontents of unequal societies. It is partly these feelings which have allowed Indonesia's largest Muslim organisation, the Nahdlathul Ulama (NU), to grow to between 20 and 40 million members (out of a population of 189 million) and prompted its leader to speak of Indonesia becoming 'another Algeria' within ten years,[41] in which discontent would turn into violent struggle. Muslim protests, such as the Tanjung Priok riot in 1984 or the murder of an infantry officer in Lampung over a land tenure dispute in 1989, resulted in violence which left 200 dead in each case.

Muslim organisations provide a cover for factional criticism of Chinese business wealth and Christian influence in the Indonesian Cabinet, in the absence of a political system which allows legitimate scrutiny of business and finance. When Muslim organisations led protests against the state-run lottery, the question of the distribution of its profits was as highly charged as that of gambling itself: another instance of the wider demands for accountability riding on a supposedly religious issue. Active proselytising by Christian evangelicals in East Java and elsewhere has meanwhile led to violence, including the burning of churches. This is not simple religious antagonism but a reaction among the 20 million Muslims who live below the poverty line and who see violence of this kind as a way of protesting at what they regard as a history of economic privileges granted to Christians by the Dutch and preserved since independence.

In Malaysia, too, the Islamic PAS has been the political receptacle of protest at an increasingly unequal society and student radicals are drawn more towards Islam than human rights activism. By holding out the prospect of an Islamic state – shorthand for a radically changed social order, the details of which are not made explicit – PAS has capitalised on the dissatisfaction of rural Malays in the relatively backward North East. The patronage network on which UMNO has relied to deliver the rural vote is being undermined as knowledge of the living standards of the urban middle class slowly permeates the countryside. The realisation that the benefits of growth have gone disproportionately to urban Malays has widened divisions within the Malay community which was previously more united in its support for UMNO. Mahathir's response has been to goad PAS towards fulfilling its commitment to an Islamic state, complete with *hudud* laws, in the conviction that the reality will alienate Muslim and non-Muslim voters alike as well as dividing PAS from the main opposition party, the Chinese-led DAP. Until those laws are fully implemented, however, the slogan of an 'Islamic state' has proven appeal in one majority Muslim state.

Religion in Singapore is perhaps the only area of private life in which the state does not intervene, perhaps reflecting the fact that Lee Kuan Yew himself is not known to have any strong religious convictions or to uphold the economic virtues of any particular faith. Were he to be 'born again', however, the Singaporean state machine could be expected to swing into campaigns for religious observance and study in much the same way as it has sought to encourage marriages between graduates and, according to fluctuating policy priorities, different family sizes.

REGIONAL DEMANDS

The support which PAS commands in the state of Kelantan indicates not only the channelling of protest into religion but also the rise of demands for greater regional autonomy. In Kelantan, these have also coalesced around the Sultan, who fell foul of Mahathir in 1992. The ensuing row was partly instrumental in prompting Mahathir to launch an offensive against, first, the legal immunity of the sultans and then, in 1994, their power to delay legislation. Regional autonomy is an acutely sensitive issue in the Malaysian states of Sabah and Sarawak, which only merged with the Federation of Malaya to form Malaysia in 1963. To win assent in a referendum on the merger the 'Twenty Points' agreement offered various reassurances to Sabahans along with federal pledges of economic development. Yet the state's economy continues to grow more slowly than Peninsular Malaysia's and the *Parti Bersatu Sabah* (PBS) fears that the guarantees of the Twenty Points may be removed. The party's leaders are suspicious of the federal government's policy of informally allow-ing immigration into Sabah by Muslims from neighbouring Mindanao in the southern Philippines. They fear a conspiracy to tilt the state's religious mix towards potential UMNO supporters and against the Christians on whose votes the PBS relies. The federal government also believes conspiracy is afoot in the state: Jeffrey Kittingan, a brother of Joseph

Pairin Kittingan, then Chief Minister of the state, was jailed for two years on suspicion of plotting to take Sabah out of the federation. An active secessionist movement would be a serious problem for the federal government, which has guarded against it by building up naval facilities off the Borneo coast at Labuan Island. More adroitly, Jeffrey Kittingan was released in time to take part in the state elections in early 1994. He subsequently broke with his brother and joined a pro-UMNO grouping as part of a majority in the state assembly. If this can restore the flow of federal development funds from Kuala Lumpur then economic dissatisfaction could be eased. But over the longer term Sabah has the potential to become Malaysia's Kashmir: there is room for argument over its constitutional position in the federation; raw materials have been exploited; its population is an ethnic and religious jumble; and its location on the country's periphery is complicated by a territorial claim from the Philippines, a claim periodically revived by rogue nationalists.

The movements fighting the Indonesian government in East Timor, Aceh and Irian Jaya are already at the stage of armed struggle. The Portuguese revolution of 1974 placed its colony of East Timor in something of a limbo. Decolonisation was set in motion but was neither a priority in Lisbon nor a process on which Portuguese policymakers were agreed. Indonesian leaders saw their chance to destabilise East Timor and pre-empt Portuguese dithering by intervening to seize the territory, with the complicity of Western governments. In an effort to forestall this, the East Timorese political movement FRETILIN made a unilateral declaration of independence in November 1975.[42] Little more than a week later Indonesia invaded the territory and a struggle has been fought for the freedom of the East Timorese people ever since – not for autonomy within Indonesia, or secession from a country they never chose to join, but for the removal of an occupying power. At no time before or after the invasion has Indonesia had the support of more than a tiny minority of the people of East Timor.

In Aceh at the northern tip of Sumatra, the *Aceh Merdeka* separatist movement has been fighting actively for independence for the region's 3 million people since the early 1970s. A similar struggle is being waged by the Papuans in Indonesia's Easternmost province Irian Jaya (West Papua). This was wrested from the Dutch in 1962–3 before a vote could be taken on independence, absorption into Indonesia or unification with the other half of the island of New Guinea, then under Australian administration. When Indonesia granted its so-called 'Vote of Free Choice' in 1969 President Suharto told one journalist that voting against integration into Indonesia would be regarded as an act of treason and UN supervision of the vote was a shambles.[43] Armed resistance began as early as 1965 and has continued ever since. Indonesia has no grounds for its occupation except its claims as 'successor state' to the Dutch. Regrettably, these claims do have considerable force under international law, which has been developed, after all, to maintain the continuity and stability of existing states and is, therefore, generally inimical to any re-drawing of international frontiers.

Besides these three movements, there are latent desires for regional autonomy or secession in several other parts of Indonesia. Bali, which was only finally brought under Dutch control early this century, has distinct cultural traditions which have been a source of tension between the Balinese and exploiters of the island, whether Javanese or foreign.[44] If given a free choice the people of Bali might well choose a greater measure of autonomy within a looser Indonesian federation, as might other parts of the archipelago. A series of regional revolts in the 1950s in Sumatra, Sulawesi, West Java and the Moluccas were a mixture of Islamic militancy and secessionist resistance to greater centralised control.[45] The fear of the national disintegration which might follow a resurgence of such movements in these provinces has led Indonesian governments since independence to resist any greater measure of federalism.

REINCORPORATION

The leaders of Malaysia, Singapore and Indonesia have not been oblivious to the alienating effects of deinstitutionalised politics. They have adopted a number of reincorporation strategies to try to offset growing dissatisfaction. The most obvious is the growth strategy, accompanied by promises of higher and higher living standards in the future. As has been argued, however, the economic outlook for these countries cannot be confidently predicted. The vulnerability of régimes which depend mainly on prosperity for legitimacy was exposed in Malaysia in the mid-1980s. An economic downturn precipitated a full-scale political crisis. Mahathir was challenged for the UMNO leadership, the party eventually split, public criticism of crony capitalism and authoritarian government mounted and Mahathir resorted to attacking the courts and jailing over 100 opponents in 'Operation Lalang' in October and November 1987.[46]

Expressions of dissatisfaction outside the electoral system have alarmed these régimes and prompted other efforts at reincorporation. In Singapore the PAP has sought to give voters a 'stake' in prosperity through the CPF and home ownership: efforts which, as we saw in Chapter 3, have not brought unalloyed benefits. The 'Feedback Unit' and town councils were set up in the mid-1980s to try to draw in the disillusioned middle class who were chafing at exclusion from any meaningful political participation, local government having been abolished in 1959. Government Parliamentary Committees (mingling MPs and outside experts) and the Institute of Policy Studies think-tank have also been part of this more consultative approach, while nominated MPs have been encouraged to broaden the range of contributions to parliamentary debates. With its limited objective of drawing more participants into discussions while ensuring that the parameters of these discussions are not stretched too far, the consultative process has tended to mean that only a small number of familiar faces has circulated through its various institutions. There is a restricted pool of the intelligentsia available which has not already received (or rejected) overtures from the PAP. The real dissenting voices remain frozen out. Likewise, nominated MPs know the limits on what they can do: any attempt to build a public following around the issues they raise would soon result in the termination of their role.[47] Consultation is an exercise, nothing more. Less formal gestures along the same lines have been made in Malaysia, where the environmentalist Gurmit Singh received the 1993 Langkawi award (previously given to civil servants) and the Federation of Malaysian Consumers' Associations has been encouraged to make an input into government thinking.

The main worry for the Indonesian and Malaysian governments is the growing strength of Islamic organisations and parties. Heading off the politicisation of these groups is more difficult because neither government dares risk alienating Muslims: incorporation is therefore essential. Suharto himself made the *hajj* (pilgrimage) to Mecca in 1991 to bolster his religious credentials and, in 1993, brought more Muslims into his cabinet at the expense of Christians. His biggest gestures so far have been associated with the Muslim intellectual organisation ICMI. Suharto approved its formation in 1990 and became patron in 1993.[48] ICMI, closely identified with Habibie, supports cultural, educational, financial and publishing activities. Its real purpose is to serve as another of the functional groups funnelling political activity into state-controlled organisations and ultimately subordinate to the President. Mahathir set up a think-tank on similar lines – the Malaysian Institute for Islamic Understanding (IKIM) – to help in his ideological juggling act.[49] A greater stress on UMNO's Islamic credentials, helped by Anwar's reputation as a former Islamic firebrand, helps the régime to shore up its support amongst Malays. It can help arrest the drifting away from the party as the old rural *bumiputra* identity decays and the Malay community divides along rural/urban and class lines. But once unleashed, Islam is hard to control. Opposition groups can use the the cover of Islam to press for changes that are not on the government agenda. And when the 100 000-strong Al-Arqam sect gathered strength amongst urban middle class Malays and within the ranks of the civil service, Mahathir banned it in 1994 (and his action was repeated in Jakarta).

Most alarming for the Malaysian ruling class are the instances where Islam clashes with the objective of economic growth. IKIM's task is to demonstrate that growth and Islam are not irreconcilable, that growth does not lead inevitably to Westernisation and depravity. The debate about the medium of instruction in institutes of higher learning goes to the heart of this issue.

When Mahathir announced that he wanted technical subjects taught in English, 18 groups in the Third Malay Intellectuals Congress were immediately up in arms at the suggestion as academics trained in Malay united with Muslim activists to oppose it.[50] The clash between Islamic teachings on the role of women and the need for more women to participate in the workforce is another example of the likelihood that the incompatible demands of capitalist economic rationality and Islamic revivalism will produce conflict rather than shore up UMNO's hold on Malay support. The AIDS debate also pits Muslims against economic and social realists in both Malaysia and Indonesia: should the spread of the disease be tackled with condoms and public education or with deportations, segregation and homilies from the Koran?

UMNO's leaders set the party a target of 2 million members by the 1995 election, as against 1.9 million at the start of 1994.[51] Anwar demonstrated his ability to galvanise UMNO right down to the villages during his campaign for the Deputy Presidency. It was, however, money that was the key to galvanising the party, with delegates' votes reportedly on sale for up to M$15 000.[52] Financial manipulation within the party will, over the long-term, undermine its function as a means of incorporating support. Debates at UMNO's 1992 general assembly were, according to *Aliran Monthly*, evidence of the 'limited tolerance of party members towards the swift rise of new non-Bumiputera businessmen'[53] and, if such businessmen are able to use their wealth to exert influence within the party, that tolerance will be even further strained. Its product will be either factionalism or disillusionment.

This has prompted a search in Malaysia, as in Singapore and Indonesia, for 'Asian values' which can be employed as an ideological prop for veiled authoritarism. 'Asian values' usually means little beyond the assertion that Asians are hardworking people who prefer strong government to the chaos of individualism, thanks to values that Westerners cannot understand and should not criticise. Yet the PAP's reiteration of 'Asian values' and 'core values' caused the party as many problems as it solved. The 'Speak Mandarin' campaign to encourage Asian values (code for instilling more Confucian teachings on the virtues of obedience) backfired on the government, for the Chinese-speaking middle class saw their chance to demand a larger share of senior positions on the grounds of their superior understanding of Asian values. Indonesia's standby of *Pancasila* is little more than a chore for civil servants that barely elicits lip service. The Malaysian government has been so intent on stripping away such 'traditional' aspects of society as the powers of the sultans and on building more shopping centres and golf courses that it is hard to resuscitate 'Asian values' outside the explicitly religious context. Mahathir's 'Vision 2020' of a future society translates principally into more material goals.

REPRESSION

Where reincorporation fails governments repress. Intellectual critics, workers and independence movements alike are confronted with arbitrary jailings and military force. Indonesia has the worst record among the three in this respect. In East Timor 200 000 people, equivalent to a third of the population in 1975, have died as a result of the Indonesian occupation. Deportations, resettlement in camps without medicine or adequate land, arrests and killings, and the use of chemical weapons have built up a terrible death toll. Forced sterilisations and the organised immigration of settlers from Java add to the insidious genocide. The massacre of at least 250 civilians[54] in a cemetery in Dili in 1991 was a reminder of the callous brutality with which Indonesian rule is preserved: for all the talk of winning hearts and minds, the reality is the shooting and bayoneting of mourners and commercial exploitation of the island by Suharto family interests and former Defence Minister Benny Murdani. The Dili massacre was also symptomatic of the military's free hand to kill opponents throughout the territories where it is in conflict with guerrillas and the population at large. Amnesty International reports that between 1988 and 1993 2000 Acehnese civilians were killed and another 1000 were arbitrarily arrested on suspicion of supporting *Aceh Merdeka*. As in East Timor the Indonesian army has used the 'fence of legs', a shield of civilians which advances at gunpoint in front of the soldiers to flush out and draw fire from rebels. The record of savagery is the same in Irian Jaya, where up to 30 000 Papuans were killed between 1963 and 1969; the Organisasi Papua Merdeka (OPM, the Free Papua Organisation) claims that 150 000 had died by 1984 and the Anti-Slavery Society believes that the total could have been 200 000.[55] Mass reprisals, the use of napalm, the murder of prisoners and atrocities against civilians have all been part of the Indonesian record. Irian Jaya's vast, sparsely populated territory has also encouraged the Indonesians to use the weapon of population transfer from overcrowded Java. In the mid-1980s, the target for 'transmigrasi' was 685 000 – enough to outnumber the native Papuans. By 1992 the programme was still going at 'full tilt' and in 1993 a new plan to move groups of 2000 or even 5–15 000 (instead of 200–500) at a time was announced and incentives were increased.[56] The intention is to destroy the Papuans' culture by overwhelming it and then to assimilate them into the Indonesian mainstream.

Yet, despite their brutality, Suharto and ABRI have failed to crush any of the independence movements. The arrests of leaders check each of them periodically, but a new generation of leadership emerges every time to resume the struggle.[57] The prospects of victory for any of the guerrilla groups remain slight, though the Indonesian army would be badly stretched if all three movements were able to intensify their activity at the same time.

The connivance of Western governments has facilitated Indonesia's repressive policies. There has been very little international condemnation of Indonesian human rights abuses, as when 5000 people disappeared in the mid-1980s. This resulted from ABRI and the police killing criminals as part of a 'shock therapy' to clean up the cities. Tattoos – taken as evidence of membership of criminal fraternities – could mean a death sentence. To deal with dissidents such as the 'Petisi 50' group, Indonesia still maintains blacklists banning people from entering the country (including over 4500 foreigners) and from leaving (over 4000). Criticism of Suharto is met with prosecutions for defamation[58] and, according to Amnesty's estimates, 200 people are in jail for their beliefs. The establishment of a Human Rights Commission has been a token gesture. Three months after it was set up in 1993 only one member had been appointed and activists were refusing to serve on it. Protests by workers or peasants are dealt with as harshly as the independence movements. In 1993 four farmers were shot for protesting at a dam project. Individual workers have been murdered for leading or taking part in labour disputes – Marsinah in East Java, Rusli in Medan – and strikers routinely arrested. The army blamed the police for heavy handed behaviour in Marsinah's case after it drew international condemnation, but both have the same attitude to dissent in any form: to crush it.

The Malaysian and Singaporean governments have not had to use armed force extensively to deal with challenges since the Malayan Communist insurgency was pronounced defeated in 1960. Repression has mainly been carried out through arrests under the Internal Security Act (ISA) in both countries. It was under Internal Security Council Regulations that Lee Kuan Yew jailed Communists in 1963. The ISA was also used against the Catholic 'Marxists' in Singapore in 1987. Malaysia's ISA allows the government to detain people for two years at a stretch, without charges being brought, on a indefinitely renewable basis. The Minister of Home Affairs in Malaysia and the President in Singapore can detain anyone whom they 'are satisfied' is a threat to national security. No genuine appeal or review procedure exists. This kind of arbitrary arrest, or 'preventive detention' as it is termed in Malaysia, has sufficed to intimidate and suppress protest.

FACTIONS AND FRACTIONS

The efforts to restrict political activity in the veiled authoritarian states have largely been successful. Popular demands have been kept out of the political arena, although this has not eliminated all political debate. Rather, it has bottled up political activity within ruling parties and the institutions of the state, which have become the arena for factional political struggles reflecting the differences between fractions of capital. In Singapore these struggles focus on the degree of relaxation that is compatible with continued economic growth, while in Malaysia and Indonesia they revolve around the allocation of state patronage to industry.

Younger Singaporean leaders recognise that they could allow a greater latitude to the opposition and broaden the parameters of political debate without provoking a dramatic loss of support for the PAP and a crisis of confidence on the part of investors. If anything, such a loosening, on the lines of that now being seen in the emerging bourgeois democracies (Chapter 6), could revive support for the PAP and increase the security of capital. Within the PAP, however, Lee Kuan Yew's hold is still sufficiently strong for him to be able to resist moves which would permit a significantly greater measure of open political competition. It could still be several years before Lee steps down, especially if he decides to run for the presidency and wins office. While his influence remains powerful in Singapore, to the extent that he is still, as James Cotton puts it, 'at the centre of the network of patronage and personal relations which animates Singapore's party and state',[59] Prime Minister Goh Chok Tong has proved more resilient than expected. His personal victory in a by-election in 1992 strengthened his hand and gave him a mandate, beyond simply having been chosen as a stopgap leader until Lee Kuan Yew's son Brigadier-General Lee Hsien Loong is ready to take over as prime minister. Given 'B.-G.' Lee's reputation for an intellectual arrogance possibly even greater than his father's, his treatment for cancer and the ambitions of other PAP politicians, it is quite conceivable that, if Lee Kuan Yew insists on his son taking over as prime minister, Singapore could see a repetition of the party in-fighting which affected the PAP in its early years.

Such factionalism would not represent fundamental disagreements about the accommodation of capital in Singapore, but it would reflect differences over the needs of capital as well as issues of political style and presentation. To the younger, more internationally minded generation of the bureaucracy and middle class, Singapore's political repression seems excessive to the point of being economically counter-productive. To make a successful transition to a more developed economy, in which free information flows can enhance economic performance and prevent the loss of skilled workers, some political loosening is important. 'B.-G.' Lee has shown no signs of being willing to countenance such a relaxation. Yet a political strategy based on repression of labour is no longer central to the progress of the Singapore economy and its importance will diminish as more Singapore companies carry out their labour-intensive manufacturing offshore. It also creates a needless source of potential friction with Western governments, whose willingness to challenge Asian human rights and labour conditions rubs up against Lee Kuan Yew's role as the self-appointed custodian of 'Asian values' of political intolerance.

Questions of political succession in Indonesia have become interwoven

with those of the strategy of accumulation as a result of the close dependence of a group of capitalists on privileges granted by the Suharto government. These privileges confer very considerable benefits on Suharto's cronies
and those connected to his family's businesses, often at the expense of other
fractions of capital (both domestic and foreign), which incur additional costs
from monopoly prices or bribes and which have to cede stakes to these
privileged capitalists. The large scale subsidisation of state industries, particularly those associated with Habibie, also causes conflict among fractions of capital. It is reflected in the pressure to curb state support to this
sector, applied through both the international agencies and the domestic Indonesian media. Political factionalism therefore turns on the questions of
cutting down the influence of the Suharto family and on curbing the growth
of state industry, with an eye to a more 'rational' redistribution of state
financial aid.

Leading businessmen close to Suharto have begun to seek protection in
the public arena. Prajogo, one of Suharto's closest cronies, obtained a public share listing for his Barito Pacific Timber in 1993 in order to give the
company the legitimacy of publicly audited accounts and of a body of investors, including foreign interests. The reasoning was that a future Indonesian government might hesitate to strip him of his assets for fear of alarming
foreign investors. Other cronies are likely to seek similar protection as the
end of Suharto's sixth term approaches in 1998, as well as salting away
assets overseas as an extra precaution. Suharto's son Tommy is expected to
start listing his Humpuss Group companies during this period.

Whatever happens as 1998 approaches will necessarily affect the position
of the armed forces. ABRI has been testing its strength as a political force
since the setback of seeing State Secretary Sudharmono installed as vice
president over its candidate in 1988. It was successful in securing the selec-
tion of its former commander, Try Sutrisno, as vice president in 1993. But
Suharto rebuffed ABRI in having a civilian, the Information Minister Harmoko,
appointed leader of Golkar late that same year. Although ABRI is divided
between officers who are ready to accept a role as professional commanders
under ultimate civilian control and those who wish to preserve the 'dual
function' and remain an integral part of the ruling class, the latter view is
the stronger one and leads ABRI officers to argue that they should be the
final arbiter of the succession to the presidency.[60] It is the succession which
will test ABRI's power conclusively. ABRI could enlist wider support against
any attempt by the Suharto family to entrench its interests in the state beyond 1998 by passing the Presidency to a family member.

The succession question in Indonesia is complicated by the fact that there
is no tried and tested mechanism for selecting Suharto's replacement. More
than half the members of the *Majelis Permusyawaratan Rakyat* (MPR), the
body which elects the President indirectly, owe their appointments to him.

While the ruling class may strive for what one diplomat describes as an 'aura of constitutionality' in the succession it is just as likely that ABRI, or factions within it, may use students or other groups to orchestrate disorder. This would give them a pretext for imposing a military figure as successor. Such a scenario is more likely if Suharto tries to place one of his associates – such as his son-in-law Colonel Prabowo Djojohadikusumo – in the job or even hints that he might try to stay on himself beyond 1998. Two of Suharto's children have joined the executive board of Golkar to give themselves formal political positions and some measure of protection during a transition, a move that could also indicate an intention of intervening in the succession. In trying to block the creation of a Suharto dynasty, ABRI would find allies among local and foreign business interests and within the Indonesian middle class. Some ABRI officers have already been making appeals for wider social support through calls for democratisation as they manoeuvre against Suharto.[61] But in installing a candidate of its own or even supporting the President's brother-in-law, army commander Wismoyo Arismunandar, ABRI is less likely to enjoy similar support, for fear that the generals would use the opportunity to supplant the Suharto clique as the beneficiaries of monopolies and the essential partners in any deals.

The more bitter the in-fighting around the succession to Suharto, the greater the likelihood that other social forces will be drawn into the conflict. In industrial disputes, large and small, the military has intervened actively on behalf of capital, arresting workers and confronting them on the streets. Its resources are already employed against independence movements. In the context of serious factional conflict it is likely that, whether or not in orchestrated fashion, workers and independence movements would become actors challenging any attempt by the military to impose its choice of president. Particularly in Jakarta and Jogjakarta students are also likely to be used both by ABRI and against it. It would not, of course, be in the interests of any of the factions to provoke unrest that threatened the position of capital *per se* or seriously divided the armed forces. Neither the *pribumi* groups which have benefited from the Suharto regime nor Chinese capitalists want to see greater political democratisation that could open their wealth and power up to demands for accountability. In such an event, a closing of ranks between ABRI and competing fractions of capital could be expected. But unless that happens a period of instability is likely as a result of factional in-fighting in the years leading up to the end of Suharto's current term in 1998.

In Malaysia dissent has been stifled, criticism silenced and accountability disregarded. This has induced a degree of complacency in the leadership. Mahathir, Anwar and the second echelon of UMNO politicians, such as Muhyiddin Yassin and Muhammed Taib, believe that they are exempt from any democratic controls. If dissent, criticism and demands for genuine accountability were to surface Anwar can be expected to deal with them in exactly the same way as Mahathir. As well as backtracking on reform of the UUCA Anwar is now in favour of retaining the ISA, under which he was detained in the 1970s as a student radical. Having made an opportunistic switch to join UMNO he has embraced the party's traditional methods of social control.

Factionalism is another tradition of UMNO's internal politics. The Malaysian brand reflects a fairly straight contest between fractions of capital seeking to benefit from state patronage. The rivalry provoked by the fraction grouped around Anwar Ibrahim echoes the contest which split UMNO in 1987, when Mahathir and the Razaleigh-Musa faction contested the party leadership. Although this earlier battle resulted in the emergence of *Semangat '46* as an independent party, the subsequent open electoral contests between the two parties have not been on issues of policy so much as a reflection in the open political arena of a tussle for a redistribution of state patronage.

Anwar's rise to the position of Mahathir's heir apparent quickened in 1993 with his successful campaign for the party's vice-presidency. Yet within six months of his victory press reports[62] suggested that his supporters were growing restive at the thought of having to wait a matter of years before Anwar acquired the Prime Minister's powers of patronage and they received their payoff. The more Anwar is pushed – perhaps to contest the UMNO Presidency and the Prime Ministership in 1996 – the more the envy of his swift rise as a 'helicopter politician' is likely to grow and the greater will become the fears of those business interests outside his circle, particularly those grouped around former Finance Minister Daim Zainuddin. Mahathir may dig his heels in if pushed: the composition of Cabinet after the elections in 1995 will test how far Anwar has obtained Mahathir's acquiescence in his ambitions.

Political struggle is likely to remain at the level of factionalism in all the veiled authoritarian states. In both Indonesia and Malaysia working class consciousness has not developed beyond the initial emergence of trade union consciousness (that is, the readiness to struggle for better wages and conditions). Even this development has been retarded by the determined opposition of the state apparatus.

At the political level the working class is still prone to diversion into religious organisations and protests of the kind described above and to manipulation by nationalists or on ethnic lines. Where a social democratic party does exist, in the form of Malaysia's Democratic Action Party (DAP), its appeal is vitiated by ethnic and religious factors. As Crouch puts it, 'Divided along communal lines, the Malaysian working class has never been united politically to fight for class interests',[63] a conclusion echoed in Hua Wa Yin's *Class and Communalism in Malaysia*, which traces the use of communal sentiments to prevent the emergence of class politics from the earliest days of the Malaysian state. These divisions make it very difficult for the DAP to co-operate further with the other opposition parties, PAS and *Semangat*

'46, which have their strongest bases in the North and North East of Malaysia. Both of them have made a political appeal to Muslim fundamentalism that alienates the DAP's ethnic Chinese support. An alliance with *Semangat '46* would undercut the DAP's urban Chinese support, yet stressing its Chinese identity would frustrate any hopes it has of building support among urban working class Malays on a class basis. The DAP's best hope[64] is for the opposition to deny the BN the two thirds parliamentary majority that would allow it to change the constitution at will.

Among the Indonesian working class the rapidly growing trade unions remain divided from other currents of dissent and vulnerable to exploitation by factions for their own ends (whether discrediting ABRI or calling for more openness or less privileges for 'Chinese' conglomerates). The rise in workers' support for the PDI is likely to continue in future elections as Sukarno's daughter Megawati capitalises on her father's enduring popular appeal and nationalist credentials. This may lead her to make some gestures in the direction of opposing foreign influence in the economy and on other nationalist issues. But the suggestion that Megawati's election as PDI leader enjoyed the backing of ABRI and her reportedly cordial relations with Suharto's children[65] imply that additional support for the PDI would only feed into factional conflict, rather than putting radical demands on the political agenda. Nor is Abdurrahman Wahid's Nahdlathul Ulama (NU) a force working for decisive economic and social change, despite Wahid's other position as chairman of the Forum for Democracy. The NU serves to head off Islamic fundamentalism and, as such, it ensures that fundamentalism does not militate against capitalist efficiency in the way that it threatens to do in Malaysia. The Forum for Democracy may have enjoyed tacit military support when it was launched in 1991[66] and can be understood partly in the context of factional competition with Suharto's patronage of ICMI. Nevertheless it is a political channel outside the state-controlled institutions, attracting the support of the thin layer of middle class activists who seek a more open, less arbitrary society as a better arena in which to advance their own interests. However, it does not follow that they would make common cause with workers and peasants for wider redistributive objectives.

In Singapore even trade union consciousness has been suppressed in a highly regimented system. The PAP is, nevertheless, losing working class support, evidenced in its falling share of the vote in parliamentary elections. The focus of reforms on co-opting the middle class back into a dialogue with the PAP has overlooked working class voters. This may lead to the attrition of the PAP's majority and a situation in which the PAP leadership is forced to choose between a renewed onslaught on opposition candidates, the media and individual voters or constituencies that have rejected the PAP, or an approach which is more overtly conciliatory towards complaints about the high cost of living and the burden of taxation on lower-paid workers.

Such a debate clearly feeds into the emerging factional debate within the PAP between 'B.-G.' Lee's uncompromising stand and the more responsive attitude of others in the party, but it is limited to just that – a tactical debate within the ruling party. There is no sign of the Singapore working class mounting an autonomous, radical challenge, nor of the growing population of migrant workers organising on economic or political issues. Singapore remains the most stable of the three veiled authoritarianisms.

5 Market Stalinism: Burma, China, Laos, North Korea and Vietnam

Many years after being patronised by their counterparts in the Soviet Union, China's Communist leaders had the satisfaction of seeing their erstwhile comrades in Moscow tumbled out of power while they remained clinging to it as tenaciously as ever. The encouragement which Mikhail Gorbachev's visit to Peking had given to democracy activists in the spring of 1989 can only have added to their *schadenfreude* at his fall. China's leaders and apologists proudly tell the world how right they were to have sought *perestroika* without *glasnost*. Stalinism consequently survives in China, through the Communist Party's control of social organisations and individual lives alike and the repression of the working class and peasantry who are nominally the masters of the system.

REVOLUTIONARY LEGITIMACY

The governments of China, Vietnam, Laos and North Korea draw for their legitimacy on the same kind of revolutionary heritage as that which Stalin was able to distort for his own ends. The Chinese Communists who emerged triumphant after long years of struggle against the Japanese and the Nationalist Kuomintang government of Chiang Kai-shek had led a popular peasant movement. Although democratic control was never part of Communist rule after 1949, Mao and the other veteran Long March leaders had an enormous political capital to dissipate. In the capitalist China of the 1990s the 'early Mao' of the guerrilla struggles in the 1930s and 1940s is still invoked by the Communist Party. The Vietnamese Communist Party has been able to draw on a similar stock of revolutionary legitimacy from its role in leading the struggle against the French, the Americans and their puppet régimes in the South. So too the Lao People's Revolutionary Party (LPRP), whose Pathet Lao guerillas led the overthrow of the American-backed Royal Lao government in 1975 after a 12 year struggle.[1] Even Kim Il Sung's regime in North Korea grew out of the popular Korean People's Republic set up in 1945 by those who had opposed Japanese rule. The Korean War of 1950–53 began as a revolutionary struggle to liberate the South,[2] even if it degenerated into being part of the global struggle in which the US and its allies fought China and the Soviet Union. In Burma, General Ne Win was among the Thirty Comrades led by Aung San who received military training in Japan during the Second World War and emerged as the architects of Burma's transition to independence.[3] Although always overshadowed by Aung San's popularity, and now completely eclipsed by that of his daughter, Aung San Suu Kyi, Ne Win nevertheless had some claims to legitimacy based on his wartime role.

ONE-PARTY RULE

Historical experience in Vietnam, Laos and North Korea has diverged but political control is maintained by parties which drew material support and ideological direction from Moscow or Peking. In Burma, though the Communist Party has been out of power and has engaged in armed struggle since 1948, from 1962 to 1988 the governments of the Burma Socialist Programme Party (BSPP) used Marxist as well as Buddhist and nationalist images and slogans[4] in what could be characterised as a 'pagodas with electricity' definition of socialism. Eccentric as the 'Burmese way to socialism' was, the political control exercised by Ne Win has had the same Stalinist reach and intent as formal rule by a Communist Party. Under the State Law and Order Restoration Council (SLORC), which took over the running of the country in 1988, the socialist elements in the state ideology have been further diluted, but political control has remained as tight as ever and Ne Win is still the most powerful man in Burma.

It is the structure of the state in these countries which provides the closest analogies to Soviet rule. An inflexible state designed to serve the repressive needs of the ruling party cannot, by definition, accommodate the pressures for change which arise out of economic growth and increasing inequality. Strictly limited accommodation of new interests and demands has been achieved only through the decay and erosion of parts of this state apparatus. As growth continues so it will further corrode the institutions of the Stalinist state, though not, as liberals predict, simply by putting these countries 'on the road to bourgeois democracy'. Corrosion affects the army as much as any other institution, dividing it into those elements which profit from economic reforms and those which are left behind. The armed nature of the struggles which brought these régimes to power and which have, especially in the case of Burma, sustained in power, have made the military an important component of the state. Changes which weaken the link between the ruling parties and the armed forces therefore have serious implications for stability.

All five of these régimes are characterised by one-party rule and a denial of pluralist politics within the ruling party. Intra-party democracy has been confined to gestures and short-lived periods of relaxation in central control. At times Chinese Communist Party leaders have discussed party reforms as a way of helping to further economic reforms, but discipline has been reasserted in moments of wider political uncertainty.[5] In Vietnam, likewise, Nguyen Van Linh, Communist Party General Secretary from 1987 to 1990, introduced reforms to increase flexibility and decentralisation within the party as part of a modernising mission but these measures were suffocated by an entrenched majority in a party which still fears greater open debate.[6] Kim Il Sung established his supremacy in the Workers' Party of North Korea in the 1960s and secured it by placing family members in key positions. At the time of his death, a dozen of Kim Il Sung's relatives held senior positions. These included vice-president Kim Yong-Ju, two deputy prime ministers, Prime Minister Kang Song-San and the chairman of the Supreme People's Assembly, Yang Hyong-Sup.[7] Changes in the leadership of the Lao People's Revolutionary Party (LPRP) following President Kaysone's death at the end of 1992 were limited to a seamless transition within the politburo, in which the generation who led the revolution of 1975 retains power.[8]

FREEDOM OF EXPRESSION AND ORGANISATION

Limitations on freedom of expression and organisation in civil society parallel those on intra-party democracy. The Vietnamese Communist Party has made purely superficial gestures in the direction of disentangling the party and the state. Under the 1992 constitution the government of Prime Minister Vo Van Kiet is to take more executive responsibilities for day-to-day affairs and the National Assembly is to be more active in discussing policy, while the party assumes a guiding strategic role. However, only two out of 44 prospective independent candidates were allowed to stand among the 602 contesting the National Assembly elections in 1992.[9] After the elections the chairman of the assembly was elected unopposed, as were the President and Prime Minister.[10] Pluralism is still subordinated to the Communist Party's determination to retain its leading role.

Constitutions have been just as much of a formality in China. Changes in the political climate meant the minting of new constitutions in 1954, 1975, 1978 and 1982.[11] The expedient manner in which constitutions are treated by the Chinese Communist Party has also been chillingly demonstrated in Tibet. Its status as an 'Autonomous Region' has been violated by a policy of genocide which even the Communist Party General Secretary Hu Yaobang was moved to describe as 'plain colonisation'.[12] Any legal guarantees given to Hong Kong are likely to be regarded in the same cavalier fashion by the Chinese leadership. Elections in China itself are correspondingly meaningless. Candidates for the National People's Congress (NPC) are pre-selected and its legislative functions are delegated to a Standing Committee of 130 trustworthy members.[13] A few 'quantitative' indicators of greater democracy have been introduced, such as the modifications to Prime Minister Li Peng's reports on government work to the NPC, which has flexed its muscles occasionally on issues such as the Three Gorges dam project. But power remains highly concentrated and centralised. The critical decision to crush the students' and workers' movements by massacring the protesters in Tiananmen Square was taken by just five men, the members of the Standing Committee of the Politburo.[14] The leadership has allowed genuine political debate for brief periods, but only for tactical reasons, as when Mao flushed out critics in the Hundred Flowers movement in 1957 and when Deng encouraged democracy activists to back him in his struggle against the Gang of Four in the aftermath of Mao's death. Once these movements had fulfilled the leadership's requirements they were suppressed. Wei Jingsheng, advocate of the 'fifth modernisation' of democracy was jailed for 14 years in 1980, while thousands of the intellectuals who spoke out in the Hundred Flowers movement became victims of 'anti-Rightist' purges.

Like China's NPC, the National Assembly in Laos has become bolder in criticising and amending legislation[15] and, as in Vietnam, the executive has been given more leeway within the party's strategic guidelines. But the LPRP fixedly maintains a one-party system, which its leaders argue is preferable to the upheavals experienced in Russia. Nor could Kim Il Sung countenance a multi-party system or any other measure of greater political freedom for fear of criticism spreading like wildfire through the brittle, tinder-dry framework of his régime. The 687 members of North Korea's Supreme People's Assembly have been nothing but a rubber stamp for the Workers' Party. Burma's brief experiment in democracy under SLORC has also remained unconsummated since the elections in May 1990. SLORC had hoped to divide opposition to its rule by sanctioning the establishment of more than 200 parties. The overwhelming victory by Aung San Suu Kyi's National League for Democracy, which won 392 of 485 seats contested,[16] was more than SLORC and Ne Win could stomach. She was placed under house arrest and SLORC has subsequently sought to undermine the NLD and to divide its other opponents in the Democratic Alliance of Burma. Aung San Suu Kyi continues to enjoy widespread popular support while the murderous and increasingly fractious SLORC régime has very little support outside the ranks of those who have profited from its encouragement of privately-owned businesses and the armed forces, which are its mainstay.

Where constitutions are instruments of policy judicial protection for human rights is negligible. China had no Ministry of Justice between 1959 and 1979.[17] Legal reforms in the Deng era have not affected 'the one underlying principle . . . that party control is sacrosanct and law is one of its tools'.[18] The Chief Justice of the Supreme Court doubles up as head of the

Central Committee's Political and Legal Commission and chief party disciplinarian.[19] Broad definitions of 'counter-revolutionary' activity strip any dissidents or protesters of legal protection. Courts have consistently been used to silence critics,.whether senior officials, students or workers. They play the same role in Vietnam, handing down long sentences to dissidents. In Burma Aung San Suu Kyi remained in detention beyond the expiry of a judicial order, in mid-1994. The law serves only as a convenient mask for authoritarian rule.

Independent criticism and the media are also stifled in all the market-Stalinist economies. The political uncertainty surrounding the succession to the Chinese leadership prompted a tightening of media controls in 1993 and 1994.[20] The selling of TV satellite dishes was virtually banned in late 1993 and commercial operators were put under pressure to limit hostile news coverage, to which Rupert Murdoch succumbed in dropping the BBC's news service from the Star TV network. Journalists have received heavy jail sentences in an effort to intimidate their colleagues. A Chinese journalist was given a life sentence in 1993 for leaking details of a speech by Jiang Zemin, General Secretary of the Communist Party, to its 14th Congress.[21] Early in 1994 a Hong Kong journalist, Xi Yang, received a 12-year sentence for disclosing the policies of the People's Bank of China on gold sales and interest rates, and the official who provided the information to him received a 15-year sentence, as part of a strong message to Hong Kong about the limits to free speech.[22] Occasional bursts of artistic freedom cannot obscure the Communist Party's belief that intellectuals and journalists, as much as the law, should be instruments of control.

In Vietnam the vintage language of Stalinism is applied at times to the press, which Communist Party General Secretary Do Muoi described in 1992 as a 'shock force on the ideological and cultural front'.[23] To a greater extent than in China, however, the Vietnamese Communists do let artists off the leash and have used the press in anti-corruption campaigns directed at Party members. The publication of magazines and novels with a sexual or violent content has also been allowed. Even so, the 1993 censorship law banned works 'hostile to the socialist motherland, advocating violence, divulging state or party secrets, falsifying history or denigrating the gains of the revolution'.[24] In Laos, foreign newspapers now circulate more widely in the capital, Vientiane, but writers remain under party 'guidance'. North Korea remains tightly sealed against the outside world, with Voice of America broadcasts being jammed since 1993 to prevent news percolating in through radios illegally acquired in border trade with China while domestically-produced radios are fixed on AM frequencies. Both press and television in Burma are controlled by SLORC.

Regional and provincial autonomy are also denied. One of the aims of Ne Win's seizure of power in 1962 was to prevent the granting of greater autonomy to ethnic minority provinces. Since then his various régimes have fought to crush ethnic struggles. While a series of peace deals have been struck with some rebel groups SLORC's new draft constitution will not grant significant autonomy. There was even a proposal, at the convention drafting the document, to reimpose Burman names for all provinces. The Lao leadership has been similarly wary of allowing too much autonomy to ethnic groups in a country with a long history of sporadic regional conflicts (particularly between lowlanders and highlanders). In Vietnam the legacy of war and the economic resurgence of the South have fed the leadership's suspicion that growing regional differences will erode its political hegemony. There have been gestures, such as bringing more Southerners into the politburo, but the party continues to operate double standards by stifling criticism more rigidly in the South.

China has the worst record of abuses in the treatment of minorities. Like the Russians, the Chinese extended their frontier into the uncolonised expanses of Central Asia in the nineteenth century. The territory of Xinjiang (Sinkiang) then brought under their control now has a population which is 46 per cent Uygur, most of whom are Muslims, and 36 per cent Han Chinese.[25] The ethnic and religious complexion of the province have put it in 'the frontline for Chinese worries about its outer empire'.[26] These worries can be traced back to an uprising in 1962 and have prompted Peking to encourage economic growth in the area in order to buy off separatism.

Tibet has seen the worst carnage of all the territories in what is still a Chinese empire. Since China invaded in 1951 dubious claims of historical suzerainty[27] have been used to justify the importation of rule by Peking's satraps. Nearly one and a quarter million Tibetans have died as a result of torture, murder, forced abortion, infanticide, starvation and labour camps.[28] The destruction of Tibetan culture, which Chinese leaders have tried to attribute exclusively to the period of the Cultural Revolution, began earlier, though it certainly intensified during those years, and continues today. All minority cultures inside China itself have come under attack, as examples of the 'old' practices that the Red Guards were intent on stamping out in those years and on other pretexts since; and Tibet has received the same treatment. Yet despite this sustained ideological and political onslaught most ordinary Tibetans appear to remain loyal to the Dalai Lama.[29]

The Chinese aim is to overcome this resistance by swamping the population. The Dalai Lama reported in 1994 that there were 7.5 million ethnic Chinese in Tibet, outnumbering the 6 million Tibetans,[30] and that population transfer shows no sign of slackening. China's Lhasa Development Plan, issued in 1980, reportedly calls for the destruction of all Tibetan buildings in the capital apart from a few tourist landmarks.[31] Armed resistance ended in the 1970s, but demonstrations shook Chinese rule in the late 1980s and helped refocus international attention on the plight of the Tibetans. Senior

Chinese leaders reportedly met this challenge in 1993 by planning to speed up population transfer and trying to foster dissent among Tibetan exiles.[32] A resolution of the Tibetans' struggle for freedom may well come only in the context of a much wider reconfiguration of the Chinese state. The dynamics of this process have already been set in motion partly as an unintended consequence of economic reforms. By granting much greater economic autonomy to the provinces the central authorities have already ceded control of important areas of policy. This clearly has the potential to lead on to a more explicit denial of political authority, setting up the possibility of open conflict.

MASS ORGANISATIONS

To supplement state/party control of the institutions of civil society these régimes still rely on the Stalinist props of mass organisations. Direct recruitment had brought large numbers of workers and peasants into the Workers' Party in North Korea by 1983[33] and the huge crowds assembled during the mourning for Kim Il Sung were evidence of the régime's ability to mobilise its citizens. The Chinese Communist Party numbered 52 millions in the early 1990s.[34] However all the parties in these countries have been suffering increasing problems with recruitment and membership. Anti-corruption purges have affected the Chinese party, while the Vietnamese party reduced its numbers by 20 per cent in the late 1980s to eliminate supposedly disreputable elements.[35] Recruitment has grown more difficult as party standing and connections become less important for obtaining employment and other opportunities.

Other mass organisations have lost their former effectiveness as means of mobilising support and exercising social control. The official trade unions in China were used in this way but now that the growth of private business is bypassing the old nexus between state enterprises and these unions, and there is pressure from the working class for unions that will provide more potent weapons in struggles over wages and conditions,[36] they are no longer a reliable buttress of the state. Vietnam's National Homeland Front has lost credibility just as the Communist Party has. Only in Burma is there a serious effort to revive and maintain the role of mass organisations. The Union Solidarity and Development Association (USDA) was set up in 1993, offering privileged access to state resources and services in the hope of drawing in a mass membership.[37] USDA provides SLORC with part of the turnout it needs for mass rallies, such as those held to back the new constitution, but it is a hollow pillar of support for the régime.

REPRESSIVE APPARATUSES

Although the formal role of mass organisations has thus declined, the Stalinist repressive apparatus continues to intrude on the lives of ordinary citizens. Street committees and the day-to-day monitoring of the actions and opinions of individuals are still a feature of life in Burma, North Korea and areas of Vietnam and they remain important components of the ideological transmission belt in China, disseminating the latest thinking of the leadership down to household level. The People's Armed Police has meanwhile been increased in number as the People's Liberation Army (PLA) shrinks.[38] In North Korea, classes in *juche* and an informer network are used to instil and police ideological conformity. Ordinary people will run away to avoid incriminating contact with foreigners and prison camps held 100 000 of Kim Il Sung's opponents at the time of his death. Strict controls on movement within the country have been unintentionally reinforced by a fuel crisis, but shortages also led to food riots.[39] Military plotting had reportedly resulted in the execution of officers involved.[40] In Burma, some easing of surveillance allows a little interaction between ordinary Burmese and foreign visitors, but any two Burmese who do not know one another will not openly criticise the government. As SLORC tries to create a semblance of normality the universities were reopened in 1992 after closure in 1991, but there is still a noticeable military presence in the cities, dissidents continue to be jailed and thousands of political prisoners remain in detention.

The changing patterns of life in a market economy are eroding some of the power of the street committees. As people move to the fast-growing areas in China and start work in private enterprises they elude the once ubiquitous state. The decay of co-operative institutions in rural areas also means less social control. Defiance of regulations on personal life – such as the one-child policy – becomes far easier once away from the prying eyes of organised informers. But more serious defiance is still met with arrest and punishment. China's political dissidents are whisked in and out of jail to a chorus of international and domestic condemnation or congratulation, according to the signal the Chinese leadership wants to send to the world. In 1993 Wei Jingsheng was released ahead of the voting on Peking's bid to stage the 2000 Olympics, only for its defeat to signal another bout of rhetorical intransigence on questions of human rights and dissidents. The executions of workers after the Tiananmen Square massacre showed the readiness of Communist Party leaders to kill those whom they fear most. The massacre itself left between 1000 and 1500 people dead in Peking[41] and hundreds more outside the capital in disturbances that touched cities as far away as Chengdu in Sichuan. Detentions and executions – mostly of workers – continued through the summer and autumn of 1989 and revealed that there are few if any limits to what those leaders would do to retain power.

Ne Win too showed that he would recognise no limits to repression when his soldiers killed 10 000 Burmese during the upheavals which led to SLORC's seizure of power in 1988.[42] Students, monks, workers, farmers and some members of the armed forces took part in a series of demonstrations demanding democracy and began to take control of the running of the economy, through Strike Centres and People's Committees.[43] Ne Win turned first General Sein Lwin and then to the civilian Maung Maung to provide more acceptable masks for his continued political control but their inability to stabilise the situation forced him to resort to the army to reimpose his rule in the form of General Saw Maung and SLORC. Calculated killings drove protesters from the streets and singled out students. Besides the 10 000 who died at least an equal number fled to join the various guerrilla struggles around the country.[44]

Burma and China have seen the most violent suppression of political protest among the market-Stalinist countries. The Vietnamese Communists have not yet been tested by large demonstrations and have been able to pick off individual activists. Amnesty International's Vietnam representative, for instance, received a 20-year jail term in 1992.[45] The number of political prisoners now admitted to by the government is less than 300[46] (against 90–100 000 after reunification).

DECLINING LEGITIMACY

All these régimes are experiencing declining legitimacy. Memories of the revolutionary struggles which brought them to power are fading, while disillusionment at the outcome of those struggles sets in. As the vanquished imperialists return to Vietnam, triumphantly flaunting their wealth, criticism of the jettisoning of revolutionary principles is brushed aside. Thus, for instance, the 'Hanoi Hilton' prison, where revolutionaries were held by the French, is being torn down to make way for a luxury hotel and shopping complex owned by a Singaporean enterprise.[47] Nguyen Co Thach, a former foreign minister, was one of the few who publicly dissented from the commerical hyperbole surrounding the end of the US trade embargo early in 1994. 'The latecomer buffalo will drink polluted water'[48] he remarked acidly as American companies scrambled for contracts. While the honeymoon period of initial contacts with freespending foreigners persists, Thach may well remain in a minority, but the debates reported within the Vietnamese Communist Party in 1993–94 reflected his brand of ambivalence over the wider consequences of this capitulation to international capital.

Muddled ideological formulations have become the hallmark of the Vietnamese and Chinese leaderships as they struggle to reconcile 'socialism' with a subservient position in the international economic order. Gobbledegook such as a 'socialist-oriented market mechanism under state management'[49] rubs shoulders with the theory advanced by the then-General Secretary Zhao Ziyang in 1987 that China was in the 'initial state of socialism'. During this stage, as Gordon White points out, 'a wide range of economic forms and policies were admissible as long as they fostered economic growth'.[50] Political systems which not only fail, as they have for many years, to live up to socialist standards of civil and political rights, but which also start to uphold the rights of entrepreneurs with no formal connection to ruling parties over the interests of workers, are certain to lose any residual legitimacy. Particularly among that half of the Vietnamese population that is under the age of 20, for instance, invocations of the glorious deeds of the war years are ineffective when the veterans of that struggle are so visibly marginalised and unemployed. The 'workers' paradise' of North Korea has managed to shore up its myths only by rigidly excluding information about the outside world, but once the seal is broken the ideological props of the régime will crumble on contact. Already food riots and growing lawlessness are indicative of dissatisfaction at economic catastrophe and the Kims' monstrous personality cult. *Sotto voce* grumbling about economic problems – especially inflation and unemployment – and political repression has become the norm in Burma as people wait for a chance to turn the tables on SLORC.

As legitimacy decays, the market-Stalinist régimes have come to rely principally on economic growth to bolster their credibility. Even in North Korea, where any kind of change carried high risks for the Kims and their clique, economic contraction and a looming crisis of legitimacy prompted overtures to foreign investors as early as 1984. But, before we consider the unexpected political consequences which growth has produced, it is worth noting the 'hearts and minds' efforts to head off dissent.

POLITICAL CONCESSIONS

Party leaders have responded to diminishing credibility with various 'drives' to clean up party discipline, root out corruption and restore morale. This is a direct response to the popular unrest which corruption provokes. One of the main demands of the protesters in Tiananmen Square in 1989 was for the ending of corrupt practices within the Chinese Communist Party. The same practices have provoked peasants to riot in their thousands across China, where they have been met with the mobilisation of army units. The ineffectiveness of 'rectification' campaigns directed at this behaviour is plain to see from the fact that they have been waged since the early 1980s. The opportunities are simply too great in China's market-Stalinist economy and senior Party figures and their accomplices are seldom targeted, except where disciplinary action becomes part of wider factional in-fighting.[51] Often all that happens is that hapless minions are shot, anti-corruption hotlines attract thousands of denunciations and a handful of prominent scapegoats are jailed. The same problems are apparent in Vietnam, where ministers have been tried but the root causes have not been dealt with. In Laos too middle-level functionaries have been penalised most. Corruption contributes to a pervasive climate of cynicism that can easily turn to anger. In Burma and North Korea, corruption is a relatively minor issue in the much wider condemnation of the failings of their régimes. Nevertheless, it is becoming more important in Burma as the military's involvement grows in business and more foreign investment is attracted to the country and in North Korea as a result of the collapse of the economic system and resulting shortages which force even formerly well-off officials to take a chance on corrupt dealings.

Attempts to head off those protests which have been sidetracked into religious movements (as in the veiled authoritarian states) have demonstrated more flexibility. The Chinese authorities have been harshest where religion and ethnic unrest coincide, as in Xinjiang. Muslim protests over schoolbooks in Qinghai were met with state violence that left nine people dead in late 1993.[52] In Tibet the rulers have applied the principle that religion is more controllable if it is regulated. Monasteries are being rebuilt and young men are able to become monks with permission. Whether this will work in the longer term is not so clear, as the Chinese can expect little gratitude. The Catholic church in China has been under the same pressure to submit to state regulation and control, with priests who refuse being detained and beaten. Seven Christians were arrested early in 1994 as new laws regulating religion were given their first test.[53] Some greater latitude has, however, been granted to try to check the rise of millenarianism, which made an appearance in Western China in late 1992 and which has a natural constituency among the growing dislocated rural population.

In North Korea Protestant and Catholic churches have been allowed to open since the late 1980s[54] to provide a safety valve for some of the despair that living conditions induce, but any coalescing of political opposition around a religious pole would be likely to be promptly squashed. In both Vietnam and Burma widespread religious beliefs and the political role played by religious organisations in the past have made the authorities wary of too heavy-handed an approach to dissent from these sources. A high percentage of the Vietnamese are nominally Buddhist and Buddhist monks played a leading part in protests against the Diem régime in the South in the early 1960s. The Vietnamese leadership has tried to balance making concessions with retaining control of religious movements. General Secretary Do Muoi has been visiting temples and the Catholic Phat Diem Cathedral, while religious building, publishing and begging have all been sanctioned.[55] Concessions have not satisfied Buddhist critics, however, who continue to agitate for the release of detainees and the restoration of the Unified Buddhist Church, replaced by a state-sponsored body in 1981.[56] Nor have they prevented violent clashes and the upsurge of religious cults, one of which led to 56 deaths in October 1993. The biggest cult, the eclectic Cao Dai, claims 4 million adherents. Catholicism also needs to be appeased, prompting the Vietnamese government to despatch a mission to the Holy See in 1992.[57] Buddhist monks have been a rallying point for the opposition to government in Burma since the days of British colonial rule. They were in the forefront of the clashes with the various governments which held power during 1988. An uneasy truce has since been patched up between SLORC and organised Buddhism. Muslims have, however, been persecuted, forcing nearly 300 000 to flee to Bangladesh in early 1992.

For SLORC the most important deals are those which it has struck with ethnic minority rebels. Almost from the moment of independence from Britain in 1948 the Karen have been fighting for an independent state in South East Burma.[58] Their struggle spread to other minorities including the Karenni, the Pao, the Mon, the Shan and the Kachin. In combination with the insurrection of the Communist Party of Burma (CPB), these created a permanent backdrop of armed struggle and crisis for the Burmese state. Those who fled the urban repression in 1988 swelled the numbers of ethnic rebels by another 18 battalions.[59] SLORC's first priority in creating the appearance of normality was stabilising the cities; meanwhile, it kept up the offensive against the ethnic minorities, notoriously pressing villagers into service as porters on whom appalling casualty rates were inflicted. Since 1989, however, the insurgencies have progressively been suspended with truces. The CPB lost support from Peking after 1988 and, following a series of mutinies, its forces dissolved into their ethnic constituents.[60] These have since made deals with SLORC to suspend fighting in exchange for supplies.[61] Others groups including the Shan State Army and the Pao National Army have followed suit. Most importantly for SLORC, the 6000 strong Kachin rebels agreed a truce in October 1993, leaving only the Karen as the major force opposing it in the field.[62] By January 1994 the Karen were in talks and in February so were the Karenni, though talks with the Mon broke down in July that year. Overall, SLORC's strategy of striking separate deals with each group appeared to be paying off. These deals are, it should be remembered, truces in which the acquiescence of the rebels rests partly on their ability to engage in profitable cross-border trading. They provide no more of a lasting solution to ethnic minority demands than SLORC's constitution will to demands for democracy.

Concessions have also been made by market-Stalinist régimes with a view to enlisting the support of the middle class and students. The various phases of liberalisation in the media and in cultural life in Vietnam and China have been intended to win back the support of these groups. In Burma, too, drawing

back the intelligentsia and businessmen from abroad has also been an element in economic development strategies, baited with the promise of a more
relaxed political climate. If these promises are to be honoured – and they
have been thoroughly dishonoured in China in the past – then they carry
with them considerable political risks from the opening up of channels of
criticism. In most cases, market-Stalinist régimes have sought the capital
and technical expertise of emigré nationals without the trappings of political
liberalisation.

POLITICAL DYNAMICS OF GROWTH

At the centre of their efforts at relegitimation have been strategies for economic growth. Whether through meeting specific targets for *per capita* income levels and growth rates, or just through the spread of consumer goods,
Stalinist leaders hope that the economy will resurrect their popularity. But
any strategy of economic development based on a greater role for the private sector has a hidden political dynamic which runs counter to the objective of Stalinism. As economic change proceeds it undermines market-Stalinist
legitimacy further. Partly this is a consequence of the awareness of relative
deprivation in the increasingly unequal societies described in Chapter 3,
combined with the rising expectations which growth has created. But it is
also the result of specific social and economic changes that lead to more
uncontrolled and uncontrollable activity. As we noted above, the repressive
apparatus of street committees is less effective now that population movement is under way on a huge scale in China. Since 1985 the right to move
temporarily to the cities has enabled millions of peasants to flout the *hukou*
restrictions on residence[63] and the system has decayed further since.[64] Most
of the workers in the huge Shenzhen labour market are there unofficially:
up to 150 million people are roaming China in search of work, outside Communist Party control of the *minutiae* of their daily lives. Another 68 million
will join the urban workforce by the start of the next century bringing total
unemployment to as many as 268 million, according to the Ministry of Labour.
An urban underclass has already been formed and it was probably this which
constituted the backbone of resistance to the PLA units entering Peking to
crush protest in Tiananmen Square in 1989.[65] It also feeds the explosion of
crime in the rapidly growing provinces. Guangdong's 'frontier' problem of
rising crime, including the kidnapping of investors and cross-border robber-
ies in Hong Kong, can be traced to the conditions of insecurity in which
this new floating population lives. In concert with corrupt officials and security personnel, criminals have created a free-for-all in which the government is unable to preserve personal security or equality of opportunity.
Campaigns against 'social vices' are as ineffective as those against party

indiscipline. As communications and transport improve so more people are drawn to the cities by hopes of wealth and opportunity and by the return of rural/urban income inequalities. Vietnam is only a few years behind China in this respect. Hanoi and Ho Chi Minh City are already pulling in opportunistic or desperate peasants and creating an urban underclass of beggars, prostitutes and casual labourers.

Where these people do find employment in the formal economy it is far more likely to be in the expanding private sector rather than the stagnant state sector. Jobs, income, welfare and housing are no longer in the gift of the Communist Party, nor can they any longer be withdrawn as the penalty for political dissent. While the Chinese Communist Party has tried to bolster party cells in workplaces and universities since the Tiananmen massacre, it has much less clout in private sector workplaces. As more workers and peasants are told to fend for themselves in the economy, the idea of taking responsibility for the organisation of their lives can easily spread to the political sphere.

Private industry and foreign investment bring other problems for market-Stalinist régimes. One is that foreigners tend to insist on legal protection for their investments. In societies where the legal system has served party political purposes the idea of placing the law above party authority is anathema to bureaucrats, yet foreign investors and their lawyers are adamant that legal loopholes must be plugged as the price for the commitment of long term investment capital in all the market-Stalinist systems. Binding joint venture agreements, contracts with suppliers, intellectual property protection and properly documented tax codes all crop up as issues. Some investors may ignore them on the grounds that nothing will be enforceable, but China may well yield to the pressure and set up special economic courts to try to insulate the foreigners' demands and practices from the rest of the legal system. If this happens, the door will be ajar for Chinese citizens to begin demanding that courts also respect their formal civil and political rights; and Vietnam will be under severe pressure to follow suit. Western investors argued in 1993 that Vietnam had a matter of two or three years in which to introduce the kinds of legal guarantees they wanted.

Such investors would prefer to avoid unsettling political effects in the search for a disciplined, cheap labour force. For all the talk in the West of the benign effects of trading with and investing in market-Stalinist economies the intention of these capitalist interests is not to disrupt the economic and political relations on which their profits rest. Only when the desire to promote the development of the domestic market in such countries takes precedence over the quest for cheap labour do they want to see purchasing power spread more widely through the economy. But political change which might see the emergence of forces resistant to multinational influence in the economy would be most unwelcome to foreign investors.

The effects of economic change also reach deep inside ruling parties, dividing them over the question of how far to pursue economic reform and resulting in public debates on the pace of reform, such as those in Vietnam in 1993 and 1994. At the mid-term conference in January 1994 there was talk of 'economic restructuring along the line of industrialisation and modernisation'[66] but the specifics were unclear, betraying the division within the leadership on how to proceed. Changes in the upper reaches of the bureaucracy in North Korea indicated that the same kind of debate was taking place in the last year of Kim Il Sung's rule. The reappearance of Kim's brother, Kim Yong-Ju, was interpreted by some analysts as preparing the way for a joint leadership with Kim Jong Il and as a means of bridging the divide between the younger Kim and party conservatives. The transfer of 'reformers' among senior officials was also pored over, but the biggest bout of speculation on future economic direction was that triggered by Kim Il Sung's death. At that point, it was still unclear to commentators outside North Korea whether or not Kim Jong Il wanted to endorse economic reform and, if he did, how long it would take before he felt confident enough to set it in motion. In Laos, meanwhile, resistance to economic reform has been apparent at provincial level and among older party members and senior military figures.

The more embedded the state is in industry the more disruptive are the shock waves of change. Where bureaucrats derive their power base from the scale of the industrial operations they control they are resistant to change which endangers these operations. Economic reform tends to be to the benefit of light industry and at the expense of heavy industry. It also promotes private industry over state industry. In China, Vietnam and North Korea, where the Stalinist legacy is an agglomeration of state-owned heavy industrial plant, a fault line in the bureaucracy is clearly exposed by the reformers' drive to close loss-making plants. The issue of bankruptcy becomes a bureaucratic battleground, as advocates of heavy industry within the party are put under pressure to resist closure both by their own interests and, from below, by workers. The regional pattern of heavy industry opens another fault line. In China it is concentrated in the North East and in the factories of the 'Third Line' built in remote Sichuan away from American atomic weapons. Cuts in heavy industry mean further relative gains for the prosperous coastal provinces.

In Vietnam heavy industry was built in the North during the years of partition and reliance on Soviet aid. Closures there aggravate the growing gap in the relative incomes of North and South. They also heighten the fears of older bureaucrats that destabilisation and 'peaceful evolution' might undermine the régime. Thus a generational divide becomes a further factor in party fragmentation. Older bureaucrats tend to be tied more to heavy, state-owned industry; younger ones are more comfortable in the murky interstices of the state and the private sector. This process is most advanced in China, apparent in Vietnam and in its early stages in North Korea, where heavy industry was downgraded in late 1993[67] to the disadvantage of those provinces which have benefited most from the concentration of industry. With little industry to speak of, it is not a significant divide in Burma or Laos. Resistance to reform within the LPRP is focused more on the adverse social consequences of new economic development than on defence of certain industries and bureaucratic powerbases.

The overall result is to set up opposing camps of winners and losers within the state and party. The winners are those elements of the party, and army, which are involved in the new market economy, whether at regional, industrial or enterprise level. Alongside them are the new class of entrepreneurs. In the losers' camp are army units which have seen budgets cut without being able to replenish funds from commerical activity, bureaucrats in the wrong sectors or regions or enterprises (up to one million of whom may lose their jobs in China[68]) and state industry employees (60 to 70 million Chinese workers are at risk of unemployment). Each of these groups uses its position within the party, or the pressure it can exert on the party, to urge or to resist reform. Severe intra-party contradictions develop, as simultaneously preserving social control and implementing economic reform become more and more difficult.

The armed forces become just as divided as the ruling parties. By the end of 1993 the Vietnamese armed forces operated over 300 enterprises, occupying around 70 000 troops (12 per cent of regular forces)[69] and were beginning to seek joint venture agreements with foreign investors. Whether the proceeds are used for officers' perks or new equipment, divisions are clearly emerging between those who prosper and those who do not. The same splits have appeared in the Burmese armed forces. Drugs and smuggling, rather than industrial production, are the main source of income and factionalism is the result, as greed and enrichment create jealousies. Officers are shifted around commands when their venality upsets the generals in Rangoon who are the biggest profiteers.[70] The enterprises of the PLA in China represent a more extreme version of what is happening in the Vietnamese case. It controls over 20 000 of them and has become a vital partner for foreign investors in several areas of the economy.[71] The alliances being forged with business interests complicate the future for an already divided and factionridden institution. In 1992 Deng Xiaoping removed Yang Shangkuan from the Presidency and dismissed his half-brother Yang Baibing from his post as head of the army's General Political Department, on suspicion that they had been plotting to control the choice of the next effective Communist Party leader. Since then, the nominal party leader Jiang Zemin has been manoeuvring to assert his formal control of the PLA through his chairmanship of the Central Military Commission. This jockeying for power is echoed in the politicisation of the army as elements are drawn into an alliance with party factions, nascent domestic capitalists and foreign capital. Political leaders are consequently anxious that the involvement of the army in business may prevent them using it as a unified repressive force.

TRANSITION TO VEILED AUTHORITARIANISM?

The new hybrid ruling class of bureaucracy, military and capital in market-Stalinist states can and does fulfil the conditions for accumulation in the short term. But it exposes more vividly the frailty of the 'socialist' legitimacy still claimed by these states. As legitimacy wanes and economic change splinters ruling institutions all these régimes face considerable political uncertainty. For the leaderships a metamorphosis into veiled authoritarianisms is probably the most appealing outcome. Not only do bureaucrats in North Korea admire Singapore, but Lee Kuan Yew's success in retaining power behind the facade of democracy also has an appeal to the Vietnamese politburo. The role of the armed forces in Indonesia makes its system a more attractive model for SLORC in Burma, which has modelled USDA on Suharto's Golkar. Chinese leaders are loath to acknowledge any alternative model, but reformers within the Communist Party looked favourably on the concept of 'new authoritarianism' (essentially Singapore, but also South Korea and Taiwan before the changes of the late 1980s) as a system that attracts less international opprobrium.[72] Any such remodelling of these régimes would be principally for international consumption in face of human rights pressure and the threat of trade sanctions.

The Vietnamese Communist Party probably has the best chance of making this outward transformation while retaining power in the medium term. The economy has registered consistent growth and inflation has been brought under control. Although the benefits of growth are being shared unevenly the resulting tensions have not yet become acute. Income disparities – whether regional, rural/urban or between private and state industries – are not yet so great as to create a widespread backlash. The rich endowment of offshore oil gives the government financial room for manoeuvre not available in North Korea or Burma. International aid – albeit with conditions – has been relatively large and foreign banks are ready to lend capital. Since the withdrawal from Cambodia, ASEAN governments have been supportive of the Vietnamese régime and accepted Vietnamese membership of ASEAN from July 1995, offering some economic advantages within the ASEAN Free Trade Area (AFTA) and less tangible political dividends from reintegration into the region.

Inside Vietnam the Communist Party has at least attempted to withdraw from the state and to give the appearance of debate within the National

Assembly. It still has some residual legitimacy in the North, from the wars of independence and reunification. Ho Chi Minh remains above the fray of daily politics as a symbol of the party's paternalistic and patriotic devotion, and nationalism can be invoked against China, with the disputed territory of the Spratly Islands providing the issue on which Vietnam may, literally, do battle. The Communist Party is further strengthened by the divided character of its opponents. Emigré bomb plots do not attract public support, nor is there an obvious common organising focus for redundant state enterprise workers in the North, would-be separatists in the South, marginalised ethnic minorities in the central highlands and disgruntled peasants in the Red River delta.

Nevertheless, the Communist Party is growing afraid of the destabilising effects of peaceful evolution and of emerging pluralism. The very division of the opposition makes the party more fearful that any political liberalisation will lead to uncontrolled disintegration. No 'responsible' opposition exists with which it can hold a dialogue and to which it can make cosmetic concessions. Its international 'friends' are now governments which welcome the opportunity of more trade and investment links but have little interest in preserving a specifically Communist régime. Thailand, Singapore, Taiwan and the like will support any government which allows them to exploit Vietnamese labour and resources, unlike the former Soviet patrons who were willing to provide financial support and had an ideological stake in the maintenance of explicitly Communist rule. None of these problems is yet critical for the Vietnamese Communists. But beyond the medium term, especially in the wake of a probable severe upheaval in China, their position is likely to look exposed and increasingly untenable. Vietnam might come to resemble Poland, with a fragmented array of political groups emerging, each representing sectional or regional interests, but with a substantial rump of Communists.

What happens in Vietnam will have profound implications for the fate of the Lao People's Revolutionary Party. If the Vietnamese Communists lose their political monopoly the LPRP is unlikely to be able to retain its exclusive hold on power. The Lao leadership has followed the Vietnamese model in much of its economic and financial reform and it is also likely to be exposed to similar political consequences. The traditional alternative to a Vietnamese alignment – a closer relationship with Thailand – is unlikely to give the LPRP another crutch to lean on. Neither business nor the military in Thailand has anything to gain from shoring up a Stalinist régime in Laos; on the contrary, the weaker the Lao government is the more opportunities they will have to pillage natural resources. But so long as the Vietnamese Communists remain in power political developments in Laos are likely to continue to lag behind those in Vietnam. Without so many of the political problems of dismantling the state sector the major challenges are those presented by the dissatisfaction of workers in the new industries in Vientiane and by the long term problem of regional antagonism to central government. Neither is likely to become chronic in the near future.

For the other three Stalinist régimes succession crises open the prospect of marked instability in the near future and a much smaller chance of a transition to veiled authoritarianism. In all three the outcome is highly unpredictable, but neither unified Communist control nor military rule in Burma can be expected to remain intact. SLORC has tried to guarantee the military's involvement in the future Burmese state by drafting a constitution which gives it a leading role in society and establishes military, political and administrative experience as qualifications for an elected president. This constitution was forced down the throats of a specially assembled convention and has no popular legitimacy. The qualifications for president, which include a requirement of 20 years' continuous residence, have been framed specifically to disqualify Aung San Suu Kyi. In reality, constitution-writing provides no mechanism to guard against the outbreak of serious factional fighting in the army once Ne Win dies.

As in the veiled authoritarian regimes, Ne Win has accumulated considerable personal power and patronage during more than 30 years of ruling Burma. It is unlikely that competitors for power in the military would want to see that inheritance pass undivided to Ne Win's apparent appointed successor, General Khin Nyunt, the military intelligence chief and SLORC Secretary. A power struggle, aggravated by the divisions within the army caused by private business dealings, could open a chink in the régime's repressive front. Once that happens popular leverage can begin to be applied. Differences between the army leadership and its rank and file, among whom Aung San Suu Kyi has some support, would increase the chances of the military régime beginning to crack. The lack of depth to political culture and Aung San Suu Kyi's own political inexperience do not, however, bode well for the future in the event of SLORC's collapse. Aung San Suu Kyi could play a similar role to Cory Aquino in the Philippines as a rallying point for opposition to military rule, but the reversion to 'normal' politics which Aquino and the People Power movement ushered in is not possible in a country where political life has been suffocated for more than 30 years. More likely is a situation analagous to Romania, where it was sections of the former state bureaucracy which moved into a political vacuum. Alternatively ethnic rebels could see a virtual political vacuum as the opportunity to press for independence. Either way Aung San Suu Kyi could find herself the figurehead of a régime locked in internal struggles.

The other possible outcome is that the military leadership, conscious of the popular desire for revenge for the killings of 1988, recognises the risks of in-fighting and, rather than hanging separately, prefers to hang together. Having dampened down the ethnic insurgencies, at least for the moment, they are better placed to face down urban unrest during a transition period. There is very little room for compromise in between the extremes of continued army rule or its overthrow. The constitutional drafting exercise did try to create the impression of a functioning political life, but the essence of its deliberations was a stark choice between accepting instructions from the generals or being silenced. Aung San Suu Kyi's own refusal to strike a deal with SLORC has helped to preserve implacably opposed positions[73] and any talks between SLORC and the UN can be expected to be little other than an attempt to find a back way out of international isolation.

There is a good chance that the stalemate will break with Ne Win's death. If not, foreign interests may end up determining the path of political development. Few Burmese believe they can despatch the SLORC without international help and pressure. Students pitted themselves against the régime in 1988 and paid a terrible price. What they and other opponents now observe, sadly, is that ASEAN governments are pursuing a policy of 'constructive engagement' and grooming it for eventual ASEAN membership.[74] In early 1994 Japan was meanwhile looking for a political pretext on which to resume aid.[75] SLORC thus evades the international pariah status visited on it after 1988, while Singaporean investors and Thai logging companies make money. Japanese, European and US companies have also been active, if more discreet. That, in turn, helps SLORC build a slightly broader base of support within the urban middle class. More foreign exchange earnings help ease shortages, whether of fuel or fertiliser. Ironically, it may take another bout of demonstrations and violent repression on the streets before pressure on the issue of human rights is once again brought to bear on SLORC, on companies which trade with Burma and on governments inside and outside Asia. Denying SLORC the comfort of trade and investment and condemning it internationally would strengthen the hand of its opponents. Changes in the Chinese leadership which cut off the support of its closest international ally would also help the cause of greater political freedom.

In China the moment of succession after Deng Xiaoping's death will be enormously testing for the Communist Party. Supreme authority within the Party has rested with Deng since 1978, yet by the early 1990s he no longer held political office. Aspirants to that authority have to add it somehow to the offices they hold. At the same time widespread hopes have come to rest on the changeover. Although Deng's death was being 'discounted' by financial analysts by the end of 1993 all the contending groups – regional, ethnic, army, industrial, party, student and peasant – see the impending moment of transition as a chance to strengthen their position during a period of a weakened leadership. The weakness of leadership rivals, none of whom commands a following among all these groups, will heighten expectations if each tries to drum up wider support by using the media and building coalitions of interests. Alternatively, recognition of their lack of a mass following may incline them to try to arrange a collective leadership. Some of the precedents for this move suggest that it would be futile, as it was in the USSR after Stalin's death, in Yugoslavia after Tito's or in China itself following Mao's. There is no reason to believe that a collective party leadership would be any more capable of managing the Chinese economy or balancing interests and demands than the same group of bureaucrats were when accountable to Deng. If anything they would find it even harder to address sensitive questions such as the reform of state industries and face the political consequences of large scale redundancies and divisions within the Communist Party. The difficult decisions on economic policy discussed in Chapter 2, postponed during the prelude to Deng's death, are thereby delayed even further.

The longer Chinese leaders refuse any measure of *glasnost* the more it becomes apparent that they have not avoided demands for political freedom, but merely bottled them up. To employ another Russian parallel, if the massacre in Tiananmen Square is equated with the shootings at the Winter Palace in 1905, then China has still to face its 1917. Whereas in 1905 Czarism could still call on the loyalty of peasants and the revolution was crushed in St Petersburg, by 1917 the industrial working class had expanded rapidly in Petrograd and Moscow and Czarism has lost the loyalty of the peasantry. Likewise, in 1989 Deng and the PLA were confronted principally with protests in Peking (in which workers played a far more significant part than students' accounts suggested[76]) and other cities while peasant unrest was limited. When China's leaders face the next challenge to the state they are likely to find larger numbers of restless urban workers ready to demand change and more of the peasantry alienated. The prospects are greater than before that the opposition can coalesce, even if only through a shared distaste for a Communist Party which has outlived its popular support as assuredly as the Soviet party had in the 1980s.

As in Eastern Europe a transition may be mediated first through existing institutions and reformist leaders. The former General Secretary Zhao Ziyang, for example, might be cast as a Hans Modrow or a Karoly Grosz[77] and an invigorated NPC could at last become a transmission belt for change from below rather than for commands from above. Such institutions and leaders should not be expected to play more than a transitory role in a moment where demands are likely to escalate rapidly. Economic, social and political grievances in China are so widespread that they cannot be contained by an unrepresentative body. Yet the outcome of their eventual expression is unclear, for the possibilities range from prolonged chaos to a managed devolution of power to the provinces.

Chaos may involve both rural and urban unrest, army factionalism surfacing in open conflicts and regional breakaways, all precipitating the flight of thousands of people who would far outnumber the Vietnamese exodus of the 1980s. Managed devolution would see the provinces expanding the degree of autonomy that they already enjoy, applying decentralised economic management to inherently more manageable economies, entering more international agreements as quasi-independent entities and formalising their economic divergence in intra-provincial trade agreements. This process could facilitate the integration of both Hong Kong and Taiwan within a looser structure and enable Guangdong and Fujian to make use of the membership of international bodies which Hong Kong and Taiwan belong to; it could even allow the Dalai Lama to negotiate greater autonomy for Tibet while still submitting to Chinese policy on defence and foreign relations. In the coastal provinces where the economic base of the Communist Party – state industry and the preponderance of the peasantry – has been eroded, its political monopoly would come to an end: elsewhere it might cling to power. Given the sheer volatility of contemporary China, leadership manoeuvrings could be a starting point for either of these outcomes, or any other in the range between them, for once party upheavals are set in motion social forces will become engaged in a haphazard fashion. The formal and informal centralisation of power within the Communist Party means that if order is seen to have disintegrated in Peking (as in Petrograd in 1917) then a free-for-all will rapidly follow elsewhere. The speed of action and degree of organisation of other forces then becomes determinant. If Communist regional bosses are quick to make tactical concessions to workers, peasants and students and take the initiative, managed devolution is more likely. If those bosses fall out amongst themselves and enlist mass support, while the PLA disintegrates in the event of its effective decapitation, then chaos is more likely. In any event, the chances of the quiet tones of liberal democracy being heard above the turmoil are slim. Other Asian governments, greatly fearing chaos in China, have enlarged their navies partly in preparation for the flight of huge numbers of people. As in the case of North Korea they would be prepared to support virtually any Chinese régime which appeared to be capable of preserving order and avoiding a mass exodus.

As for North Korea, the succession to Kim Il Sung has set in motion major changes, possibly violent and chaotic, almost certainly leading to reunification with the South in a matter of years rather than decades. Immediately after Kim Il Sung's death it was not clear what constellation of forces existed within the leadership of the Workers' Party and the army. Although Kim Jong Il assumed all his father's offices, his particular star is likely to burn out in a matter of months or years, consigning him to the same historical dustbin as 'Baby Doc' Duvalier, sometime dictator of Haiti. Kim Jong Il's following is assured neither in the Workers' Party, where high level factionalism includes his stepmother and half-brother and where his mass following is vitiated by a lack of charisma and genuine revolutionary credentials to match his father's, nor is it secure in the army despite his efforts to cultivate senior officers.

If the Kim Jong Il regime does embark on economic reform it would only prolong its demise briefly and could even accelerate it. Access to information about the world outside North Korea, from which its citizens have been rigorously excluded (unlike their counterparts in the former East Germany), would expose the lies on which the state is built. A successor régime from the same Stalinist mould would also have difficulty in limiting the political effects of reform. As in China, reform would divide the bureaucracy, army and people at large and its momentum 'once begun, is bound to accelerate to the point where pressures for reunification become irresistible', according to Aidan Foster-Carter.[78] That dynamic also has grave implications for the emergent bourgeois democracy in South Korea, to which we turn in the next chapter.

Leaders of South Korea fear either chaotic collapse or bloody repression in the North. The latter is what Kim Il Sung was preparing for in his pursuit of a nuclear device to guarantee against intervention by South Korea, the US or the UN in domestic affairs. If Kim Jong Il or other leaders order the murder of thousands of people to protect themselves (assuming the armed forces obey such orders) they want to be able to do so without military threats from across the border and a nuclear device gives them a protection which Saddam Hussein lacked. Such a policy might be tolerated by the leaders of South Korea, whose principal concern is to find any régime in the North with which it can co-operate in a kind of 'managed collapse' which would allow companies from the South to begin exploiting the cheap labour and raw materials in the North without the South having to take fiscal or political responsibility for administering the North. Whether the people of South Korea would be willing to see their fellow Koreans killed in large numbers by a Stalinist dictatorship while their own government stood by is less likely.

The alternative, or the prelude, to repression is a descent into anarchy as the economy collapses and starving people take to the streets. This choice cannot be avoided if the economy continues to shrink at 5 per cent a year. In the absence of organised opposition groups, anarchy might play into the hands of former officials of the Workers' Party, but chiefly it would lead to demands in the South to assume the economic and political burdens of reunification.

APPENDIX: CAMBODIA: MARKET STALINISM AND ABSOLUTE MONARCHY

The Cambodian government which took power following the democratic elections organised by the UN in May 1993 is the most peculiar hybrid in Asia, comprised of ex-Communists and royalists. Of the two prime ministers, Prince Norodom Ranariddh is the son of Prince Sihanouk, whose 'enlightened despotism'[79] led the country towards disaster between 1954 and 1970, and the other, Hun Sen, is a former Khmer Rouge official and prime minister of the State of Cambodia (SOC), the one-party, Vietnamese-backed state created in the 1980s out of the ashes of the Khmer Rouge's rule. The co-operation of two leaders from such disparate backgrounds is governed by a shared desire to extract as much profit as possible from the international aid flowing into Cambodia and from the liberalisation of the economy.

The modern history of Cambodia is one of unbridled opportunism amongst political groups that has extended to cooperation between royalists and the ultra-nationalist Khmer Rouge. Having been overthrown in the 1970 coup by Lon Nol, Sihanouk sided with the Khmer Rouge to win his way back to power. During the Khmer Rouge dictatorship from 1975 to 1978 Sihanouk was the nominal head of the state of Democratic Kampuchea while Pol Pot and his confederates caused the deaths of between 1 and 2 million people, from a population of 7 million, as many as 300 000 of whom were executed.[80] The Khmer Rouge fled Phnom Penh after the Vietnamese invasion at the end of 1978 and, although Democratic Kampuchea continued to enjoy recognition from Western powers, Cambodia became the People's Republic of Kampuchea under the control of Heng Samrin and his colleagues.

This new Cambodia 'took on the familiar contours of the Communist party-state'[81] with controlled elections, but also addressed itself to economic stabilisation and the reconstruction of social services such as education.[82] During the 1980s, a subsistence economy expanded, the prospect of more broadly based growth appeared and the State of Cambodia (as it was renamed in 1989)[83] consolidated its hold on the countryside. A civil war was, however, continued by the Coalition Government of Democratic Kampuchea (CGDK), comprising the Khmer Rouge, the right-wing Khmer People's National Liberation Front (KPNLF) and the royalist *Front Uni National pour un Cambodge Indépendent, Neutre, Pacifique et Coopératif* (FUNCINPEC). Sihanouk's participation in this coalition was secured at the urging of the China and the US[84] which, together with the ASEAN countries, supported the CGDK. Thailand provided bases while China and the US contributed arms but, despite this backing Vietnamese troops were withdrawn gradually as the Cambodian forces demonstrated their ability to resist the CGDK and restrain it in border areas.

This withdrawal removed the last pretext for international intervention in Cambodia and, at the same time, the switch in Vietnamese policy towards closer economic integration with ASEAN, necessitated partly by the collapse of Soviet aid, opened the way for negotiations on a political settlement. Under the Peace Agreement signed in Paris in October 1991 the United Nations Transitional Authority in Cambodia (UNTAC) took over the running of the country to prepare for the May 1993 elections.[85] The UN also supervised the return of 370 000 refugees from Thailand. One of UNTAC's other main responsibilities was to disarm the State of Cambodia (SOC) forces and those of the Khmer Rouge, FUNCINPEC and the KPNLF. In the event the Khmer Rouge refused to co-operate with disarmament but, while UNTAC's firepower was present in Cambodia, did not go so far as to provoke serious armed action by UN forces. The elections proceeded as planned, although the UN concluded that they were only 'reasonably free and fair', given that UNTAC was unable to supervise the SOC's discharge of key functions in the electoral process[86] or, allegedly, to prevent SOC forces intimidating voters into supporting the Cambodian People's Party (CPP) headed by the SOC Prime Minister Hun Sen. A 90 per cent turnout gave FUNCINPEC 45 per cent of the vote, the CPP 38 per cent and the Buddhist Liberal Democratic Party 3 per cent.

The fact that the elections were conducted in even a reasonably free and fair environment defied the predictions of many observers who had expected full scale civil war to prevent this happening. The confused post-election situation testified to the unpreparedness of many participants for negotiations based on election results. An abortive secessionist attempt staged in Eastern Cambodia by Sihanouk's son Prince Norodom Chakrapong was intended to strengthen the hand of the CPP in these negotiations but revealed the underlying fragility of the UN's arrangements. Neverthless, FUNCINPEC and the CPP reached a power-sharing agreement in September 1993, with FUNCINPEC's Prince Norodom Ranariddh and Hun Sen as first and second prime minister respectively and Sihanouk as king. The coalition government subsequently oscillated between fighting the Khmer Rouge and seeking talks with it[87] before passing legislation in July 1994 outlawing the organisation. Sihanouk was unwilling to give his assent to this legislation, signalling his desire to play an active as well as ceremonial part in government. Constitutional provisions could even give Sihanouk extraordinary powers on the basis of the support of two thirds of the members of the legislature. The inept military performance of the coalition government reflects continuing division that is 'not so much a tussle about policy as it is a shameless scramble for the perks and privileges government jobs can bring'.[88] This in-fighting led to another attempted coup in July 1994, led once again by Chakrapong. The elaborate and expensive UN operation has achieved very little except to change the composition of the government and bring in additional factions to help carve up the spoils.

The medium-term outlook for Cambodia is unpromising. Sihanouk was receiving treatment for prostate cancer in 1993 and 1994 and his death is likely to be followed by renewed factional in-fighting and a succession struggle for the throne. The press is being intimidated by murder and the closure of papers which criticise the government, while at local level the state apparatus continues to be controlled by SOC functionaries. The Khmer Rouge have demonstrated their military ability to resist the government and there are grounds for believing – despite denials – that the Thai armed forces continue to support them. A large arms cache was discovered in the border area in December 1993. The Thai military are also unwilling to abandon long-running commercial deals with the Khmer Rouge and the Thai government is reluctant to see a strong Cambodian state that could more effectively challenge its aspirations to hegemony in Indochina. Members of the Thai military were implicated in the July 1994 coup attempt.[89] Unless the Thai conduit for arms to the Khmer Rouge – including those from China – is cut off completely, the Khmer Rouge are highly unlikely to be defeated militarily. That means that civil war is likely to continue indefinitely and that the Khmer Rouge will continue to control large parts of the country outside the cities,[90] where peasants will remain at the mercy of an organisation that has yet to be held to account for its barbarous rule in the 1970s. Outside areas under Khmer Rouge control, corrupt and incompetent administrators are likely to continue their depredations at the expense of ordinary people.

6 Emerging Bourgeois Democracies: Hong Kong, South Korea, Taiwan, Thailand

The events of May 1992 in Thailand were the most dramatic upheaval in Asia in the first four years of the decade. They echoed the struggle for democracy in South Korea in 1987–88 and the overthrow of the Marcos dictatorship in the Philippines in 1986. Inconclusive elections held in March 1992 to replace the National Peacekeeping Council appointed by the military were followed by the usual horse-trading in the search for a prime minister. When one candidate was rejected because of US suspicions of his involvement in drug smuggling General Suchinda Kraprayoon, then commander of the army, broke a pre-election promise and stepped forward to take the job. Civilian protesters confronted troops on the streets of Bangkok and, in three days of fighting that left over 50 dead and more than 500 missing,[1] compelled Suchinda to relinquish the prime ministership after barely six weeks. For the optimists this signalled the end of the Thai military's decisive role in domestic politics, a role which has been played out in 18 coups since the end of absolute monarchy in 1932. More realistically, however, the Thai military are unwilling to exit the political stage and will not do so until structural reforms are implemented to curb their influence within the state. Nevertheless, the bravery of the demonstrators in May 1992 did reduce that influence, if only temporarily, and advanced Thailand on the path to bourgeois democracy.

By this we mean a system in which the bourgeoisie has developed to the point where it exercises political power by virtue of its economic power and its influence, direct and indirect, over the state apparatus and the political parties, while allowing those parties to compete within an increasingly 'democratic' framework, a system familiar in much of Western Europe since 1945. Political competition turns on questions which do not threaten the fundamental interests of the bourgeoisie (its ownership of the productive capacity of the economy and its right to exploit labour), but which may require some measure of compromise on related questions in order that democracy is seen to be functioning. Neither the bourgeoisie nor the working class can push the state to act exclusively in its interests without endangering the stability of the state. Political debate turns around such 'distributional' issues as the funding of welfare or defence, or the allocation of local and regional government powers. The resulting diversion of part of the surplus that would otherwise flow into company profits may not be in the interests of individual companies, but it does help secure the functioning of the system as a whole by improving the health, education and well-being of the workforce.

Our contention here is that the bourgeoisie is greatly expanding its share of political power, as against its former partners in the 'traditional' sectors of the economy and society, and that, in parallel, the institutions and practices which, in these four economies, functioned to uphold pre-capitalist social relations are giving way to larger measures of formal democracy. Substantial political change occurred during the 1980s and has continued in the 1990s. At the start of the 1980s both South Korea and Taiwan were military dictatorships, while Thailand was in a phase of military control. However, both the advance and the process of expansion could be reversed. In Thailand, the military's resurgence could set them back, while Taiwan's relations with China and reunification in Korea could both have similar effects. It is in this sense that we speak of 'emerging' – but not secure – bourgeois democracies.

The inclusion of Hong Kong in this chapter may appear at first sight strange, since it has had a history of colonial government since 1841 (interrupted by Japanese occupation from 1941–45) without the kinds of upheavals witnessed in South Korea and Thailand in recent years. Yet in economic terms it has developed to an extent which would allow bourgeois democracy to function much as in the other three cases and the recent political reforms have enlarged formal democracy by increasing the number of members of Hong Kong's Legislative Council who are elected, directly or indirectly, by large numbers of the colony's inhabitants. Although the domestic bourgeoisie may be reluctant to take advantage of this opportunity to expand its political influence – preferring to court influence in Peking and not antagonise the Chinese leadership – the intention of the colonial administration and its international backers is to create a bourgeois democracy. However, even this limited measure of political freedom is likely to be terminated once sovereignty reverts to China in 1997. Hong Kong's bourgeois democracy will have scarcely emerged before it is snuffed out.

The emerging bourgeois democracies differ from the veiled authoritarian states on both economic and political grounds. Although Taiwan, South Korea and Hong Kong are often grouped with Singapore as Newly Industrialising Economies, and Thailand with Malaysia and Indonesia as Little Dragons,[2] there are differences in the structure of the economies which contribute to different political arrangements. Malaysia and Singapore are both heavily dependent on foreign capital while in Indonesia the interests of a narrow fraction of capital have to be closely defended. Although the emerging bourgeois democracies are also recipients of foreign investment, this has been relatively less important to the development of South Korea and, since the 1980s, of Hong Kong and Taiwan, which have become net exporters of capital. There has therefore been less need to ensure 'stability' to the same extent as in Malaysia and Singapore, where the respective governments regard it as one of the principal attractions to foreign investors. In Thailand, where foreign capital has been central to the emergence of manufacturing exporting, the need to control labour through a heavily repressive political system has been reduced by the abundance of the labour supply which, in contrast to Singapore and Malaysia, allows employers to circumvent the threat of rising wages by relocating capital or bringing cheaper upcountry labour to manufacturing centres. Unlike in Indonesia, in none of the four emerging bourgeois democracies has there been acute factional in-fighting prompted by the special privileges accorded to a handful of businessmen. This makes it easier to allow a greater measure of open political debate without fear that it would be exploited to the same degree in factional conflict.

MILITARY RULE

The removal of generals as heads of state or ruling juntas in South Korea, Taiwan and Thailand is the most visible symbol of the changing balance of forces within the state. The longest-lasting period of military rule was in Taiwan, where the Kuomintang (KMT) imposed martial law in 1949 and kept it in place until 1987. Chiang Kai-shek, military dictator of Nationalist China from 1928 to 1949, remained in power in Taiwan until his death in 1975 and kept in being Taiwan's claim to be the legitimate 'Republic of China' (a claim which lost much of its international credibility after Taiwan left the United Nations in 1971 in protest at China being given its permanent seat on the Security Council). When he fled the mainland in 1949 Chiang brought some 2 million of his defeated soldiers and camp followers to Taiwan, which then had a population of around 6 million. A large army was maintained as part of the strategy of recovering the mainland and this remained an important part of Chiang's political base. He was succeeded by his son Chiang Ching-kuo, who had served as Minister of Defence and who, as security lieutenant to the then-governor of Taiwan province in 1948, was, according to Simon Long, 'more than anyone else. . . . responsible for the merciless suppression of the Taiwanese home-rule movement in the aftermath of the February 28th uprisings'.[3] This is a reference to the origins of KMT rule on Taiwan, which began with the killing of between 10 000 and 20 000 (and possibly up to 100 000) indigenous Taiwanese, including the cream of the island's intelligentsia, in the '2/28' incident, on 28 February 1947.[4] A 'White Terror' followed in the 1950s and 1960s. The state of war with the People's Republic of China was used to justify arrests, assassinations and discrimination against anyone suspected of Communist sympathies.[5] These included any left-wingers as well as activists calling for an end to the fiction of the Republic of China's claim to the mainland and for the establishment of an independent Taiwanese state. Not until the 1980s did discrimination cease against the families of victims of '2/28'. Although not in uniform, Chiang Ching-kuo had all the necessary credentials with the military to enable him to succeed his father. This standing probably also helped him in taking the initial steps towards dismantling military rule by ending martial law in 1987, just before his death. Military controls over the press, assembly and movements in and out of the country were all abolished at this time. Chiang Ching-kuo was then succeeded as president by the civilian Lee Teng-hui and, in 1989, opposition parties were officially allowed.

South Korea endured three periods of dictatorship, first under the civilian Syngman Rhee (1948–60) and then under Generals Park Chung Hee (1961–79) and Chun Doo Hwan (1980–88). Considerable savagery marked the taking and retaining power by each dictator in turn. Rhee sickened some of his Western backers because of the way in which his régime killed large numbers of its opponents during the Korean War (1950–53).[6] The popular nationalist leader Kim Ku was among those whose death was instigated by the rightwingers close to Rhee.[7] During the Park dictatorship the military were brought into the state in large numbers to oversee economic planning, run enterprises at board level and take up a significant proportion of non-economic government jobs.[8] Park's rule grew more illiberal as it proceeded and at the moment when he was assassinated he was preparing to order the massacre of protesters in Pusan and Masan. His successor imposed his authority after ordering just such a massacre, of 2000 workers and students, in Kwangju in 1980.[9] The Chun dictatorship followed up this use of force with measures to stifle university life, religious movements and the press, as well as 'new labor guidelines, the most restrictive and oppressive in South Korean history'.[10] Chun's successor, elected in 1987, was another former general, Roh Tae-Woo, who presided over a period of gradual liberalisation. Roh's ruling Democratic Justice Party merged with the opposition parties led by Kim Young-Sam in 1990, to form the Democratic Liberal Party. When Kim was elected President in 1992 he inherited the military-bureaucratic base of the Roh régime, though mobilising popular support on his 'radical' credentials.

Ever since 1932 Thailand has experienced irregular cycles of military rule. Often bloodless, the military takeovers have usually meant simply a restructuring of the balance of power among the armed forces, business leaders and the bureaucracy within the state, rather than the repression of uprisings and rule by terror. There have been exceptions: 350 students were killed in the demonstrations which brought about the fall of the 'Three Tyrants' (Thanom Kittikachorn, Praphas Charusathien and Narong Kittikachorn) in 1973, and more died three years later in the Six October massacre, as troops, police and a right-wing mob stormed Thammasat University and ended a period of civilian rule.[11] A period of relative stability under General Prem Tinsulanonda from 1980 to 1988 saw the defeat of coup attempts in 1981 and 1986 before the election of the civilian government of Chatichai Choonhavan. This was removed in the most recent successful coup, in February 1991, and replaced by the National Peacekeeping Council under a former diplomat. Anand Panyarachun. With the defeat of Suchinda's attempt to snatch the premiership in 1992 the generals are once again sidelined, to the advantage of private capital and the bureaucracy.

ECONOMIC CONDITIONS FOR BOURGEOIS DEMOCRACY

A necessary but not sufficient condition for the emergence of bourgeois democracy is the economic rise of the commercial and entrepreneurial bourgeoisie, which underpins its assertion of greater political power against former allies and current rivals alike. In none of these economies, however, has this meant either struggle or alliance with the landowning classes, the main historical rivals of the bourgeoisie in Europe, for they virtually ceased to exist in Korea and Taiwan in the years immediately after the Second World War, have not been of great consequence in Thailand this century and never existed in Hong Kong. But it does mean wrestling with the military and the bureaucracy, a struggle in which the working class, including the middle class, also become actors.[12]

The economic rise of private capital enables it to wage its struggle more effectively, although its rise is not a seamless and unified progression. In Taiwan, as we saw in Chapter 2, the KMT channelled foreign aid and state subsidies into supporting both 'mainlander' enterprises (owned by capitalists who fled to Taiwan in 1949) and those owned by the major families on Taiwan, who used their compensation from land expropriation to build industrial fortunes. But much of the dynamic growth of the economy came from the small- and medium-sized enterprises which were excluded from state support (especially credit) but which were highly successful at exporting. By the late 1980s both Taiwanese-owned large businesses and smaller companies were pressing for reforms that would institute bourgeois democracy. The former were ready to challenge the power of 'mainlanders' within the KMT, while the latter backed the Democratic Progressive Party and its attacks on the KMT-controlled state as a wasteful drain on the island's resources, playing a Taiwanese nationalist card against 'mainlander' capitalists who were beneficiaries of state aid.

In South Korea the rise of private capital to the point where it can dispense with state control, which was the counterpart of subsidisation, was reflected most graphically in the challenge for the presidency by the Hyundai boss Chung Ju Yung. Although reluctant to discard the financial support and market protection which business has received from the state, the owners of South Korea's largest corporations believe they are now capable of taking decisions about the future direction of their companies without guidance from the military-bureaucratic state. Samsung's effort to establish a presence in passenger automobile manufacture is a case in point. No longer willing simply to fund the ruling political party in order to guarantee continued access to state financial support, large capitalists want the upper hand in the relationship between business and the state. During the first two years of Kim Young Sam's presidency, this struggle was played out in regulatory tussles as the bureaucracy resisted the pressure to cede its control over the economy and corporate activity and Chung was driven out of political life by prosecution. Nevertheless his campaign for the presidency demonstrated the willingness of some sections of the bourgeoisie to use the wider political arena created by democratisation to pursue their objectives. Kim has had to respond by lacing his programme with populist measures directed against the bureaucracy and the armed forces, particularly on the issue of official corruption. He has also offered promises of help to small- and medium-sized enterprises which, as in Taiwan, have enjoyed far less state support, in an effort to ensure that support from this section of the bourgeoisie does not accrue entirely to the opposition Democratic Party.

The commercial and entrepreneurial bourgeoisie has reached a similar point of development in Thailand after the sustained rapid growth of the 1970s and 1980s. However, as yet, 'the capitalist class has not been able to fully establish its control over the state's apparatus or its cultural and legal hegemony'[13] according to Hewison. As with much of the history of the 1980s in Thailand, current political developments can be understood as a continuation of private capital's struggle for this control against the military and the bureaucracy. As Hewison and Christensen point out, the private bourgeoisie has been effective in forming lobbying groups to institutionalise the pressure it applies at local and national level. Since the early 1970s representatives of four business and finance groups – the Board of Trade, the Thai Chamber of Commerce, the Federation of Thai Industries and the Thai Bankers Association – have been making an input into economic policy via the National Economic and Social Development Board and sectoral trade associations have grown in number from 48 in 1967 to 233 in 1987.[14] The Joint Public–Private Consultative Committee formed in 1981 facilitated business lobbying on broad issues like tax and tariff reform. In the provinces, businessmen have sought local elected office to achieve stronger influence *vis-à-vis* the local bureaucracy.

In Hong Kong domestic private capital was long overshadowed by the colonial capitalists of the great trading houses. Since the 1960s these trading houses have been gradually eclipsed by an indigenous entrepreneurial bourgeoisie which grew up out of the industrial and exporting achievements of the 1960s and 1970s. Colonial capital has been of diminishing importance in the 1990s, although the domestic bourgeoisie has been more anxious to seek an accommodation with China than to press for greater leverage over the state in Hong Kong, which it recognises, quite rightly, will be of marginal importance once China resumes sovereignty. Co-operation with the Chinese Communist Party is the antithesis of greater democratisation: the pressure for political reform has come, therefore, from those fractions of foreign capital which see less chance of being able to enter relations with the CCP on the same favourable terms enjoyed by trusted Chinese 'compatriot' capitalists. The creation of a formally more democratic political system in Hong Kong will, they believe, give them a greater opportunity for influence and create an arena in which they will be able to seek to uphold the commercial law on which Hong Kong's financial services industry, particularly, is based. In pushing for this, they have had the active support of sections of Hong Kong's middle class, which fear a loss of status and privileges as a result of the CCP's disregard for the rule of law. Foreign capital itself is also divided on this point. Probably a larger fraction has already co-operated successfully with the Chinese régime and believes it will be possible to continue to do so in post-1997 Hong Kong, leaving a minority actively supporting Governor Patten's reforms. Its marginalisation within the Hong Kong Chamber of Commerce has been increasingly apparent in the 1990s and the departure of Simon Murray, the former *taipan* (managing director) of Hutchison Whampoa and a prominent figure in the Hong Kong business community, was connected to his support for political reforms.

As a counterpart to the enhanced economic strength of private capital, repression of the working class has become less important for economic development strategies in South Korea, Taiwan, Thailand and Hong Kong. Taiwanese and Hong Kong companies have transferred operations run on low costs and heavy discipline to China. Not all capitalists will acquiesce and in Thailand, the least developed of these four economies, unenforced wage rates and other conditions are characteristic of an economy which still depends on absolute cost advantages. Equally, in South Korea, while Samsung has reduced normal working hours to 7a.m.–4p.m.,[15] there are periodic calls by other businessmen for a return to low wages.

Nevertheless, while these economies prosper there is room to accommodate the welfare demands that arise in a more democratic system. In Taiwan, for instance, a debate on pensions began in earnest in the election campaign of 1993, during which the DPP's promise of a monthly pension of NT$5000 for the over-65s drew similar proposals from the KMT. The DPP's pledges to help the disabled and to provide crèches to promote women's employment suggest that it would like to move Taiwan towards the welfare state model which prevailed in Western Europe in the 1950s and 1960s. As it did so the KMT could not avoid competing on the same ground and introduced a universal health care scheme in 1994.[16] Taiwan is furthest advanced in this regard, but the same kind of debate will follow as bourgeois democracy becomes more firmly established elsewhere. The colonial administration in Hong Kong proposed establishing a modest old-age pension scheme in mid-1994. For rapidly growing economies redistribution through the welfare state is not necessarily a problem even though business appeared initially opposed to the Hong Kong scheme. Highly productive capitalist economies such as Sweden or the Netherlands were able to support high levels of welfare provision into the 1980s. Only since the crises of the 1980s has that provision been reduced in order to restore profitability.

The risk in Asia's bourgeois democracies, however, is that the advent of a welfare system will coincide with a difficult period of economic adjustment and faltering growth. As we argued in Chapter 1, the upgrading strategies and the increased reliance on the China market by Taiwan, South Korea and Hong Kong have left these economies exposed to a considerable risk of losing their competitive positions or their market. If the economic conditions underpinning bourgeois democracy deteriorate, its sustainability could be called into question, much as the emerging bourgeois democracies in Europe in the 1920s and 1930s were undermined by the economic crisis of the inter-war years. Relatively fragile political institutions, only recently released from military or colonial tutelage, could experience severe strains as economic strategies calling for a restoration of competitiveness through an assault on wages and conditions run into newly articulated demands for improved social spending.

POLITICAL CONDITIONS FOR BOURGEOIS DEMOCRACY

Although the bourgeoisie and the middle class have intrinsically opposed interests, the alliance between them, supported by mass action by workers and peasants, has been an important factor in securing political change in South Korea, Taiwan and Thailand. The decisive push to remove military rule in both South Korea and Thailand and the steady pressure for change in Taiwan came from just such an alliance. In South Korea President Chun, having announced that he was considering a direct election for his successor in 1988, decided instead to continue with the electoral college under the terms of President Park's widely detested Yushin constitution. Demonstrations began in early 1987 around the issue of a direct election and quickly drew in a wide coalition of interests opposed to military rule. Students, workers, the urban poor, religious groups, farmers and small shopkeepers all participated in protests that reflected their own dissatisfaction at wages, housing, agricultural prices and the Chun family's self-enrichment.[17] The democracy struggle was soon supplemented by wage struggles. Disputes spread rapidly through the big *chaebol* plants across the country. In face of this unprecedented coalition of interests, Roh Tae-woo, the candidate of the ruling Democractic Justice Party, yielded where Chun had refused.

Roh's concession split the opposition, drawing some protesters into supporting one or other of the two opposition candidates for the presidency (Kim Young-Sam and Kim Dae-Jung) who themselves further divided the opposition vote. This left the working class isolated in its conflict with the *chaebol* bosses, a struggle which was once again confined to the economic sphere of wages. The existence of moderate opposition parties led by the 'Two Kims' with their middle class following enabled Roh to make a concession which, although it was clearly extracted under duress, did not threaten the fundamental interests of the bourgeoisie. Both the Kims, for all their radical pedigrees, were leaders of parties which welcomed the continuation of capitalism, albeit while urging some reallocation of state economic patronage to small and medium industries. This was also apparent when they contested the presidential elections again in 1992 and radical working class demands were once more subordinated to the interests of capital.

In the same way, the eventual outcome of the May 1992 events in Thailand was filtered through political parties that accepted the limits of bourgeois democracy. As in South Korea, it was a broad alliance of middle class and working class protesters which forced Suchinda to concede the Prime Ministership. The middle classes were well-represented in the demonstrations, given the relatively high incomes in Bangkok and the relatively small proportion of industrial workers in the total population (only 6 per cent). But there was a broader age and class background among the protesters than in 1973 and 1976, when a student vanguard confronted the military. In the elections in September 1992, the anti-military ('angel') parties won a majority. The best that can be said of them is that they shared the view that Suchinda should not be Prime Minister. The party which gained the most seats was the Democrats, Thailand's oldest political party, which traces its origins to the 1940s and was the principal anti-military party in the 1950s and 1960s. Its record of involvement in governments has, however, meant co-operation with other parties and even with the military, as in 1986.[18] Having the Democrats lead the coalition which emerged from the elections meant that whatever limited radical challenge had existed in May 1992 was safely smothered in conventional politics. The participation of the Palang Dharma Party (PDP) in government added a novel element, though also one that canalised protest in a fashion that did not challenge the bourgeoisie. Indeed, the PDP's support has been built on the issues of the environment, traffic and corruption which have given it a strong power base in Bangkok. These concerns are not inimical to capital and, especially in the case of improvements to Bangkok's infrastructure, could be substantially to the benefit of industry.

Once in power, the coalition's generally inept performance, its internal factionalism, splits and realignments and its failure to prosecute Suchinda or anyone else responsible for the killings showed how quickly the 'People Power' momentum of May 1992 was dissipated. Nevertheless, the Democrats and PDP differ from other Thai parties in having left behind the patron–client relationships which have dominated Thai elections. In place of building support on the basis of the immediate material benefits which their MPs can bring to their constituencies and straight cash payments, both parties have campaigned more on issues. Moving away from the cash nexus of electoral bribes takes these parties closer to the Western European model of bourgeois democracy, but certainly not towards radicalism. In fact, the commercial and entrepreneurial bourgeoisie in Thailand draws advantages from a system in which it is able to bring its influence to bear on elected politicians at the centre rather than having to compete for influence over MPs against local godfathers – the crime bosses whose rackets provide the cash for electoral bribery outside Bangkok and the Democrats' stronghold in the South of the country.

Taiwan has witnessed the same pattern of broad-based struggle and its distillation into support for parties which accept the limits of bourgeois democracy. The KMT's decision to lift martial law came after more than 10 years of protest led by intellectuals, nationalists and political activists. As Long observes, 'The far-reaching restrictions on freedoms of expression and association under martial law, provided a natural cohesion to what was in fact a highly fragmented opposition movement'.[19] In leading this struggle, the DPP drew support far beyond its base among the native Taiwanese with their resentment of KMT carpetbaggers and the memory of the 2/28 incident. Yet once competing freely in elections, the DPP could not retain the support of all the opponents of martial law who had mustered under its banner. Removal of this single organising issue deflated the party. While the DPP remains the core opposition party, the China New Party has been able to siphon off support on the question of policy towards the mainland. The signs at the end of 1993 were that the DPP had, for the moment, reached the natural boundaries of its electoral support. Party chairman Hsu Hsinliang stepped down after failing to achieve the gains he had forecast in county elections and was replaced by former detainee Shih Ming-teh.

In late 1993 the DPP announced that it was affiliating to the Liberal International, a body grouping it with the German Free Democrats and other Western liberal parties and placing it clearly at an equivalent point on the political spectrum: in favour of improved social spending as a better way of incorporating working class support for bourgeois democracy while firmly endorsing private industry as the backbone of the economy. Its strong orientation towards the owners of small and medium-sized businesses, from whom it obtains the relatively little corporate funding that it receives, is indicative of its selective class base. The DPP's willingness to tone down its rhetoric on the question of independence – something which could provoke a serious confrontation with China and upset a lot of corporations' plans – is further evidence of the party's desire to co-operate with the bourgeoisie as was Shih's early indication that he had no intention of leading the party back towards the radical street protests and direct action of the 1970s.

Hong Kong is different in that there has been no mass agitation for political change of the kind seen in South Korea, Taiwan or Thailand. The extension of democracy since 1991 has not been as a result of demands from within the colony, where only a section of the middle class has actively pursued political reform. The changes introduced under British administration have enjoyed widespread passive support, but the impetus has come from the administration and the influence of international capital. The limited extent of the political freedoms introduced under the Patten reforms was apparent from the Governor's own words. He described them as 'not a great step forward towards democracy for Hong Kong. They aren't even a small step'.[21] Patten's tinkering with constituencies falls well short of entrenched political freedoms won by, and ultimately defended by, mass action. The British government's refusal to endorse a human rights commission for Hong Kong indicated that its priority is not to defend individual rights against the tyranny of Peking but to ensure legal and political protection for business. It also reflected a desire to return to the path of normal relations with Peking after the recriminations generated by the Patten reforms.[22] This path was never abandoned completely as, even during acrimonious exchanges, Patten continued to lobby for the renewal of China's most favoured nation status in the US in recognition of the economic dependence of Hong Kong business on China. The resumption of talks on the new Hong Kong airport and other economic issues in 1994 pointed to a desire for business as normal, even if the Chinese response in the talks was less than enthusiastic as the year progressed.

In the absence of an active fight for greater political freedoms, the party system which has developed in Hong Kong is fragmented and immature. The Chinese authorities have backed a number of Hong Kong parties with confusing names – the Liberal Democratic Federation, the Hong Kong Progressive Alliance, the Democratic Alliance for the Betterment of Hong Kong

(DAB) – in an attempt to ensure that the Legislative Council elected in 1995 is a weak and divided body. The more parties, they reason, the less the chance of the Democratic Party – which favours more powers for an elected assembly and distrusts the Chinese Communists – gaining more seats. The 'conservative' – that is pro-China and pro-business Co-operative Resources Centre – transformed itself from a loose grouping of Legislative Council members (mostly appointed, not elected) into the Liberal Party in 1993 in acknowledgement of the need to compete in a more active fashion under the Patten reforms. The test of the respective parties' strengths in the District Boards (local government) elections in September 1994 saw the DAB take 37 of the 346 seats while the Liberals managed just 19 of 90 contested. The Democratic Party took the largest share – 77 seats – and the pro-democracy Association for Democracy and People's Livelihood a further 29. However, turnout of 33.1 per cent indicated the limited confidence of voters in institutions overshadowed by China's plans to dismantle them.

The Democratic Party itself grew out of the merger of the United Democrats and Meeting Point, the former of which is typical of political parties in the early stages of bourgeois democracy. Its leading figures are chiefly liberal professionals – drawn from the law, education and journalism – with a sprinkling of trade unionists, embodying perfectly the twin functions of accommodating capital and supporting economic growth while also gesturing to an electoral base with measures to enhance welfare and worker protection.

As yet no party in the Asian bourgeois democracies has built a mass base on the articulation of working class interests. The major parties in South Korea share a commitment to a competitive economy and have not endorsed trade union conflict over wages. The Minjung (Masses) Party obtained less than the 3 per cent of votes needed for representation in the National Assembly in the 1992 elections. Its nationalisation programme had little appeal even in the industrial cities of Ulsan, Masan and Chang-won where its efforts were focused.[23] Umbrella organisations such as the National Democratic Movement Federation and its successor, the National Alliance for Democracy and National Reunification, have gone some way towards creating a framework for unity on the left.[24] But there is still no effective mechanism linking trade union struggles to parliamentary elections and a general political mobilisation. Anti-imperialist protest directed at the US military presence in South Korea is largely a student affair unconnected to strikes at major industrial plants. Regional patterns of voting also cut across political behaviour, dividing the working class vote.

In Taiwan a division between mainlanders and native Taiwanese is similarly reflected in voting patterns, cutting across class lines. Both the KMT and DPP draw substantial working class support. A Labour Party was set up in 1987, but by 1989 it had only 1000 members, 200 of whom left to found a more radical Workers Party. A Communist Party fielded candidates in the

July 1994 village mayoral and council elections.[25] Individual radicals have followings numbered in hundreds, indicating that working class demands are unlikely to feature prominently in national politics in the near future. Hong Kong, likewise, has no significant political party with a programme shaped by radical demands.

In Thailand, the political base for a socialist party is still years away. Trade unions in the public sector were far and away the most active until they were banned in 1991. Even if their legality is restored working class consciousness will remain limited. The small percentage of the workforce employed in industry restricts it, in the first place, and among that workforce many still identify principally with their homes in the countryside. Very few identify themselves as lifelong industrial workers and very few consequently are committed to a long-term struggle to improve conditions. As a result it is extremely difficult for umbrella organisations of the left, such as the Campaign For Democracy (CFD), to assemble a wide coalition of support. The CFD remains a body of urban intellectuals with a poorly developed political base.[26] Its appeal is further vitiated by the rural/urban divide in Thai society. The regional differences in income and education allow the persistence of traditional patron–client electoral politics in rural area. They also mean that the CFD and its urban supporters tend to be campaigning on very different issues to those which affect the countryside. Traffic, welfare and the environment feature in the cities, commodity prices, water shortages and roadbuilding in rural areas. Neither the CFD nor any other political organisation has yet managed to bridge this gap.

EXTENDING BOURGEOIS DEMOCRACY

Bourgeois democracy is distinguished from veiled authoritarianism partly by the direction of political change. Whereas the veiled authoritarian states are becoming more repressive, with less room for expression of the economic and social pressures generated by economic growth, accountability and free expression are being extended in the emerging bourgeois democracies to accommodate these pressures, within limits that have yet to be seriously tested.

Further electoral reform is one of the frontline issues in the extension of accountability. The elimination of vote-buying and the introduction of direct elections for more offices are the principal demands of reformers seeking competition that is visibly fairer and therefore corresponds more closely to a claimed 'democratic' status. These reforms will make it easier to break the crude cash nexus between business or criminal interests and politicians, particularly at local level. They also improve the electoral chances of parties not entrenched in the state – in the way that the KMT and Kim Young-sam's DLP are – and enlarge their scope for using state power in the event of winning elections. Cleaning up electoral bribery has its counterpart in attacking civil service corruption and thereby reducing the volume of state economic patronage that is dispensed without reference to elected politicians and their backers.

In Taiwan, the main focus of the DPP's demands for further electoral reform has been the direct election of the president, creating a system closer to the French or US models. To achieve this the National Assembly forfeited its main function of electing the president, leaving it with responsibility for amending the constitution, redrawing the Republic of China's borders and impeaching the president. This reform does not necessarily improve or reduce the DPP's chances of winning election to the office but will give the winner a stronger mandate. At a time when relations with mainland China are likely to be difficult and complex, a directly elected president who has campaigned on an explicit policy towards the mainland could claim a firmer mandate for carrying out that policy. Although President Lee Teng-hui has said previously that he will not stand, the change to the electoral procedure may give him the pretext for doing so when the elections are held early in 1996. With KMT support in long-term decline the sooner a presidential election is held the better Lee's chances of winning and therefore of being able to preserve the interests of the KMT against a DPP victory in the Legislative Yuan (which debates legislation and scrutinises the budget).

The last piece of tidying-up of the electoral system would be abolition of the provincial layer of government left over from the days when the KMT pretended that it was the legitimate government of the whole of China. Rather than abolish this layer, the KMT introduced direct elections for the provincial governorship in 1994 and reintroduced it – after a gap of 30 years – for the mayors of Taipei and the second city, Kaoshiung.[27] At the constituency level bribery still needs to be rooted out. The KMT began to address the issue seriously as its support appeared to weaken in the county and mayoral elections in 1993. Despite this, the rules on campaign finance have been consistently ignored, and KMT candidates spent several hundred million NT dollars in the 1993 polls.[28] Spending limits in elections to the Legislative Yuan are regularly breached, compelling legislators to devote their energies during their term of office to servicing their backers. If limits on campaign spending are enforced, they will help break the link between the KMT and business at local level. This relationship has, in the past, meant that seats in the Provincial Assembly, the Legislative Yuan and the National Assembly have been rotated amongst local business factions. Further curbs on vote-buying will accelerate the KMT's loss of its ability to guarantee election in every instance, increasing the extent to which these factions are compete openly, backing other parties or even running 'independent' candidates against official KMT candidates.

Kim Young-sam is acting in a similar way to limit campaign spending in

South Korea. Parties have traditionally sold candidacies to individuals who can foot the bill of 3–4 billion won for getting elected. Businesses have been pressured into political donations to the ruling party while being warned off giving to the opposition. Kim Young-sam's proposal for limits of 45 million won in National Assembly elections and 11.6 billion won in presidential elections was intended to stop the most blatant practices.[29] Another measure, to allow military personnel to vote outside their barracks, should allow greater freedom of choice.

A campaign against vote-buying has been one of the tactics used by the PDP and the Democrats in Thailand. Their aim is to extend their brand of issue-based campaigning outside Bangkok and into the rural areas of Central and North East Thailand where politicians build support on the basis of the favours they can do for constituents. By attacking the vote-buying relationship, reformers hope to break this nexus and open the way for themselves. To complement this, improved public scrutiny of the budgets of government departments and investigation of party funding would help ensure that resources are allocated by parties which win elections. A 'sunshine law' similar to those in Korea and Taiwan would open the personal finances of officials and politicians to inspection although the prospects of reform along these lines look dim under the Chuan administration.

In Hong Kong Governor Patten's proposals have focused on the electorate and the number of directly-elected seats in the Legislative Council. In March 1994 the first batch of reforms lowered the voting age to 18, abolished appointments to local government councils and created single-seat constituencies for all elections, including the 20 out of 60 seats on the Legislative Council (LegCo) that are directly elected. This package was accepted by the LegCo despite the failure of Britain and China to agree on it. The second stage of Patten's reforms, passed by a narrow majority in the LegCo in July 1994, gave 2.7 million workers the vote in nine 'functional' constituencies and provided for another 10 LegCo members to be elected from among 346 elected members of district boards. On this basis a majority (39) of the Legislative Councillors elected in 1995 would be able to claim a popular mandate, something of which the Chinese Communists are very wary. Having consistently opposed Patten's reforms, China has decided to scrap all elected bodies after resuming sovereignty in 1997. The District Board members elected in 1994 will be replaced by appointed members, while the future franchise for LegCo is unclear. The more LegCo tries to assert itself and implement social welfare measures before 1997, the more it will arouse the opposition of the domestic bourgeoisie[30] and of the Chinese Communist Party, which is already hand-in-glove with Hong Kong business[31] and has no interest in supporting the enlargement of workers' rights in Hong Kong. If, on the other hand, it remains a compliant body serving the interests of business, the Chinese are likely to look more favourably on it post-1997. In

short, if electoral reform proves effective, it will rebound on the people of
Hong Kong; if it proves ineffective, it will be irrelevant anyway.

MEDIA AND JUDICIARY

Another feature of emerging bourgeois democracies is the relaxation of controls over intellectual and cultural life, again in contrast to the tighter restrictions in the veiled authoritarian states. Greater freedom of debate does
not necessarily threaten the bourgeoisie and, if anything, provides a useful
safety valve. Taiwan is at an interesting stage in its liberalisation. The KMT
still controls substantial parts of the media through party and government
ownership of broadcasting stations (TTV, CTV, CTS and BCC) and a KMT-
controlled company acquired the main independent newspaper publishing
group in 1994, though the DPP is launching its own TV channel, funded by
small businesses.[32] Language is a highly sensitive issue in films and popular
music, as use of the Taiwanese dialect has long had political overtones,
being regarded by KMT leaders as tantamount to support for independence.
More performers are using it and a wider Taiwanese cultural revival – including puppetry, music and dance – is under way. This parallels the growing tolerance of debate around the question of independence, advocacy of
which is no longer a capital offence. The laws against sedition no longer
provide penalties for non-violent acts and it was claimed in 1992 that there
are only five people on the blacklist of those banned from entering Taiwan.
  State control of the media was put under the spotlight in Thailand during
the events of May 1992. Army-controlled TV stations censored reports of
the fighting in Bangkok to ensure that rural areas were kept in ignorance as,
reportedly, was the king, who had to have details of the events in the capital faxed to him while his military minders were distracted. In the press
there was plenty of self-censorship, though there were also honourable exceptions, especially *The Nation* newspaper. In the aftermath of the defeat of
Suchinda's bid for the prime ministership, the armed forces' control of TV
stations has become another test of the bourgeois parties' ability to root out
military influence in the state. In Hong Kong, champions of press freedom
are on the defensive. Newspapers are subject to government licensing but
have been able to criticise Chinese policy freely while film censorship is
more concerned with sexually explicit material than political views. But it
has been very apparent from formal and informal pressures that the Chinese
authorities want to limit these freedoms. Some media owners have already
capitulated, dropping broadcasts or encouraging self-censorship that is 'sensitive' to the Chinese government in the press. The Hong Kong government
has tried to institutionalise a greater measure of media freedom by making
Radio Television Hong Kong an independent body. It also gave financial

support, in the form of advertising, to a new English language publication, *Eastern Express*, launched in 1993. Such defences are intended to complement the law in providing a check on Chinese Communist dominance of business after 1997. They offer scant protection against the onset of politically-inspired controls in the media, which could be imposed on the grounds that Hong Kong newspapers and television broadcasts are obtainable in Guangdong and therefore constitute an 'interference' in China's domestic affairs. The colonial administration will also leave behind substantial reserve powers for the new SAR government to censor, control and suppress publications in an emergency.[33] Abuse of these power to eliminate independent media would mean one less defence against arbitrary rule.

The judicial system is still of very limited value in defending or extending political freedom. In South Korea the judiciary is beginning to show any signs of independence, after years of pliably serving the needs of military rule. A decision in 1992 that the bugging of conversations between prisoners and their families is illegal was the first significant ruling against the government. The decision in 1993 overturning the government's action in dismantling the Kukje *chaebol* in 1985 was welcomed by business groups as a sign that the law could be used to defend their interests more effectively.[34] Structural reforms could give the judiciary independent funding and allow the Supreme Court greater scope for activism by prioritising those cases which it wants to review though, given the continuation of highly repressive labour laws, this independence is most likely to be of benefit to business.

In Thailand courts are largely irrelevant to questions of political freedom and are leaned on to supply whatever verdict the government of the day requires. The Supreme Court, for instance, struck down as unconstitutional a committee which investigated the 'unusual' wealth of politicians. In Taiwan, similarly, most people believe that judges can be bought and the courts have served the purposes of the KMT. The appointment of a new head of the Judicial Yuan by a future DPP government might improve standards, but it will be a long time before courts lose the reputation of favouring the rich and powerful. Hong Kong's final Court of Appeal has been left with just one foreign member, opening the way for post-1997 pressure to limit its role in the defence of political freedoms. Local courts will, in any case, not have the final say in interpreting the Basic Law (the mini-constitution for Hong Kong after 1997) as this will reside with the Standing Committee of China's National People's Congress.

LIMITS TO BOURGEOIS DEMOCRACY: BUSINESS–GOVERNMENT RELATIONS

Bourgeois democracy, by definition, implies a tension between the political power of the bourgeoisie and the popular demands arising out of the electoral process. The extensive involvement of the state in economic development and planning in Taiwan, South Korea and Thailand makes this one of the testing grounds on which this tension is played out. Hitherto representative institutions have not been pushed very far in examining this relationship, indicating that the state's economic activities remain largely insulated from popular demands, partly as a result of institutional weaknesses and partly as a result of the broadly similar nature of opposition and ruling parties in bourgeois democracies.

The Thai parliament meets for a total of less than 14 days a year, doing little apart from debating confidence motions and passing the budget drawn up by the Budget Office, the National Economic and Social Development Board and the Bank of Thailand. It has no role in scrutinising the conduct of economic policy in general or the award of specific contracts.[35] Once individual ministers have been appointed, their decisions are questioned only when the government changes and a new minister decides to reallocate the contracts awarded by his predecessors. The Taiwanese parliament has become more effective than in the past at questioning economic policy, but the effect has largely been to create deadlocks. The DPP's use of parliamentary procedure in its criticism of the corrupt ties between business and government has virtually put a stop to major deals. The law on disclosure of assets by officials and legislators, passed in 1993, should give DPP legislators access to abundant further ammunition with which to attack state–business connections. This is not because they have any principled objection to state support for industry, but out of their desire to cause maximum political embarrassment and to stake a claim for the reallocation of that support to the party's own backers in small and medium-sized industries. Thus it is not the principle of state–business relations that is under question, but their particular form.

A similar outcry over corruption was used by Kim Young-sam to attack ties between bureaucrats and business in South Korea, though this offensive, like economic policy as a whole, has been conducted by the President alone rather than by the legislature. Accordingly anti-corruption efforts have been directed mainly at Kim's personal opponents in the bureaucracy, business and army.[36] His own supporters have largely escaped the net, while former ministers, Roh loyalists within Kim's party and untrustworthy army officers have been prosecuted and purged. The selectiveness of Kim's actions does not in itself endanger business–government relations but it is likely to mean that influence will have to be used more subtly. As in Taiwan, financial support for industry is likely to be reallocated to business interests which back Kim, including small and medium-sized industries.

In Hong Kong, LegCo has always represented the colony's business interests and has never sought to criticise or inhibit business in any way. The advent in LegCo of the Democratic Party has not had much impact. The Democrats argued for better worker protection in the form of a committee to monitor the treatment of strikers returning to work after the Cathay Pacific cabin staff dispute,[37] but have not seriously challenged the government's willingness to let business and finance operate freely. However, because of the relatively low level of direct state intervention in the economy there have been fewer instances of assistance to individual companies than in South Korea or Taiwan. In this respect the construction of the Chek Lap Kok airport in the 1990s has been unusual. Large numbers of contracts on this project have been awarded to British firms, leading to accusations from Chinese officials that Britain is milking the colony dry before its administration ends[38] and pointing up the divisions between the interests of the new domestic bourgeoisie and the colonial bourgeoisie.

THE ARMED FORCES

Kim Young-sam, the DPP and the Thai 'angel' parties have all sought to extend civilian control of the armed forces and other elements of the repressive apparatus. In doing so they are pushing at a door which is already at least partly open. In bourgeois democracies, repression is no longer so important in controlling social forces and the military's hold on a substantial portion of productive resources is increasingly challenged by the commercial and entrepreneurial bourgeoisie. Its position within the state becomes the subject of conflict. In no instance, however, is this a straightforward matter.

In South Korea the military has been closely interwoven with the rest of the state since Park's coup in 1961. He appointed army officers to run state corporations and created the huge Korean Central Intelligence Agency (KCIA) to monitor and suppress dissent at all levels. The civilian administrations of 1960–61 and 1979–80 were both toppled by generals who saw the military as the best means of guaranteeing the conditions for further economic growth. Kim Young-sam recognises the threat of military intervention against his administration and dismissed generals in the Hanahoe group of officers who believed it was their right to act in this fashion.[39] He also moved against Park Tae Joon, chairman of the Pohang Iron and Steel Company (POSCO) and one of the most prominent military–business figures from the Park Chung-hee era.[40] Park, who was both a rival to Kim in the DLP and a symbol of military dominance of the economy, was forced into exile by charges that

POSCO had used money secretly for political purposes. Now one of the world's most successful steel companies, POSCO has been part-privatised, driving home the diminished economic muscle of the armed forces. Kim cannot, however, dispense with a repressive apparatus entirely, as has been shown in the violent strike confrontations since he took office. He therefore had to balance the diminution of the armed forces' political and economic role with more generous spending on modernisation and a reorientation for the KCIA, now renamed the National Security Planning Agency (NSP), towards external intelligence gathering. Kim's policy is also trying to satisfy demands among his own electoral base for bringing the army and the NSP to book. The Kwangju massacre and other incidents, during 30 years of dictatorship and domestic repression, have not been forgotten. High-profile sackings and a new civilian director for the NSP go some way towards appeasing public anger and fear, but Kim may find it difficult to satisfy the expectations of army commanders and former protesters alike. The ultimate test of relations between the army, the civilian government and the population at large will come when Koreans face collapse or carnage in the North. In circumstances in which a radical challenge could be mounted against the military, capital and the US, Kim Young-sam can be expected to call upon the armed forces to provide stability in the North and the South and, indeed, may be displaced by them.

In Taiwan the KMT is implanted in the armed forces at every level through its party commissars. The KMT used the armed forces as part of its propaganda machine and channelled their votes into particular constituencies to give it majorities. The assertion of civilian control is consequently a DPP priority, both to secure its own party position and to mollify those of its supporters who want justice and retribution against individual officers and the institution of the military. As in South Korea, the DPP is offering the sweetener of 'professionalisation', the promise of spending more on expensive armaments, as the price for reducing the army's numbers and political influence. To defuse popular pressure on the issue the KMT wound up the Garrison Command which had had responsibility for censorship, spying on critics of the government and arresting dissidents. But, as in South Korea, the question of reunification (with the mainland) will thrust the role of the military into a much wider test of the whole basis of the state.

The reining-in of the military in Thailand is likely to be especially difficult. The frequency of its intervention in politics since 1932 is not just a persistent bad habit. It reflects institutional weaknesses which have periodically incapacitated the state and produced policy deadlocks in which the military has acted to sort out squabbles amongst bureaucrats and business interests. It has been allowed to play this role partly because political institutions have had very little popular support. Against this background the events of May 1992 can be seen as a watershed. The bad habit reappeared, but after

elections rather than after a period of ineffective government, and it provoked mass demonstrations rather than the resigned acceptance which greeted
so many other previous coups. On this argument political parties can now
mobilise widespread support against a discredited military and the generals
cannot ignore them as factors in constructing or removing régimes. Changes
in the top ranks of the military have removed Suchinda and his cohorts,
replacing him with a general who accepts a more professional, externally
oriented role for the armed forces.

Arguments of this kind are not new. 'As time passes, General Suchinda's
sincerity is becoming increasingly apparent'[41] wrote one Western stockbroker
a year before the Bangkok massacre. The belief that military dictators will
tamely accept a new role is probably ill-founded. Field Marshal Phibul made
a comeback as prime minister in 1948 despite having allied Thailand to
Japan during the Second World War and led it into a humiliating occupation. Air Chief Marshal Kaset, Suchinda's co-conspirator in 1992, is planning a similar comeback and building a political party as his front. Suchinda
lurks offstage in the hope of staging a return. If the military is to be rooted
out of politics there must be structural changes within the state. Decentralisation of power to the provinces would undercut the power which regional
military commanders exercise; the boards of state-owned companies need to
be purged of their military members (an issue which the Chuan government
soon stopped forcing); the size of the army needs to be cut; military influence over foreign policy – particularly over Cambodia – has to be reduced;
and the military's power in the Senate has to be curbed. Two years after the
May 1992 events, Chuan's government was still struggling to limit the Senate's powers and battling to prevent the military-backed ('satanic') parties
from changing the constitution to allow appointment of the prime minister
from outside parliament in future (the back door through which officers slip
into the job). Bourgeois democracy is far from secure in Thailand.

Institutional weakness at another level threatens to undercut it further.
The king played the role of final arbiter in May 1992, intervening to insist
that Suchinda and the PDP leader Chamlong Srimaung (acting as representative
of the demonstrators) settle their differences. Drawing on the widespread
respect he enjoys throughout Thai society and by humbling both Suchinda
and Chamlong in his presence the king was able to pacify a conflict which
threatened to destabilise the country very seriously. Had he not intervened
at that stage, both the military and the demonstrators were preparing for an
escalation of conflict[42] and splits could well have emerged within the military itself, in which Suchinda and his 'Class 5' cohorts are just one faction
of the officer corps.[43] While King Bhumibol fulfilled his function by ar-
ranging a compromise, under which Suchinda resigned as Prime Minister
and an interim administration came in to organise fresh elections, his son
the Crown Prince, who is less popular, sympathises more closely with the

military. It is unlikely that he would be able to arbitrate in an acceptable manner if he becomes king. Without an ultimate arbiter between the army, bureaucracy and bourgeoisie, conflicts will be harder to resolve.

THE FUTURE

Whereas South Korea, Hong Kong and Taiwan all face potentially destabilising effects from relations with neighbouring states, Thailand is largely immune to disturbance originating outside its borders. Cambodia's civil war may threaten a return of refugees to the Eastern border areas but there is very little risk of the conflict involving Thailand any more than in the past. Its principal effects will be on border trade and in allowing military leaders to claim that the national security implications of the war entitle them to re-assert influence in foreign policy and government generally. Serious unrest in China would affect Thailand, along with other ASEAN countries, but less than those with a coastline on the South China Sea.

In the short term the greatest chance of change in Thailand is probably from a recrudescence of the military challenge to bourgeois democracy. As the Chuan administration sinks further into the morass of indecisive bickering which has characterised so many of its predecessors, military leaders begin to wonder if they can re-emerge and reconstruct a régime in which the armed forces will once again play a leading part, securing those of its positions in the state which have appeared to be under threat. Suchinda and Kaset may look for an acceptable guise and work in concert with the military-backed 'satanic' parties to do this: the obstacle they fear is a mobilisation on the scale of that in 1992. But, after two years or more of uninspiring and ineffective leadership that mobilisation would not be easy to organise, as the PDP's attempts to resuscitate it on the issue of elected provincial governorships demonstrated. Likewise, the muted public reaction to the pro-military parties' thwarting of constitutional changes in 1994 showed the difficulties in reviving the pro-democracy coalition. Perhaps in the context of a crisis over the royal succession – in which military officers aligned themselves with the Crown Prince against the popular Princess Sirindhorn[44] – it is possible to imagine widespread public protest. But, provided the military acts with a modicum of subtlety, it has a good chance of reasserting its political role (especially if the Cambodian civil war deteriorates). This would clearly be a setback for bourgeois democracy, both for the advance of the commercial bourgeoisie and for the greater political freedom and account-ability which has accompanied this.

Such a setback is likely to prove temporary, if the process of rural economic growth to which we referred in Chapter 1 continues. Even a slowdown in the economy resulting from infrastructure and skill constraints and the slackening of foreign investment would be felt most acutely in the Bangkok area, resulting in a new pattern of growth in which the provinces and the domestic market would be more prominent. Rural economic growth would also help create a larger middle class and a natural constituency for the bourgeoisie's parties in these areas, displacing the local godfathers and vote-buying relationships on which the pro-military parties have relied more heavily. Moreover, growth in the provinces undermines the economic importance of the military in rural areas, where infrastructure and development since the 1960s have often been under military auspices.[45] Longer term, the growth of labour, both organised in trade unions and as a political constituency is also more likely to lead towards bourgeois democracy with its scope for concessions to the working class rather than towards the continued centrality of the military.

Both Taiwan and South Korea are societies with deep fault lines. Events in China and North Korea respectively will expose these fault lines and threaten to destabilise bourgeois democracy in both countries before it can become firmly embedded. Taiwan's divide goes back to the '2/28' and the arrival of the KMT's carpetbaggers on the island after defeat on the mainland. The KMT has tried to smooth over the events of '2/28', with commemorative efforts, an apology and offers of compensation – stopping short only of putting anyone on trial. DPP representatives now play down the massacre, arguing that events 50 years earlier should not undermine a tolerant society. As the overwhelming majority of the population – 87 per cent, according to the DPP – the native Taiwanese can take control of the island's future and, in Lee Teng-hui, they already have a native-born president. In local government DPP county chiefs have worked successfully with bureaucrats appointed by and loyal to the KMT. The party's representatives believe that this will be possible at national level, though they also call for an eventual reduction in the percentage of the civil service drawn from the mainlander population. A DPP election victory could put this relationship to the test in the near future. If it does not work and KMT officials are obstructive it could easily provoke a resurgence of tension between mainlanders and native Taiwanese. But the most likely cause of such a resurgence is open conflict over relations with China.

There is a lack of consensus on this issue within Taiwan. The KMT itself is deeply divided between a 'mainstream' faction which believes in 'one China' and the ascendant faction grouped around Lee Teng-hui which is willing to contemplate formal renunciation of the Republic of China's claim to the mainland (the claim has not been officially voiced since 1991). This division helped precipitate the split which led to the formation of the China New Party, which favours direct trade and transport links with the mainland, the creation of a more powerful China and reunification talks – policies which appeal to those sections of the bourgeoisie with trade and investment links to the mainland. The KMT's underlying preference is for a continuation of the *status quo* which allows *de facto* independence without questioning the *de jure* claim to be the legitimate government of all China. This is rapidly becoming untenable as business interests seek closer economic integration with the mainland and are pulled into increasingly formal relations with PRC bodies, while the DPP capitalises on the separate sense of identity which has developed in Taiwan since 1949 and moves towards policies that are closer and closer to implying independence. The crumbling KMT position makes the future look very uncertain. Any decisive action by a government in Taiwan will inflame internal divisions. The DPP now recognises this and probably would not press for immediate formal independence if it won an election. Its willingness to co-operate with the KMT in jointly promoting Taiwan's re-entry to the UN is indicative of its willingness to compromise. The KMT and the DPP may find common ground in pushing *de facto* independence as far as possible without making a formal declaration. Apart from the internal effect such a declaration would have, it would also provoke a reaction from mainland China. The PRC government has never formally renounced the use of force to seize Taiwan whose leaders are highly conscious of the possibility of invasion (or blockade) in the event of a declaration of independence.

China is an alarming unknown in other ways. Its internal upheavals are liable to have severe polarising effects on Taiwanese politics. Unrest and repression play into the hands of mainlanders who can claim that they demonstrate the illegitimacy of the Communist régime and the need for the restoration of the 'rightful' KMT government, perhaps even by intervention. But they also strengthen the hand of independence activists who argue that a murderous régime can never be trusted or negotiated with and that independence is the only safe course. The scale of upheaval could easily turn this from a theoretical debate into a practical problem: refugees fleeing China would put the Taiwanese authorities in a very difficult position. This was demonstrated by 12 aircraft hijackings from mainland China to Taiwan in the space of 15 months in 1993 and 1994. In the heyday of ideological confrontation defecting fighter pilots were rewarded with their weight in gold. Today compliance with international law means that hijackers are handed back to China and passengers are not given a choice about staying. But how would Taiwan react to boat people setting out across the Taiwan Strait? If conflict in China were to replicate the events of Tiananmen Square across the country, the political debate between mainlanders and the independence lobby would be hugely magnified in Taiwan. No policy would be able to keep the peace simultaneously with China and with both sides of a divided domestic population. Heightened military tension would certainly play into the hands of the armed forces, but it would also highlight the lack of consensus on their role: is it to assist in the 'recovery' of the mainland that

Chiang Kai-Shek dreamed of, or to defend the island against Communist invasion?

In this context the advance of bourgeois democracy would begin to look highly vulnerable. Civil liberties are always at risk in times of crisis. Presidential power is likely to be promoted over parliamentary. Residual powers against subversion and dissent would be more widely invoked against individuals and civil disobedience. At best the *status quo* would be frozen; at worst military dictatorship would be reinstituted. Upheaval in China is likely to last until the turn of the century, much as the changes in the former Soviet Union have turned into a prolonged collapse. Only in the long term, as suggested in Chapter 5, does a looser federation of Chinese provinces perhaps hold out the prospect of reunification for Taiwan on terms that would allow bourgeois democracy to remain in being.

South Korea also faces profound upheavals. As the North collapses the lack of consensus on policy towards the North and on the form of a reunified state will be exposed. This lack of consensus − not yet fully articulated − betrays deep divisions over the role of the US in Korea and over the unsettled scores from the years of military rule. The role of US occupying forces at the end of the Second World War was to crush a Communist-led resistance movement which had fought the Japanese occupation. President Truman's adviser, Edwin Pauley, was quite explicit in saying that 'Communism in Korea could get off to a better start than practically anywhere else in the world'.[46] A popular strain of anti-Americanism has been sustained since the Korean War by the presence of US bases and the cultural insensitivity of individual US servicemen. Within the student movement the US presence has served as a highly visible proxy for criticism of militarism within South Korea and is seen as an obstacle to reunification. The complicity of US military commanders in the Kwangju massacre, by allowing Korean army units to be withdrawn from the front line to take part in the operation, reinforced the radicals' conviction that the role of US forces was as much to support the state internally as to protect it against external threats. Anti-Americanism has become tied to anti-militarism and the demands for a full accounting to be made for the Kwangju events. Just as with '2/28' in Taiwan, South Korea's leaders have tried to draw the sting of Kwangju by promoting commemoration and giving succour to the victims, through declaring a national holiday and providing medical assistance.[47] But, like their Taiwanese counterparts, they have stopped short of bringing Chun, Roh or military commanders to trial. The unpredictable events in the North are, however, likely to pull the US and the domestic military once again to centre stage and, in doing so, reawaken that the opposition coalition of 1987 around the twin poles of anti-Americanism and anti-militarism.

The wayward behaviour of the leaders of North Korea amplifies the uncertainty in the South about the course of action to adopt. In the early 1990s

Roh Tae-woo was able to hold together a consensus around his policy of *Nordpolitik*.[48] This had its origins in initiatives in the 1970s aimed at improving relations with the Soviet Union and at promoting peaceful relations with the North. As *Nordpolitik* yielded results in better ties with Communist states the North was drawn towards the highpoint of its relations with the South, the February 1992 agreement on non-aggression, exchanges and co-operation.[49] But even as this was being put in place, the experience of German reunification began to raise doubts in the South about the cost of reunification and growing fears about North Korea's construction of a nuclear weapon chilled the diplomatic atmosphere.

There are powerful economic attractions for Southern companies in the North. Wage levels barely a tenth of those in the South make it one of Asia's last great untapped reserves of cheap labour. Northern raw materials allied to Southern technology could extend the life of such industries as cement and steel. But the financial burden of reunification would fall much more widely on Southern taxpayers. Among the estimates of the cost of reunification are figures of US$90 billion, US$200–500 billion or even US$2048 billion in the year 2000.[50] The economic consequences of raising this kind of sum, particularly on taxation and interest rates – as seen in Germany – have caused political leaders to hesitate. How much better, in their eyes, to contrive a means for Southern companies to exploit labour and raw materials in the North, but without the destabilising economic burden of reunification.

While leaders in the South backpedal, the dynamics of the collapse of Stalinism in the North will force them into uncomfortable choices. Ideally Southern leaders would like to see a régime, whether led by Kim Jong Il or some other figure, which would embark on economic reforms. This would allow Southern companies to invest and closer economic ties to develop, without entailing the costs of reunification. Various 'commonwealth' schemes have been floated by academics and politicians to create an overarching framework for co-operation between independent states.[51] It is surely unlikely that such arrangements could last. As the experience of East Germany has illustrated, the momentum of events is very difficult to control once the latent desire for reunification is allowed its first expression. With 10 million families separated by the Korean Demilitarised Zone, the individual demands for contact would be immense once the first visits are allowed. Why should businessmen have the freedom to visit the North, invest and trade there when humanitarian contacts are denied? It would be very difficult for a Southern government to resist domestic pressure to expand a relationship with the North beyond commerical exploitation. The right to family visits is an issue which could mobilise large numbers of ordinary Koreans. A purely economic relationship is also likely to be unsustainable in the North. No matter how insulated Southern investment is in special economic zones, the influx of technology, goods and individuals would fracture the illusion of the 'Workers Paradise'. After years of castigation of the South as a puppet of US imperialism any régime in the North associated with Kim Jong Il or the Workers' Party would have severe ideological problems in justifying dependence on the South.

The collapse of the North would also present difficult choices to leaders in the South. If Kim Jong Il and the Workers' Party lost control, the South would have little alternative but to accept the financial cost of reunification. Whether through co-operation or collapse, large numbers of people would be mobilised in the South behind demands for immediate reunification, regardless of the financial or human cost. In that process, a unified Korea would be recast politically and bourgeois democracy could be overwhelmed. Reunification could be a polarising experience, dividing Koreans along class lines. Many Koreans from the North, who would be even less prepared for the social conditions of capitalism than their counterparts in Eastern Germany, would have difficulty adjusting to their first taste of the exploitation that companies from the South have in mind for them. Once information regarding labour conditions in the South permeated the North, demands for comparable pay could soon be expected to follow while, in the South, workers are unlikely to accept unquestioningly the preservation of a low wage economy in the post-reunification North at the expense of their jobs. Equally, the bourgeoisie in the South would find it hard to accept the enfranchisement of the adults in North Korea's population of 20 million, especially not in the circumstances of considerable social disorder or the rapid loss of the economic advantage of cheap labour in the North. The military would inevitably be pushed into a much more prominent role in a period of intensely strained relations. Whether behind a civilian figurehead or not (and probably with US backing) a military régime which made 'order' its watchword in South and North alike could take power with the support of the *chaebols* in the South. The bourgeoisie would be ready to dispense with bourgeois democratic institutions if confronted with a coalition of anti-American, antimilitary and pro-reunification interests. Yet a reversion to military rule is the one thing that could reawaken the coalition of 1987–88 and present a serious challenge to the state.

Political institutions in Hong Kong face a palpable and immediate threat from the deep-seated antagonism of China's leadership. Deng Xiaoping's implacable opposition to the Patten reforms was loyally echoed by the next echelon of leaders, including Zhu Rhongji. Zhu's 'liberal' economic credentials did not stop him cracking the Stalinist whip on the question of political changes that could create a more popular elected legislative body in Hong Kong. The view expressed by Chinese officials during talks with Britain summarised their attitude to liberties in the colony: 'we've got sovereignty after 1997',[52] implying that they regard this as *carte blanche* to run things as they please despite Hong Kong's supposedly semi-autonomous status as a Special Administrative Region. The Chinese plan to dissolve all elected bodies after regaining sovereignty and threats to sack the judiciary and executive in 1997 if Patten persisted with his reforms[53] reinforced the point that Hong Kong will have virtually no protection thereafter. There will be a token British participation in the Joint Liaison Group until the year 2000 and Hong Kong will enter whatever international agreements it can in its own right, but Chinese government respect for such niceties is minimal.

The symbolic importance of 1997 diminishes as Chinese leaders work to undermine Hong Kong instutions ahead of that date. The establishment of the 'second stove' – a shadow body of advisers ready to become a government – has been under way since 1992.[54] The acceleration of the formation of the Chinese-run Preliminary Working Committee (PWC) in late 1993 was designed to undercut further the significance of the elections in 1994 and 1995 in Patten's new constituencies and under new election rules. The PWC, which will set the rules for Legislative Council elections after 1997, is a rival centre of power to the Governor and his councils. A shadow chief executive will be in place ahead of 1997. Businessmen and professionals keen to court favours from the next rulers of Hong Kong have been selected for the advisory bodies and the PWC. This collection of lackeys and opportunists will be an important element in post-1997 Hong Kong, at ease in dealing with a Chinese government bureaucracy that finds itself on better terms with capitalists than with workers. As Lu Ping, the Communist head of China's Hong Kong and Macau Affairs Office, remarked revealingly during the arguments with Patten over functional constituencies: 'Do you think a cleaner, an ordinary worker in the textile industry, can represent the interests of the textile industry? I don't think so'.[55] His comment echoed almost exactly that of a Hong Kong property developer and China adviser, David Chu, on the enlargement of the franchise in the functional constituencies: 'The floor sweeper, everybody, will be voting in my construction constituency. They will outvote me, but they will not represent me. Indeed, my interests are likely to be misrepresented'.[56]

Hong Kong's political institutions are weakly implanted precisely because they did not grow out of a mass movement but out of the ambitions or afterthoughts of British politicians and officials and the lobbying power of international business. Even the limited attempts to shape a bourgeois democracy are being muffled by Chinese threats. Civil servants are told their 'mistakes' may be overlooked after 1997, to instil the fear that comes from having their actions monitored. Solicitors are running scared: many of the territory's leading firms refused to act for Democrat leader Martin Lee for fear of losing business from bodies linked to Peking. Revision of legislation to bring it in line with Hong Kong's Bill of Rights is being dragged out, possibly through Chinese pressure.[57] Much of the territory's legislation will, at the present rate, not be 'localised' (translated and agreed) quickly enough to remain in use after 1997. Critics of the Peking régime fear that a black-list is being assembled. Moreover, the colonial government is likely to leave behind extensive reserve powers that could easily be abused, whether over the licensing of newspapers or the holding of demonstrations (permission is needed for a gathering of more than 20 people). The test of the last of these will be the annual commemoration of the massacre in Tiananmen Square, which draws a substantial crowd every year. The tenth anniversary in 1999 may be expected to become a major political event, which would severely test the nerve of the authorities.[58]

The Chinese Communists will be ready to place political order above econ-omic advantage. Bureaucrats and their offspring do hold extensive stakes in Hong Kong's stock market and property market and, in mid-1994, up to HK\$48 billion was held in the territory's banks by individuals and entities from the PRC.[59] It has been widely assumed that this economic stake will inhibit them from taking action that might upset the territory's volatile econ-omic confidence. However, they are likely to be willing to sacrifice econ-omic interests if political order in China proper is seriously threatened by a democratic bacillus from Hong Kong. Sun Yat-sen's success in fomenting revolution in the South East corner of China early this century is not forgot-ten in the Communist Party and the Party's leaders know that if they lose political power they will not be able to regain it, whereas in a corrupt po-litical system fortunes lost in Hong Kong can be rebuilt.

The advent of Chinese Communist rule and the corrupt practices that come with it will trigger departures within the business community. The largest Hong Kong capitalists, such as Li Ka-shing of Hutchison, are important enough for Peking to win over, but medium-sized companies have little to gain from a new administration. It is the owners of these enterprises who are best placed to buy themselves passports and take their cash to Canada or Aus-tralia, or just about anywhere else. Insofar as bourgeois democracy is en-trenched in Hong Kong it has relied on middle class professionals and smaller capitalists as important reservoirs of support. These are the groups which will feel most threatened by Chinese rule and which have the greatest ability to decamp with their skills and their capital. The working class, which has been scarcely organised or mobilised, would be left facing that rule with the same resignation with which it has experienced colonial government.

7 Elite Democracies: Bangladesh, India, Pakistan, the Philippines and Sri Lanka

The Sri Lankan capital, Colombo, is a 'security-conscious' city. In the space of one year Navy Commander Clancy Fernando, former Defence Minister and opposition leader Lalith Athulathmudali and President Ranasinghe Premadasa were all blown up or shot in the city centre. As elsewhere in South Asia the response of the military has been to station more soldiers with obsolete weapons on street corners, institute checkpoints and supplement the dress uniform guards at the president's palace with commandos in jungle fatigue lurking in the shrubbery. Yet, amid this ineffective officiousness, personal information about public figures is readily available: taxi drivers know where the leading politicians live and the way to speak to them is to find their residential number in the Colombo telephone directory and phone them up. The home of Prime Minister Sirimavo Bandaranaike is as much a landmark as the Bhutto compound in Karachi. The reason lies in the small size of the Anglophone and Anglophile ruling class, within which family squabbles and personality clashes are widely known and discussed and knowledge of one another's education, interlocking business interests and marriage ties is taken for granted.

All the élite democracies of Asia are characterised by a small ruling class and (with the exception of Sri Lanka) large populations – over 900 million in India and over 100 million in Bangladesh and Pakistan. In the Philippines and Pakistan landowners comprise an important part of the ruling class, as does the military in Pakistan. The bourgeoisie is strongest in the Philippines but has elsewhere been largely dependent on the state, rather than dominant. Relative economic failure and high levels of state ownership have thwarted the emergence of a bourgeoisie on similar lines to that in Taiwan or South Korea. The bureaucracy itself, through its control of state industry and banking and of foreign aid flows, is one of the most important components of the ruling class in South Asia as a whole. In that sense we cannot yet talk of these countries as bourgeois democracies. Nor, in the methods by which they seek to incorporate subordinate classes do they resemble the bourgeois democracies' increasing ability and readiness to do so through social spending.

They do, however, resemble the bourgeois democracies in having political systems – inherited from the departed colonial powers – which were intended to fullfil the twin requirements of assisting capital accumulation and containing and accommodating popular demands through institutionalising them. The British and American administrations passed on systems which functioned in what were then the two most advanced capitalist countries in the world. Yet with economies which bore no resemblance to British or US capitalism the states of South Asia and the Philippines had little chance of accomplishing the two objectives simultaneously. Since independence they have never been very successful at either and have tended to oscillate between the two. Occasionally popular demands are accommodated: more often those demands are repressed in the interests of the ruling class or fractions of it. As an alternative to making economic concessions, the ruling class has also used electoral manipulation and populist appeals which obscure economic issues and prevent economic demands being effectively articulated. These states differ from the veiled authoritarian states in allowing more open debate although, precisely because this can lead to popular demands which are economically unsustainable, élite democracy has been suspended on several occasions and replaced with outright authoritarian rule.

THE COLONIAL INHERITANCE

Britain and the US bequeathed political structures in the 1940s that were images of their own parliamentary and presidential systems. Those structures allowed local business and landed interests to strengthen their political positions ahead of the end of formal colonial rule. In the Philippines landowners were already entrenching themselves in political power before the Americans purchased the colony at the end of the Spanish–American War of 1898. The new colonial administration did not then scatter its own officials throughout the archipelago but enlisted those landowners in its service. Their control of the state machine at the lower levels put them in poll position to win elections firstly to provincial and then to national assemblies.[1] Since 1946 presidential elections in the independent Philippine Republic have replicated the non-ideological character of their US models, being contests between coalitions of these powerful landed interests. This system produced political leaderships as indistinguishable as Democrats and Republicans until Marcos introduced martial law in 1972. He ruled as a dictator from then until his overthrow in 1986, reallocating wealth to favoured cronies at the expense of some of the traditional landowning clans.[2] Once Marcos was disposed of, following the People Power uprising of 1986, these families and their allies took care to rewrite the constitution to limit the powers of his successors, ensuring that vested interests could once again be protected by obstruction in Congress. Although President Ramos, elected in 1992, has toyed with ideas of further political reform, the Congress remains firmly controlled by landed and business families.

A similiar political culture evolved in Ceylon, as it then was, under British rule in the 1930s. Elections to the Legislative Council began in 1931 and local landowners were quick to capture influence. After independence in 1948 they used patronage to consolidate their position.[3] In contrast to India they stepped into a virtual political vacuum. There had been no mass agitational independence movement. The Ceylon National Congress, the counterpart of Jawaharlal Nehru's Indian National Congress, had co-operated throughout with the British. There was the Trotskyist Lanka Sama Samaja Party (LSSP), which emerged in 1935 and acquired a following among rail and dock workers in Colombo, but the British jailed its leaders during the Second World War. This allowed the landowning class to assemble hastily its election vehicle, the United National Party (UNP), in time to fight the pre-independence elections in 1947. Politics did change dramatically in 1956 when S.W.R.D. Bandaranaike's Sri Lanka Freedom Party (SLFP) made a nationalist appeal to the Sinhalese Buddhist majority. Bandaranaike combined this with the network of support he had constructed among local 'intermediaries', mostly petty-bourgeois traders, businessmen and small farmers, with whom he had cultivated links during his time as Minister of Local Government (1936–47 and 1947–51).[4] This combination won a comprehensive victory over the neo-colonial business and landowning interests represented by the UNP but it also inflamed ethnic divisions and led eventually to a bloody civil war.

The contrasting, vigorous momentum for independence in India brought experienced politicians to power in 1947. Besides leading the internal struggle to expel the British Congress politicians had served in various provincial legislatures and as provincial premiers after 1937. While the leaders of Congress accepted financial underpinning from the Tatas and the Birlas, India's richest industrial families,[5] they were also infused with a commitment to state socialism that derived from their experience of the misery of the Great Depression of the 1930s, the industrial achievements in the Soviet Union and the teachings of a generation of Fabian scholars. This commitment ensured, however, that the upper ranks of the bureaucracy became an important part of the Indian ruling class after independence. It was not democratic planning that Congress pursued, but the organisation of economy and society by an enlarged bureaucracy into which the upper echelons of the Indian Civil Service left behind by the British were neatly absorbed. The private sector was left free to operate within parameters defined by the state as the reward for the continued funding of Congress by domestic big business. As Congress economic policies failed to improve the well-being of millions of ordinary people the party saw its stock of political capital whittled away. After Nehru died in 1964, it became increasingly difficult to counterbalance the failures of the present with the battles which Congress had fought for independence in the 1930s and 1940s. By the time Congress finally lost its stranglehold on electoral politics in the 1970s, social inequalities and corrupt electoral practices played into the hands of a coterie of rival politicians. But these rivals have only held power briefly, from 1977 to 1979 and from 1989 to 1991. For the rest of independent India's history Congress has enjoyed a cosy relationship with the bourgeoisie and the bureaucracy. This has been reinforced by common socialising experiences, particularly in mission schools in India and in foreign universities. This has been more marked at national level, which Indians refer to as 'the centre', than in the states, where a medley of parties have held power.

In contrast, Pakistan's struggle for independence was chiefly fought by Muhammed Ali Jinnah in the councils of the Viceroy where, backed up by the threat of communal (Muslim-Hindu) violence, it enjoyed support from a colonial ruling class which had sustained itself by accentuating communal differences. Jinnah's achievement was to secure independence for Pakistan, then divided in two 'wings', East Pakistan (now Bangladesh) and West Pakistan. Although officially revered as the founder of the country, Jinnah's death in 1948 left it without the same strong ideological framework as that in which the Indian ruling class was able to operate. His speeches and writings were quarried for ideological building blocks and the first Prime Minister, Liaquat Ali Khan, produced an 'objectives resolution' for Pakistan[6] which set down principles of 'democracy, freedom, equality, tolerance and social justice, as enunciated by Islam'. The constitution finally approved in 1956 defined the country as the Islamic Republic of Pakistan and Islam has been increasingly used by the state to reinforce political control. As an assemblage of feudal provinces (Baluchistan, Sindh and the North West Frontier Province), together with the commercial city of Karachi (home also to many of the 'Mohajir', refugees who fled India at partition) and the relatively prosperous Punjab, Pakistan has never had a cultural coherence to supplement Islam as a unifying force. This has, however, been offset by a continuity with strong British administrative structures. In West Pakistan, the landowning class with whom the British had collaborated maintained their feudal power and position and co-operated in a loose alliance with the bureaucracy and the military. The form of régime which this alliance has taken has varied as these factions have had their ups and downs since 1947, but in West Pakistan, now Pakistan, this triumvirate has remained in place, only recently having had to adjust to the rise of a bourgeoisie.

In East Pakistan, experience diverged from the start, as Hindu landlords fled to India. This made political competition more open than in West Pakistan. But the most important differences between the two 'wings' were economic and cultural. Exploitation and neglect of the East by businesses and government fuelled calls for greater autonomy which coalesced initially around the Bengali (Bangla) language issue. Strikes and protests were led by the Awami League, which won a majority in the parliament of Pakistan in the 1970 election. Domination by the Awami League was unacceptable the ruling class in the West, as was the proposal of its leader, Sheikh Mujibur Rahman, for confederation. At the instigation of the Prime Minister, Zulfikar Ali Bhutto, President Yahya Khan had Mujibur arrested and ordered the army to crush armed and unarmed protests in the East. The war of independence – eventually won with Indian help at the end of 1971 – gave Bangladesh a powerful unifying impetus behind the Awami League. But the destruction of war and the legacy of underdevelopment left the army and the bureaucracy as the dominant forces within the state. Coups – several in 1975 and again in 1982 – and periods of military rule have rendered constitutional arrangements short-lived and the state inchoate. Political leaders are drawn from a handful of families. Of the two principal political parties, the Awami League is now led by Sheikh Hasina, the daughter of Sheikh Mujibur, who escaped the massacre of his family during the first 1975 coup. The ruling Bangladesh National Party (BNP) is led by Khaleda Zia, the widow of General Ziaur Rahman, the President murdered in 1981. The wife of the deposed and imprisoned dictator General Ershad leads the Jatiya Party. In circumstances of relative economic failure, the search for ideological props means that political debate frequently turns around the attribution of blame for past mistakes and the desire for vengeance.

SUSPENSIONS OF DEMOCRACY

Where national or regional demands threaten to break out of the containment imposed by élite democracy they frequently provoke military intervention or the suspension of features of that democracy. The military's role has also been to repress industrial and agricultural labour with the aim of assisting accumulation. In Pakistan the army held power from 1958 to 1971 and from 1977 to 1988. During the 1980s the dictator General Zia ul-Haq did his best to reverse any social progress that had occurred in Pakistan and to thrust the peasantry back into medieval conditions of serfdom and ignorance. Islamic laws reinforced political repression with additional social control. This supplemented the power of landlords and discouraged workers and peasants from pursuing the benefits promised during the preceding administration of Zulfikar Ali Bhutto. Zia also sought to nurture a new class of entrepreneurs as the basis of a more dynamic economy in the future and therefore a more effective military. His death in a suspicious air crash[7] cleared the way for a return to fractious civilian rule. The army soon intervened again when it supported the then President, Ghulam Ishaq Khan,[8] in the removal of Benazir

Bhutto's first government in 1990. It showed more restraint in 1993, when it refrained from taking power in a situation in which President Ishaq Khan and Prime Minister Nawaz Sharif were trying to unseat one another. The army's leader, General Waheed Khan, intervened to maintain the veneer of constitutionality by persuading both men to stand down and call fresh elections, making way for a World Bank official, Moeen Qureshi, as interim Prime Minister and the appointment of the Senate chairman as President.[9]

The Indian Army, in contrast, has never intervened independently in a system in which politicians have been able to contain popular demands adequately. Where, as in some of the regional conflicts around India, containment has broken down, the army has been the tool of the centre in imposing direct rule over certain states. It also acted with Mrs Indira Gandhi when she imposed the State of Emergency in 1975 in face of economic problems, strikes and the threat of being personally disqualified from Parliament. Over 30 000 people were detained without trial during the following two years.[10] The Emergency was also intended to be the midwife to a new class of entrepreneurs, sheltered by labour laws that would enable them to emulate the growth rates of South Korea of the 1960s and 1970s.[11] It ended after splits within the Congress Party pushed Mrs Gandhi into holding an election in 1977.

Military interventions in Bangladesh have been more headstrong though generally supportive of the conditions of accumulation. Since the first coup in 1975 in which Sheikh Mujibur was assassinated, having created a one party state earlier that year, there has been a reversal of the policies of nationalisation pursued by the Awami League. The most recent period of military-led rule was that of General Ershad, from 1982 to 1990. In both Bangladesh and Pakistan some military interventions have been not so much to protect specific private sector assets or interests as to provide public order. Suppression of political in-fighting or strikes provides the conditions of greater predictability in which businessmen prefer to operate.

In Sri Lanka, as in India, the subversion of parliamentary democracy came from within the state, in the form of President J. R. Jayawardene. In 1982 he rewrote the constitution to give himself the kinds of executive powers enjoyed by the President in the Fifth French Republic, cancelled the elections then due and called a referendum to extend the life of the parliament elected in 1977 by another six years. Having secured resignation letters from all the UNP MPs, Jayawardene had considerable power over parliament. What Willian McGowan calls the 'suppression of legitimate political dissent'[12] outside parliament paved the way for racketeering, corruption, tax cuts and foreign investment to the gain of those domestic and foreign interests linked to the régime. This provoked a backlash amongst the *Janatha Vimukthi Peramuna* (JVP), a petty-bourgeois led movement which drew support from peasants in the South alienated by this régime. Its Maoist, autarkic, nationalist programme alarmed the ruling class and its attacks on military and economic targets represented a direct challenge to the state. Jayawardene's successor, Ranasinghe Premadasa, concentrated power in his own hands to an even greater extent. Originating outside the social élite yet accepted by the ruling class as a necessary evil to rid themselves of the greater evil of the JVP, Premadasa gave a free hand to the armed forces and the UNP's death squads to kill as many as 30 000 people.[13] But Premadasa also began to frame his own development strategy, which would have funnelled the benefits of government policy to a narrower clique of his cronies. This threatened to upset the traditional hold of ruling class families, and provoked a split in the UNP[14] and an impeachment attempt. In May 1993 Premadasa was providentially killed by a suicide bomber after the impeachment proceedings had failed. The stock market celebrated the return to normality with a year-long rally.

The Sri Lankan ruling class feared that Premadasa was a Marcos in the making, a monster they could no longer control. The lesson of the Philippines was an alarming one for them. When Marcos first declared martial law, he was able to bypass the logjam of legislation in Congress and concentrate economic decision-making in the hands of technocrats. Under their guidance the economy was better managed, the Bataan EPZ was set up to attract foreign investment and, for a while, the economy fulfilled the twin functions of accommodation and accumulation. But the greed of Marcos, his family and associates led him to seize assets or demand shares in Filipino companies and to break the hold of foreign companies in sectors of the economy where they were dominant.[15] To guarantee conditions of accumulation, Marcos also detained 50 000 people[16] and escalated repression in the provinces.[17] By 1986 Marcos had alienated more of the ruling class outside his own circle and had long since lost any popular support. He had outlived his usefulness to his ultimate patron, the United States and could no longer deliver on promises to the IMF. No matter how many bulletproof brassières his wife had, the emperor himself had no clothes.

When the armed forces deserted him, Marcos had to flee. Their role in his overthrow and previously in sustaining his régime when it had little else to support it had led army officers to believe they should exercise a greater influence in the state, parallel to that of the Indonesian or Thai military. This, in turn, prompted a number of abortive coup attempts during the Aquino presidency, a problem only finally resolved after former soldier and police chief Fidel Ramos became President. Ramos has struck a deal with the military which offers the prospect of modernisation and a reduction in unwelcome anti-guerrilla campaigning in exchange for a less political role.

POPULAR UPHEAVALS

The 'People Power' revolution in 1986 was an explosion of popular demands which built up as Marcos neglected virtually every constituency except the armed forces and his cronies. The same phenomenon has occurred elsewhere: prolonged failure of the accommodation function of élite democracy triggers rejection of a régime. The process of rejection is through widespread mobilisation, though broad class alliances are not then embodied in new régimes. Just as in the Bangkok uprising of 1992 or the overthrow of military rule in South Korea, popular demands are suppressed as the ruling class reconfigures itself. In the élite democracies, restoration of democracy tends to mean restitution of the same institutions of government as have existed before a seizure of power, along with the same mechanisms through which the ruling class has manipulated and controlled them in the past.

This was apparent in Cory Aquino's actions after she was inaugurated as President, just before Marcos finally fled, in a ceremony at the élite Club Filipino. Within a year peasants demonstrating for land reform at the Mendiola Bridge near the presidential palace were met by armed police who shot 19 of them dead. In the Congressional elections of May 1987 pro-Aquino candidates campaigned under the Lakas banner. To ensure the largest possible victory Aquino endorsed the most electable candidates, on a list which included two former members of Marcos Cabinets, 25 other associates of Marcos and a big slice of the élite with the right local power base deriving from their control of land and jobs in the regions, as well as extensive kinship ties.[18] Elected a year after the 'People Power revolution', the House of Representatives included 130 members of traditional political families and 39 of their relatives among its 200 members[19] – a far cry from the composition of the 125 000 supporters of 'People Power' who had defied Marcos's troops. This solid phalanx of interests was able to stifle land reform proposals. The House elected in 1992 contained 145 members with similar ties.[20]

A depressingly similar statistic emerged from the almost identical events in Pakistan. In 1986 Benazir Bhutto returned to the country after more than two years in exile to lead a struggle against General Zia's régime. Using the image of her 'martyred' father, Zulfikar Ali Bhutto, hanged by Zia in 1979, she was able to conjure up the same kind of sympathy that Cory Aquino attracted after the murder of her husband Benigno in 1983. Zia's repressive Islamic régime was rapidly losing popularity just as Marcos had. Bhutto's revived Pakistan People's Party (PPP) and the wider Movement to Restore Democracy (MRD) organised mass rallies and protests during 1986 and 1987 and in the run-up to the elections conceded by Zia in 1988. Yet when the elections finally took place in November 1988 the PPP's candidates were drawn from the familiar landowning families with the same electoral pulling power as Cory's turncoat Congressmen. Former Zia officials were inducted into the PPP in the same way that Marcos's creatures rallied to the Lakas banner. A third of PPP candidates joined the party three months before the elections, some of them offering up to 3 million rupees for one of the 700 national and provincial candidacies.[21] The MRD split with the PPP as Benazir's ambitions displaced the principle of democractic elections. The result of the 1988 election was that 230 of the 237 MPs elected were major landllords or tribal chiefs.

Equally unpopular régimes were overthrown in Bangladesh and in India. General Ershad's dictatorship was brought down by mass protest in 1990 in which the Awami League, the BNP and the Jamaat-e-Islam were all active. Indira Gandhi was heavily defeated in the 1977 elections when voters gave their damning verdict on the excesses of the Emergency. The poor who were the victims of forced sterilisation and slum clearance joined with middle class critics to eject her and her son Sanjay. Yet the election of the BNP government in Bangladesh played into the hands of domestic and foreign investors while the election of the Janata-led coalition of 1977–79 brought in a disunited government which had, in Tariq Ali's words, 'even less substantial a programme than Congress', the impotence of which was demonstrated by its repeated attacks on Mrs Gandhi and the iniquities of the Emergency.[22]

ELECTORAL MANIPULATION

Such upheavals are the exception. Most of the time electoral manipulation through patronage and vote-buying ensures that the ruling class does enough to retain control without resorting to military intervention or provoking mass uprisings. As the role of the state has expanded, especially in rural areas, so politicians are able to use it to parcel out benefits in exchange for electoral support, backed up by gangsterism and thuggery. Absolute poverty and inequalities in these five countries are among the worst in Asia (see Chapter 3) and they make voters more susceptible to overt electoral bribery as well as perpetuating ignorance and suggestibility. The actual nexus can vary considerably, from jobs in a garment factory in Sri Lanka to logging contracts handed out in the Philippines to businessmen who deliver a block of votes purchased in cash.[23] In India 'vote banks' are constructed from particular castes, with promises of special help; in Sri Lanka the Ceylon Workers Congress Party successfully bargained the votes of tea plantation workers against protection for the industry from outright privatisation. In India the decay of the Congress as a genuine vehicle of popular mobilisation has actually accentuated the need for bribery. Individual members are no longer recruited to a party built from the bottom up. Instead prospective candidates buy up blocks of memberships and distribute them among their supporters to ensure they are selected for party office.[24] When it comes to national elections, however,

Congress's grassroots organisation exists only on paper. It has little to campaign with except electoral bribery and cardboard cut-outs of the Nehru/ Gandhi dynasty. Where patronage fails gangsterism takes its place. India has coined a new term – 'booth capturing' – to describe initimidation and armed violence on polling day.

Drug money sloshes over into Pakistan's elections, funding parties and buying seats and votes in all the provinces. Feudal loyalties ensure the return of landowners and their relations in rural areas of Sindh, Baluchistan and the North West Frontier. Attempts to clean up electoral practices in Sri Lanka in the 1950s and 1960s failed in 1982 when opposition parties were unable to monitor polling booths.[25] Opponents of Jayawardene in Sri Lanka accused him of using voter impersonation and intimidation in the 1982 referendum. Opposition critics also allege ballot box stuffing and polling station closures in the 1988 parliamentary elections, but 10 000 volunteers came forward in 1994 to observe polling day procedures. Pre-election violence left around 20 people dead and voting was minimal in areas under the control of the Liberation Tigers of Tamil Eelam (LTTE or Tamil Tigers) in the north, although it reached 75 per cent nationally. Concerns over electoral manipulation are being used in support of opposition calls for the 1995–6 elections in Bangladesh to be overseen by an independent commission, a proposal which is unlikely to be accepted. Only in the Philippines were there signs in the 1992 elections that patronage and party machines were losing some of their effectiveness. Machine candidates such as the presidential hopeful Ramon Mitra were unable to mobilise votes by calling on local bosses. There are several explanations for this (including Mitra's beard), but one of the more convincing is that remittance income from relatives working abroad has made people in rural areas less dependent on the power of those bosses. The death toll in Philippine elections meanwhile fell from 151 in 1986 to 50 in 1992,[26] but the tenor of campaigning does little to dampen a violent climate.

Violence can be used with impunity because the judicial system is at the disposal of the rich. The legal systems in all these countries afford very little protection to anyone challenging vested economic interests or the politically powerful and offer no effective means of redress where democracy fails. Perhaps the greatest gulf between lofty sentiments in law and humiliating everyday experience is in the Philippines, where the preamble of the 1987 Constitution declares that it was promulgated 'in order to build a just and humane society'.[27] Its provisions include 'social justice in all phases of national development' and making all crop-lands subject to land reform. When Aquino herself agreed to fudge land reform to protect her family's 6000-hectare Hacienda Luisita it was evident that the new constitution would change little in that respect. The five years of Aquino's administration after 1987 brought few other steps towards a just and humane society. Aquino sanctioned the death squads killing Communists and their supporters in Davao, while the Presidential Commission on Human Rights which she established proved ineffective.[28] For the 50, 60 or 70 per cent of Filipinos in poverty a petition to the Supreme Court for 'social justice' in the current 'phase of national development' would hold little hope. The Court's openness to influence from more persuasive sources was amply demonstrated when one of its justices allegedly allowed lawyers from the Philippine Long Distance Telephone Company to write an opinion for him to protect its near-monopoly.[29] The long delays in the labyrinthine legal system in the countryside have been a major factor in popular support for the Communist-led New People's Army (NPA), which dispenses justice a great deal more quickly.

The same Kafkaesque nightmare confronts any ordinary Indian sucked into the legal system as plaintiff or defendant. The Indian Supreme Court has had a relatively good reputation for being free of corruption,[30] although the Court has done little to arrest its rampant spread at virtually every other level of government. Failure in this respect is paralleled in the area of human rights. The gravest abuses of human rights currently are in the Northern Muslim-majority areas of the state of Jammu and Kashmir (see below). Amnesty International has been refused permission to visit the state and has criticised the Terrorism and Disruptive Activities Act and lack of rights for detainees. The abuses in Jammu and Kashmir are against the background of the suppression of Sikh terrorism in the Punjab, where militant terrorists were hunted to extinction in 1993 having forfeited popular support by increasingly widespread killings of farmers. Kashmir has now become an important test for India's new Human Rights Commission. It announced in early 1994 that it was to investigate the shooting of more than 30 civilians by the Border Security Force (BSF) at Bijbehara in Kashmir. But a Commission composed of three former judges and a retired UN official is regarded sceptically by human rights activists. Its limited powers to compel government co-operation reinforce that concern, as does the ineffectual record of commissions on women and tribal peoples.[31]

The law in Sri Lanka has served chiefly as a weapon of oppression. The government has used far-reaching emergency powers and a sweeping Prevention of Terrorism Act to harrass Tamils and other opponents. Jayawardene also emasculated the judiciary by removing its power of judicial review. The 11 year-long state of emergency was lifted only in mid-1994, shortly before parliamentary elections. Outside the law, the UNP used political thuggery and murder against dissent in any form. Likewise a Special Powers Act has been on the statute book in Bangladesh since 1974 and was joined by an Anti-Terrorism Act in 1992. Together these give wide-ranging powers to detain opponents of the government without trial, and arrests and detentions run into several thousands annually. Suspected criminals are also taken into preventive custody in their thousands in law and order offensives.[32]

Pakistan's legal system meanwhile keeps in being the Islamic laws drawn up during Zia's rule in the interests of the reactionary landowners and mullahs. It was one of the failures of Benazir Bhutto's first government that it did not try to reverse Islamicisation for fear of alienating religious leaders. Not only did repressive laws remain in place, but Bhutto's government was brought down by use of the 8th Amendment to the Constitution. Drawn up to give Zia, as President, the right to dismiss a government, it was used to remove Bhutto in August 1990, though when President Ghulam Ishaq Khan tried to use those powers again in 1993 to dismiss the Nawaz Sharif administration, his ruling was overturned by the Supreme Court. Since returning to power in 1993 Bhutto has seen a PPP leader, Farooq Leghari, installed as President. But the 8th Amendment stands as a constitutional provision for a coup against an elected government.

The media have, for the most part, supported governments in the élite democracies. During periods of dictatorial rule press and broadcasting freedoms have been totally withdrawn. Zia, Premadasa and Ershad gave short shrift to press independence and to critics. After the worst abuses of that period were over, however, newspapers in Pakistan and Sri Lanka swung behind the government. In Bangladesh harassment of journalists and withdrawal of government advertising are used against unfriendly voices. Between 1991 and 1994, 150 journalists were arrested on charges including defamation and blasphemy.[33] State television broadcasting in South Asia serves the government of the day, with faithful reporting of the doings of senior government figures although it is being displaced by the growth of cable and satellite television.[34] In Sri Lanka access to international broadcasts has to be weighed against the fact that foreign coverage of the civil war is blacked out.

In India, there is a tradition of a relatively free press but the Emergency nevertheless saw it cowed by Mrs Gandhi. Since then it has recovered a more independent voice and the audiences for satellite television broadcasts reinforce an openness to international information flows. Newspaper proprietors and editors do, however, share the language and preconceptions of the civil service and political élite.[35] Freedom of information and exchange of views is also confined to the relatively small audiences for international news broadcasts[36] and to the 52 per cent who are literate. In the Philippines rhetoric rises to unrivalled heights and the press revels in the orotund and the sensational. But it does so in the service of its owners. Every publication of note is tied to specific corporate and political interests. Exceptions, such as the Philippine Centre for Investigative Journalism, which exposed the potential policy implications of a close relationship between President Ramos and a prominent socialite, are few in number.

THE MIDDLE CLASSES

A changing social structure is unlikely to alter the fundamentally élite nature of democracy. According to the optimistic M.S. Dobbs-Higginson in his recent *Asia-Pacific: A View on its Role in the New World Order*, 'the middle class is still likely to be the harbinger of social change in India' and 'could act as both a stabilising factor and a factor in change in Indian politics'.[37] On this argument, what India's middle class do today, their Pakistani and Bangladeshi counterparts will do tomorrow. But what are the 180 million people the Indian Planning Ministry identifies as middle class (on the basis of their spending patterns) doing exactly? Rather than embrace economic reform and opportunity the middle class are just as fearful of economic change as state enterprise workers are. This fear is reflected in growing support for the right-wing Hindu party, the Bharatiya Janata Party (BJP). The party has drawn support from a middle class which Bruce Graham (quoted in Prem Shankar Jha, *In the Eye of the Cyclone*) sees as 'being threatened from two directions: from above, by the competitive individualism and the secular values of capitalism and from below, by the first expressions of rural populism, the growing power of caste associations and the increased militancy of communist-led trade unions'.[38] In 1994 the BJP turned out this support almost simultaneously against economic reforms to open Indian markets under the GATT and against the Harijans (the 20 per cent of Hindus formerly referred to as untouchables). The petty-bourgeois, middle class and rural mass base of the BJP invites comparisons to the political base of fascist parties. Its nationalist ideology encourages envy of India's Muslim minority, accusing the government of pandering to them unduly. The BJP has helped foment the communal violence which has killed hundreds across India, as in the riots which followed the demolition of the Babri mosque.

The new Pakistani middle class is no more a force for liberal change than are the BJP's cohorts. Zia's strategy of development held out hopes of advancement to lower middle class *mohajir*, offering them a new stake in a society in which they had come to feel at a disadvantage to Sindhis. But when Zia's régime favoured Punjabis, the *mohajir* turned to the Mohajir Qaumi Movement (MQM) as a means of redressing perceived inequalities. Its demands are for recognition as a 'fifth nationality', alongside the Sindhis, Baluchis, Pathans and Punjabis of Pakistan's four provinces; it is not a force for stability or for liberal economic and political reform but one which tugs at the loose ends of the structure of the state. In Bangladesh only a tiny middle class exists – perhaps as few as 100 000 people – most of them tied to government jobs or contracts and with very little interest in social change. The student population, which is politically active, is recruited as auxiliaries for the main parties, which fight proxy battles on university campuses using their student supporters. Students are also used by party organisers at election-time, when they are needed as canvassers in the absence of wide-spread access to television or newspapers. Sri Lanka's middle class, its ranks thinned by the exile of many Tamils and preoccupied by white collar status, is likely to side with the ruling class to protect that status. In the same way, many of the Filipino middle classes have sought employment overseas, while those who remain use whatever ties they have to the ruling class to keep them precariously above the abyss of urban poverty. Only in the upheavals of the 'People Power' movement did the Filipino middle classes side with the other groups disenfranchised by Marcos. Although David Timberman's study of Philippine politics published in 1991 talked of the 'most optimistic scenario' as being 'one in which political change will be forced upon a reluctant élite by the increased power of emerging groups such as the middle class, sectoral and cause-oriented groups'[39] there has been little sign of this materialising.

RELIGION

The general failure to accommodate popular demands, whether because elected bodies are full of landowners and businessmen or their relatives and cronies, or because no other avenues are available through which to seek social justice, has the same kind of results as in the veiled authoritarian states. Religious leaders, populists and separatists provide receptacles for disillusionment, and the ruling class manoeuvres to control what is both a potentially useful safety valve and a potentially destablisiing force.

The death threats and arrest warrants directed at Taslima Nasreen are indicative of an Islamic revival in Bangladesh. She initially affronted Islamic fundamentalists by writing about Muslim attacks on the minority Hindu community in Bangladesh in the aftermath of the demolition of the Babri mosque. In a subsequent interview with a Calcutta newspaper, Nasreen made remarks about the Koran which were interpreted as implying that she thought it should be rewritten, an interpretation she rejects. Islam has also been turned against the economic and social influence of aid organisations by religious fundamentalists who are opposed to the spread of secular education and women's rights. The largest fundamentalist party, the Jamaat-e-Islam, has hitherto had a restricted appeal, labouring as it does under the enormous negative connotations of its having been on the wrong side in the 1971 war of independence. It has seized on the campaign against Taslima Nasreen as a way back from the political wilderness, aided by the willingness of the main opposition party, the Awami League, to run with the fundamentalists. The BNP government, too, went along with the fundamentalists by ordering Nasreen's arrest. Just as in Indonesia, the government seeks to use and control the Islamic extremism which feeds off material deprivation.

The Jamaat-e-Islam's counterparts in Pakistan also feed off the wider frustration at the rich, whose privileges attract resentment in the guise of religiously-inspired protest at their longstanding double standards of conduct (especially drinking). Thus, for example, 200 cars were smashed up in a riot outside the social élite's 1993 New Year's Eve party at the Punjab Club in Lahore. To date, however, Pakistan's religious parties have drawn relatively little electoral support in a country where voting is still controlled through patronage networks or divided on ethnic lines and where no important political leaders – apart from the unlamented General Zia – have felt the need to use religious fundamentalism to bolster support. This does not, of course, rule out its use in the future, with divisive consequences.

Militant Buddhism in Sri Lanka was first consciously used by S.W.R.D. Bandaranaike when he led the SLFP to electoral victory in 1956. An Oxford-educated member of the ruling class himself, he had no scruples about enlisting Buddhist nationalism as a way of mobilising voters to displace the UNP.[40] The charge that it had neglected Buddhism and the interests of the Sinhalese while allowing the English-educated and the Tamil minorities to prosper sank in among the poor Sinhalese. Bandaranaike's manoeuvre rather backfired three years later when a monk shot and killed him for not having pushed the cause far enough. Like Mahathir and Suharto, S.W.R.D. Bandaranaike found religious militancy more than he (or his successors) could handle. Increasingly linked to the Sinhalese identity, militant Buddhism has become a deeply embedded obstacle to any settlement of the island's political problems on the basis of autonomy for the Tamils. Outside the ruling class, the JVP was also successful in mobilising Sinhalese Buddhist chauvinism in conjunction with the real economic grievances of the poor South. This gave Sri Lankan politicians a nasty shock and made them wary of handing their opponents a chance to play this potent card. Yet every time they play it themselves without addressing the fundamental economic inequalities which give it that potency, they increase the likelihood that a rival – even one as uncontrollable as the JVP became – will repackage it in some telling new combination.

Militant Hinduism has never been acceded to in this way by the Congress Party in India, which has always been able to assemble sufficient electoral support from economically deprived groups, Muslims and regional strongholds. The BJP is thus able to portray itself as the undisputed champion of the Hindu cause against a secular, Westernised élite. Its only problem is finding issues broad and unambiguous enough to unite a large portion of India's Hindus. The Babri mosque, built over what militant Hindus claim is the birthplace of the warrior god Lord Ram, was just such an issue. The demolition of the mosque by a mob at the end of 1992 took the wind out of the BJP sails and left it searching for another unifying issue.

In Asia's only majority Catholic country, the Philippines, natural disasters and extreme poverty provide fertile soil for religious explanations of the world and spiritual consolations for material inadequacies. Credulity and devotion are rife. Tens and hundreds of thousands of people subscribe to such cults as 'El Shaddei' or scour the provinces for visitations and miracles. Religion feeds off their suffering. Its leaders did also – as in Latin America – take sides against dictatorship. Cardinal Sin's denunciations of the Marcos régime were an important factor in mobilising mass opposition against it and Sin intervened to resolve differences between opposition leaders Cory Aquino and Salvador Laurel in the 1986 presidential election campaign. In the 1992 presidential elections he opposed Ramos on the grounds that he was a Protestant and, more specifically, favoured birth control (in a country with one of the highest birth rates in Asia).   Once Marcos was gone, the Catholic Church reverted to its role of perpetuating the existing social order, although Sin did also oppose those 'oppressors and plunderers'[41] (Imelda Marcos and Eduardo Cojuangco) whose election could have meant a return to crony capitalism. In the southern island of Mindanao, meanwhile, the Muslim Moro National Liberation Front (MNLF) has played on a shared religious faith as well as economic grievances – encapsulated in the fact that life expectancy on the island is 14 years lower than that in Manila[42] – in its campaign for independence.

POPULISM

The gap between expectations and experience on which religions feed is exacerbated by the extravagant promises of politicians. Ramos has displayed this tendency by promising to sort out, personally, virtually every problem, from urban poverty and power shortages to the environment and terrorism. In doing so he is playing into the hands of populists; political leaders who seek to build support by appealing to ignorance, prejudices and resentment created by economic and political failure. To retain their following once in elected office, populists may find it necessary to make some concessions to workers and peasants that go beyond what sections of the ruling class would want (such as imposing nationalist limitations on foreign investment) but such measures are a tactical alternative to a military régime, which could also contradict the interests of some fractions of the ruling class. The more reality falls short of the promises of other politicians, the easier it is for populists to whip up support. They are doing so in all the élite democracies, using a rhetoric which is misleading anti-élitist to secure office for themselves.

The 1992 presidential election in the Philippines saw former judge Miriam Defensor Santiago finish as runner-up to Ramos. Her campaign focused on corruption and law and order issues, appealing to those excluded from the perks of corruption and unable to buy the justice and security they want. In

a society of corrupt police officers and heavily fortified residential compounds, the poor and powerless responded to her message. The same appeal
propelled Joseph Estrada into the vice presidency. As a film actor with a
record of frequently playing roles in which he championed justice against
crime, Estrada convinced voters he could bring the same attributes to the
conduct of national politics. His antics after the election, such as personally
ordering arrests at a press conference as head of a special Anti-Crime Commission, suggested that he saw the advantages of continuing that role in
real life. Estrada is now a strong contender to succeed Ramos as president
in 1998.

Film stars such as N. T. Rama Rao, M. G. Ramachandran ('MGR') and
Jayalalitha Jayaram have been part of the political scene in South India over
the last two decades. Jayalalitha is now Chief Minister of Tamil Nadu in
succession to 'MGR'. She has built an enormous personality cult, feeding
off the gullibility of voters who identify politicians with the roles they
play in hugely popular films. If politics is a land of fantastic promises,
who better to fulfil them than fantasy characters? This is the less harmful
side of Indian populism, in contrast to the more alarming populist appeal of
the BJP.

Elsewhere in South Asia the master populist of the years since independence was undoubtedly Zulfikar Ali Bhutto. His 1970 election slogan of
'food, clothing and shelter' (not so different from the Bolsheviks 'bread,
peace and land') has a powerful resonance even today. Benazir Bhutto has
massaged her father's apparently anti-élitist posture and his death at the
hands of the military to obscure the economic failures and political repression
which characterised his period in office. Pakistan's history of failure, economic and political, creates the conditions for populism that does not analyse
failure, but searches for a culprit (from a long list of suspects) and reinforces
the tendency to look backward which characterises political discourse in
Pakistan. Benazir Bhutto further fuels it, announcing plans to build a mau-
soleum for her father, adhering to his policies wherever possible and trying
to portray her family as a representative of Pakistan's suffering as a whole.
So long as the failures continue, so will the populist search for scapegoats
and the popular susceptibility to extravagant promises.

The same turning over of the past is used by Bangladeshi politicians for
the same reasons. The BNP has dragged out the prosecutions of General
Ershad and capitalised on salacious stories of his private life to keep alive
its populist image as the saviour of democracy. Likewise the Awami League
plays up the war of independence to embellish its own record and its leader,
Sheikh Hasina, seeks revenge for the murder of her father. In Sri Lanka
populism began with S.W.R.D. Banadaranaike's use of Buddhist nationalism. Premadasa also resorted to populist techniques in his garment factory
building programme and such gestures as the distribution of free school uni-

forms. His death represents, for the moment, the high water mark of Sri Lankan populism, but a corrupt society dominated by a small ruling class and a shaky economy are natural breeding grounds for its return. The election platforms of both the UNP and the SLFP and its allies in the People's Alliance ahead of the 1994 elections contained generous promises of state social spending. Both also promised to end political corruption, with the People's Alliance even threatening to close the airport to prevent the escape of corrupt UNP MPs fearful of being brought to justice. Following the People's Alliance's victory in the August polls, it was expected to inaugurate a social spending programme costed at around Rs.23 billion (to be financed by additional goods and services taxes).

SEPARATISM

The third channel into which discontent flows is separatism and regional conflict. Governments which refuse to meet the demands of minorities and tamper with rights under federal systems add to the general frustration at economic failure and social inequality. None of the élite democracies has been spared regional conflicts. Bangladesh, Pakistan and the Philippines have experienced fewer or less intense struggles, India has a multiplicity of conflicts, while Sri Lanka has the most savage and intense. The Bangladeshi conflict involves the Chakma tribes of the Chittagong Hill Tracts, in a classic tale of encroachment by displaced lowland settlers followed by the ultimately violent reaction of the tribes. The government strenuously denies that it has done anything other than try to integrate the hill tribes, yet since 1972 the Parbattya Chattagram Jana Samhati Samity and its armed wing, the Shanti Bahini, have been fighting for regional autonomy within a federal structure and the removal of post-1971 settlers.[43] Talks have been held periodically, as between 1985 and 1989, and resumed in November 1992. A positive sign was that the 50 000 Chakma refugees in India began returning home in 1994. Talks also began in 1993 between the MNLF and the Ramos government. At one point its guerrillas tied down 60 per cent of the Philippine armed forces, though its armed strength has dwindled considerably. A starting point does exist for talks in the form of the 1976 Tripoli Agreement, which promised autonomy to 13 provinces.[44] A 1990 referendum resulted in just four of them joining the Autonomous Region of Muslim Mindanao: enlarging the size of this region could be the basis for settling demands.

Regional unrest and repression have been much more severe in Pakistan, partly because the achievement of independence by Bangladesh has made governments more worried about any threat of further secessions. Zulfikar Ali Bhutto put down a rising in Baluchistan in 1973 which resulted in the deaths of 10 000 people.[45] The Sindh uprising of 1983 was crushed with similar ruthlessness and the army were back in 1990 to deal with MQM violence in Karachi and Hyderabad. The military presence has remained on the streets of the cities since then. As well as military repression elected federal governments in Pakistan have sought to install sympathetic administrations in the provinces, while ensuring that they retain the upper hand over such administrations. As her father did, Benazir Bhutto has destabilised potentially hostile provincial governments. She unseated the North West Frontier Province government not long after returning to power in 1993 while her rival, Nawaz Sharif, used his provincial base in the Punjab to try to dislodge her during her first administration. Provincial leaders naturally try to capitalise on conflict and rivalry at the centre, but the constant manipulation of provincial politics for the sake of power struggles at the centre only increases disdain for the political system.

The machinations of the centre have been a factor in uprisings in the Indian states of Assam, Jammu and Kashmir, the Punjab, Tripura, Nagaland and other small states of the North East. Each of the uprisings now is at a different stage of a cycle of repression, quiescence and resurgence. One fear of Indian leaders is that several struggles could assume critical proportions at the same time, further stretching the army, 20 of whose 34 divisions were already employed in internal security in 1992.[46] Their other fear is that secessionism in the South could resurface. This has remained latent after its outbreak in the early 1960s when there were demands for a separate Dravida state.

Jammu and Kashmir's accession to India only came after an invasion sponsored by Pakistan. It allotted the Indian government control of defence, external affairs and communications and was made conditional on a plebiscite[47] to be held when the law and order situation permitted. The presence of Pakistani troops occupying part of the state has enabled India to refuse to hold such a vote. The 'secessionist' politics of Sheikh Abdullah, the state's leader, prompted an intervention by Nehru's government in 1953. It manipulated a split in Abdullah's party to secure a more favourably inclined state premier. Vote-rigging by Congress from 1957–72[48] was followed by free elections in 1977, but interference from the centre featured again in 1984 and, as votes slipped towards the Muslim United Front in the 1987 elections, intervention in the electoral process pushed more young people, especially, into supporting the Jammu and Kashmir Liberation Front (JKLF) and other outlawed organisations. The insurgency in the Muslim-majority areas of the state of Jammu and Kashmir is the worst, and India currently has troops and paramilitaries estimated variously at 250 000[49], 450 000[50] and 600 000[51] fighting a mixture of armed movements, some financed and armed (though not necessarily controlled) by Pakistan. Between 1000 and 1500 foreigners are reported to be fighting alongside the guerrillas. Shootings of civilians and death in custody have contributed to Pakistani claims of as many as 40 000[52] deaths since the outbreak of the latest, and most serious, Kashmir uprising in 1990. Indian figures put the death toll at a much lower 2000 or so a year since 1990. Indian hopes that the security operation would stabilise the situation sufficently to allow elections to be held in 1994 were dashed when Home Minister S. B. Chavan extended President's Rule (that is direct rule by New Delhi) until September 1995.

Political interventions elsewhere by the centre have often been intended to exploit discontents in the states for its own ends: for example, Mrs Gandhi built up the Sikh fanatic Jamail Singh Bhindranwale in the Punjab in order to defeat the Akali Dal, the local rivals to the Congress party. Bhindranwale became far too strong for Mrs Gandhi to control, leading to the politically costly storming of the Sikhs' Golden Temple and, eventually, to Mrs Gandhi's assasination. Less dramatically, in the Gorkha area of Bengal, both the state government and the centre have encouraged autonomy demands for their own ends but without delivering, pushing local leaders towards separatism.[53] Such manipulation compounds the fears of growing centralisation, a trend which has been apparent in Indian politics since Mrs Gandhi's first intervention in national affairs in 1959–60, when she became involved in the toppling of the Communist government in the state of Kerala.[54] Use of Presidential powers to hold up bills from state assemblies not governed by Congress was another of her tactics.[55] The bifurcation of state and national politics, which has been apparent since state elections were separated from national elections in their timing in the 1960s and, increasingly, in their issues, is likely to continue. The more regional issues the greater the number of possible points of contention between New Delhi and the state govenments. Whether the issue is caste, religion, state subsidies, minorities, agricultural prices, the environment, language or foreign relations, the centre constantly runs the risk of offending some regional interest group. Economic growth accentuates state differences further. As Rajiv Gandhi found, intervening in state politics to try to knit together a patchwork of friendly governments is fraught with just as many perils. Nor can a coalition of regional parties become a stable base for a new national government. With so many regional separatist conflicts – whether latent or active – any government at the centre is bound to find itself absorbed in complicated relationships with the states. A less effective government at the centre is likely, though this may actually be compatible with continuing economic growth in the states, where local politicians can strike deals with investors.

It is the complex politics of the states of South India which led the Indian government into its entanglement with Sri Lankan internal affairs in the 1980s. The civil war in Sri Lanka has its roots in conflicts over distribution. Prior to 1956, partly as a result of the allocation of jobs under British rule, Tamils accounted for a disproportionate percentage of the Ceylonese professions and civil service. Once S.W.R.D. Bandaranaike had invoked Sinhalese nationalism in his 1956 campaign he had to deliver jobs and privileges for the majority community. Unlike in Malaysia, where it was possible to create a parallel structure of opportunities in the public sector alongside the private sector in which Chinese businessmen had prospered, the focus of Sinhalese nationalists was on dislodging Tamils from jobs in the public sector and the educational and other advantages conferred through it. It was not a case of enlarging the cake, but of redividing it. The weeding out of Tamils from the public sector and the denial of opportunities to members of a community which had previously seen education as a route to advancement caused great bitterness.

The anti-Tamil riots of 1958 and 1983, which had at least a partial economic motive in seeking to drive out businessmen and seize their assets, added to that feeling. The savagery of the 1983 riots was such that it gave the LTTE the support it needed to launch a serious armed challenge to the state. This confronted the Indian government with a difficult situation. Governments in New Delhi could not afford to be seen to be neglecting this struggle, for fear that their inaction would fuel disenchantment among the 55 million Tamils in Tamil Nadu, but neither did they want the Sri Lankan Tamils to succeed in winning an independent homeland, for fear that this would encourage Indian Tamils to seek the same goal. The problems inherent in this situation led eventually to the Indo–Sri Lankan Accord of 1987, which was intended to demonstrate that the Indian Peacekeeping Force (IPKF) was protecting the Tamil minority yet doing so within a constitutional framework that preserved the integrity of the Sri Lankan state. The IPKF episode ended, however, not by satisfying all interests, but by alienating them, to the extent that the LTTE murdered Rajiv Gandhi and the Sri Lankan government supported their attacks on the IPKF.[56] Since then Indian federal politicians have decided against further support for the LTTE and put its leader, Vellupillai Prabakaran, on trial (in absentia) for Rajiv's murder. They have been able to do so with less fear that the Tamil issue would be exploited by southern Indian politicians. Jayalalitha and other local leaders have turned against the LTTE as a result of the increase in political killings in the South.

In Sri Lanka itself the LTTE has fought the security forces to a standstill. But it has continued to send out signals indicating a willingness to discuss a compromise and welcomed the election of the People's Alliance government which made reconciliation one of its prime objectives. The new President, Mrs Chadrika Kumaratunga, and her late husband, Vijay, were the only mainstream Sinhalese politicians to visit Jaffna in the 1980s and conduct talks with the LTTE. In this respect, the outlook for peace is more propitious than for a long time. The most likely basis for agreement is a constitutional arrangement that would give the North and East of the country the same degree of autonomy as that enjoyed (theoretically) by Indian states.

However, signals from the LTTE are complicated by internal power struggles and by its past record of negotiating only to gain time to regroup. Any compromise will require resolution of difficult issues including the boundaries of a Tamil state (particularly in relation to the Mahaweli irrigation project), the status of the East coast deepwater port of Trincomalee, the question of Sinhalese settlers in Tamil areas and the appeasement of Buddhist chauvinism. The difficult long-term question is whether any formula which retains the integrity of the Sri Lankan state could actually accommodate the kinds of economic and political guarantees that nationalist leaders and the LTTE would seek. For the Sinhalese nationalists it would have to guarantee their continued domination of the economy and public sector; for the Tamils it would have to provide political guarantees that would minimise the powers of a federal government. The conditions of one side will be very difficult for the other to accept.

ARMED STRUGGLES

Sri Lanka's other armed stuggle was brutally resolved in the late 1980s when Premadasa's security forces and death squads liquidated the JVP, crushing one of the armed struggles that have, since the 1980s, been more numerous in Asia's élite democracies than in the other states of the region. Both India and the Philippines have experienced similar guerrilla struggles waged by left-wing groups around questions of ownership and distribution. The JVP drew its support from the Sinhalese in the South who had lost out in land reforms under the SLFP governments in the 1970s as well as in educational opportunities. Its ideology blended Maoism with Buddhism and anti-colonialism, proposing an autarkic society cleansed of the impurities of the modern world that sounded at times close to Khmer Rouge ideas.[57] This combination of real grievances with a programme that profoundly threatened the Western-oriented ruling class was enough to scare them into backing Premadasa.

A similar basis of support amongst the poor of West Bengal, Bihar and Andhra Pradesh has underpinned the Indian Naxalite movement. Its origins in the 1960s paralleled those of the Russian Narodnik movement in the late nineteenth century. Calcutta's middle class Maoist radicals took to the countryside to inspire peasants by terrorist acts against landlords and the state.[58] Its persistence into the 1990s, despite steady attrition at the hands of the police, is indicative of the enduring popularity of a movement based on rural class antagonisms. The same is true of the NPA in the Philippines. Its precursor, the *Hukbalahap* movement of the 1950s, fought to uphold the rights of peasants in their relations with landlords. Despite its eventual military defeat by President Magsaysay (with considerable American help[59]) the Huk movement gave peasants a measure of self-confidence and sowed seeds of resistance which the NPA was able to harvest 20 years later. As the Marcos dictatorship closed off other political channels and presided over a deteriorating economy, a crumbling government machine and growing human rights abuses, the NPA drew more recruits and expanded its area of operations. From the late 1970s and through the 1980s insurgency flourished all over the archipelago. From a peak of 25 000 guerrillas in 1988, however, the NPA declined to 13 500 by late 1992.[60] Splits in the leadership of the Communist Party of the Philippines (CPP) have been reflected in divisions over tactics and in the NPA's operations. The hardline leadership of the CPP, based in the Netherlands, has been at odds with the most active units in the field over whether to pursue an urban or rural strategy.[61] Talks with the government have amplified differences within the NPA and the insurgency has ebbed away. But its periodic resurgence and the widespread nature of the conflict in the 1980s point to a concrete social base for armed struggle.

THE POLITICS OF ECONOMIC REFORM

Armed struggle is the most extreme and therefore the least representative expression of dissent in the élite democracies; populism and regional conflicts have represented more widespread dissatisfaction prompted by economic failure. This failure has also been used by foreign capital – acting through the international lending agencies – to press for economic reforms, which themselves have political consequences. These reforms, as we saw in Chapter 2, allow foreign investors access to sectors of the economy from which they have previously been excluded and enable them to increase ownership of the domestic economic base, as well as utilising cheap labour in EPZs. They are also welcomed by a section of the domestic bourgeoisie which sees in them new profit opportunities. Thus privatisation assists not only the foreign investors queuing up to enter power generation in Pakistan or oil and gas in India or banking in the Philippines, but also the domestic capitalists who have acquired Philippines Airlines, banks in Pakistan, manufacturing enterprises in Sri Lanka or jute mills in Bangladesh. The accompanying deregulation of markets has assisted the growth of new companies in the Indian airlines sector, for instance, or in telecommunications in Sri Lanka or tourism in the Philippines. The liberalisation of financial services also presents opportunities to both domestic and foreign interests. The encouragement of portfolio investment in South Asia has seen a clutch of new brokerage firms formed in Pakistan while in Sri Lanka local conglomerates have tied up with Western firms to create stockbroking joint ventures. Indian companies have been quick to tap international capital markets to raise finance for expansion that is no longer subject to government licensing and 10 more foreign banks have been allowed to enter the Philippines after a 45 year wait.

These changes clearly do not benefit the ruling class in the élite democracies in its entirety and, in fact, can serve to divide it. A mixture of anti-reform elements appears among private capitalists, the traditional landowning class, the bureaucracy and the military. The domestic bourgeoisie is not the dominant ruling class fraction and its support for externally imposed economic reform is shaped by its hopes of strengthening its position through exploiting new opportunities and collaboration with foreign capital. The process of economic reform is only in its early stages in South Asia and the Philippines and the domestic bourgeoisie will reassess its position as that process unfolds. Indian companies are, for instance, being closely watched[62] to see if they are going to switch their financial support from the Congress Party to the BJP. This would indicate that they see greater advantage in a reversion to protection of the domestic market, regulation of the economy and acceptance of a subordinate position, dependent on the state. Some companies have been lobbying in areas where foreign investors are being admitted – such as power generation – and using the accusation of corruption to try to unseat ministers who have struck deals with foreign companies. Such industrialists welcome the opportunities of access to foreign capital and technology, but are much less sanguine about the potential erosion of their domestic market. Consequently, there have been compromise gestures by India's Congress government in an attempt to prevent too serious a rift in the ruling class. Preserving state industry keeps the bureaucrats on the side of reform and resisting IMF pressure to cut subsidies means that rich farmers and industrialists also stay on side.

In the Philippines ambivalence towards reform has already been revealed in resistance to aspects of it. The bourgeoisie's strength in the Philippines, has been reflected in Congressional obstruction and resistance to reforms – such as tax reforms and infrastructure projects[63] – and in the rejection of a renewal of the lease on the US bases. This was both symbolic and an explicit repudiation of foreign influence over the Philippine economy. Nevertheless, President Ramos has managed to push some measures through, such as the sale of oil distributor Petron to a Saudi Arabian oil company and the opening of virtually every sector to foreign investment. Resistance to reform in the Philippine Congress is, of course, also the work of landowners. Although they had to accept that US companies continued to control large parts of the economy after independence, they see their position as liable to be weakened if foreign capital becomes an alternative source of employment and economic power.

Landowners in Pakistan have opposed any extension of the taxation base to include their income or assets, bringing them into conflict with the imperatives of economic reform as set out by the caretaker Qureshi government, which called for a redistribution of the tax burden from business to agriculture. Benazir Bhutto, with her close ties to the landowning class has, not surprisingly, watered down the Qureshi proposals, reducing land tax to no more than token levels and doing nothing to push for the taxation of agricultural income in the Punjab. The Pakistani domestic bourgeoisie is, like its Indian counterpart, divided over economic reform. Those sections of it linked to foreign capital welcome the opportunities it generates but companies which have been the recipients of assistance from state banks (often in the form of unrepaid loans) are reluctant to see such relationships disturbed. The assimilation of individual capitalists, exemplified by former Prime Minister Nawaz Sharif, into a predominanly landed ruling class in the Punjab is further evidence of a divided reaction. The Pakistani military has also been resistant to privatisation of the state telecommunications company, insisting that this be accompanied by the construction of a separate, dedicated military communications network.

The army's support for the installation of the Qureshi government as a resolution to constitutional wrangling, and subsequently for the new government's programme as a reassurance to foreign investors, identify it more closely with the modernisation of the economy and the emerging bourgeoisie, at the expense of the bureaucracy and landowners. The military itself has substantial economic interests, notably through the Fauji Foundation, a charitable organisation for the welfare of servicemen and their families which is the largest capitalised undertaking in Pakistan. It controls enterprises in cement and fertiliser (two of Pakistan's biggest industries) as well as investing in power generation and other new activities. The Foundation's readiness to embrace opportunities for economic growth is another sign of the alignment of the military's economic interests with reform.

Military willingness to co-operate with civilian governments is, however, premised on the understanding that such governments will not attempt to interfere with Pakistan's nuclear weapons programme. For the bureaucracy, economic reform has already been identified as more of a threat than an opportunity. It has also opposed the diminution of its influence over the economy by obstructing privatisation of its huge fiefdom, the Water and Power Development Authority. Likewise, both government-appointed bankers and their clients have resisted the cleaning up of lending practices which were mutually beneficial.

In Bangladesh the bureaucracy has been accustomed to controlling the implementation of aid, which is now threatened by the demands of donors that this be linked to 'good governance' – that is, to projects which improve the functioning of the economy in the interests of capital. The bureaucracy fears the loss of power and privileges which it has built on control over the flow of aid and has sought an alliance with religious leaders who see their own hold over ignorant rural masses threatened by the same pressures from agencies for effective spending. In India, too, bureaucrats at lower levels do not share the enthusiasm for economic reform of those technocrats who have been trained by the IMF and the World Bank: hence the complaints of investors about their obstructive resistance.

Besides these disparate elements of resistance to economic reform within the ruling class a larger base for resistance is also being created by the effects of reform on industrial workers, peasants and the middle class, who stand to lose from the higher taxes, greater unemployment and lower subsidies described in Chapter 3. This enables disenchanted elements of the ruling class to play the nationalist card against reforms which they can easily depict as being enacted at the behest of the IMF and World Bank and therefore as an abdication of national economic sovereignty and an affront to national pride. The BJP is able to override the contradiction between its nationalism and its economic liberalism to capitalise on nationalist fears of foreign economic domination. Its '*Swadeshi*' platform, calling for greater self-sufficency, and its opposition to the GATT agreement as a betrayal of Indian interests enabled it to mobilise substantial support. On the GATT issue the BJP was able to organise some of its biggest rallies, indicating that it may have found an issue that can extend its appeal beyond Hindu chauvinism and rally nationalists, farmers and the middle classes against competition from Western goods and higher prices. The securities scandal centred on Harshad 'Bull' Mehta in 1992, in which foreign banks were implicated by a report issued by the Reserve Bank of India, gave further ammunition to economic nationalists looking to tarnish the reputation of Congress by its association both with corruption and foreign involvement in the economy. A 'case by case' approach to foreign investment has, its critics charge, become a 'suitcase by suitcase' approach, referring to the method by which a particular bribe was alleged to have been paid to the Prime Minister.

The People's Alliance, similarly, used accusations of corruption linked to the influx of foreign investment as one of its main campaigning planks in the 1994 elections. Philippines business found popular support for its opposition to the introduction of VAT that came shortly after widespread protests forced Ramos to rescind oil price increases ordered by the IMF. This kind of vocal opposition made it unclear whether Ramos would be able to continue to deliver the kinds of policies demanded by the IMF and to meet the ambitious targets set by the Fund.

Left of centre parties in India have also been able to ride on the economic nationalist bandwagon. George Fernandes, who, as Industries Minister in 1977, drove Coca-Cola out of India by demanding that it reveal its formula, split from the Janata Dal to lead his own faction in the Lok Sabha (the lower house of the Indian parliament). This is based on opposition not only to the return of Coca-Cola – this time, revealingly, in a deal with a domestic soft drinks company – but to wider foreign influence in the economy. Other left of centre parties are also enjoying a resurgence outside their traditional bases in West Bengal and Kerala. After the Uttar Pradesh state elections in 1993 the Samajwadi (socialist) Party formed the government with the Bahunjan Samaj Party, which has a strong following among the Harijans. Both the rise of the BJP's Hindu militancy, which marginalises the lower castes and Harijans, and economic reform at the expense of workers and peasants may accelerate the emergence of a parallel class/caste divide in Indian politics. The Janata Dal government of 1989–90, led by the former Congress Finance Minister V. P. Singh, sought to crystallise this divide by increasing the quota of central government jobs (including those in government enterprises) awarded to the 'socially and educationally backward' classes to 27 per cent.[64] Singh's government was then brought down, partly by the protests of middle class students fearful of being excluded from employment by this policy.

In Bangladesh opponents of reform can draw on popular dissatisfaction generated by the fact that new employment opportunities reach only a small absolute number of people. At present perhaps 1 million Bangladeshis are employed in sectors (chiefly garments) connected to the world economy. Even with reform policies designed to improve its integration into the world economy, the country's niche in that economy will never be big enough to allow more than a small proportion of the other 110 million to crowd in, while even those in the garment sector are at risk of seeing that niche disappear.

The wide social base for opposition to foreign-inspired reform policies and the opportunities for expressing it lead to offsetting populist gestures by governments implementing those policies. Hence Ramos backed down on imposing the oil price levy in 1994 while Sri Lankan governments have offered a series of compensating giveaways when they have pressed ahead with economic reform policies. Political distractions have also been used, such as Benazir Bhutto's exploitation of the Kashmir issue. In India, Rao and Finance Minister Manmohan Singh sought to mitigate the effects of reform to prevent too widespread an opposition forming. As Singh said in late 1993: 'Two things matter to ordinary people. One is food prices; the other trades unions'.[65] The Indian government has moved cautiously on privatisation and public sector redundancies for precisely this reason.

Given both the divisions in the ruling class and the possibility that popular discontent will be exploited, economic reform brings with it the risk of heightened political tensions that can run counter to foreign investors' desire for stability and docility in the workforce. Hitherto electoral manipulation has provided a relatively efficient way of preserving legitimacy without the interests of the ruling class being endangered. If divisions within the ruling class grow and elements of it begin to use the institutions of élite democracy to orchestrate mass support, then other fractions of that class may seek to close down those institutions. In other words, some of the élite democracies may be heading for another period of authoritarian rule as an alternative to open political conflict.

The manner in which the next government is installed in Bangladesh will be an important test in this regard. The Awami League's parliamentary boycott in 1994 and its demands for an independent election commission to oversee the elections due by 1996 could indicate that the party intends to launch an extra-parliamentary challenge to the BNP, particularly if it loses the elections. These are exactly the circumstances in which the military might well intervene to restore order. More serious in the long term for Bangladesh is the threat of the original Malthusian nightmare. With what used to be the safety valve of emigration closed off since 1947 the population is growing faster than its means of support. Cultivable land could shrink by as much as 13.7 per cent if the sea level rises 1 metre as a result of global warming.[66] The population will reach 140 million by 2000 at its current growth rate of 2.3 per cent a year and will not level off until it has exceeded well over 200 million. In a situation in which resources are hugely overwhelmed by human needs, Bangladesh is most likely to slide almost completely into the control of foreign aid agencies and governments. They would probably work through a local ruling class which would have no choice but to surrender the independence it has been trying to maintain in order to preserve stability. This would also promote the Bangladeshi military to a position of considerable importance within such a régime. This projection does, however, rest on the assumption that international agreement could be reached on shoring up the Bangladeshi state in spite of its location at the fulcrum of Indian–Chinese rivalry and its involvement with the competing financial interests of Japan and Western Europe.

The political dynamics of the rise of the BJP in India could yet precipitate a serious crisis and the emergence of an authoritarian régime. The trajectory of the party is far from certain. Its support has grown rapidly since the 1970s to make it the second largest party in the Lok Sabha, with 119 seats at the 1991 elections against Congress's 226. Yet it lost office in Uttar Pradesh and Himachal Pradesh in 1993 as its meaningless slogan 'Ram Raj' (literally the 'rule of Ram') translated into a disappointing experience for voters and as the Babri mosque issue evaporated. Hence the quest for wider issues to give it an added electoral appeal. Whatever new themes the BJP seeks to develop in its campaigning – stopping cow slaughter being a case in point – they are sure to heighten the sense of communal tension and push India towards greater Hindu–Muslim confrontation. The communal element is unavoidable even in the BJP's policies on the economy, where the contradiction between its nationalism and its liberalism is best glossed over by presenting policy in the mystical terms of national strength. The nation is equated with the Hindu nation and the more this is stressed, the more are the lower castes excluded. In short, a continued rise for the BJP is sure to be divisive.

However, it need not necessarily lead to an institutional crisis. This depends on the reaction of Congress, and of its financial backers. If Congress finds that both popular and ruling class backing is moving towards the BJP it can reverse its policies, jettison economic reform and, perhaps behind a leader from the Nehru–Gandhi dynasty, reassert its own historic claim to be the champion of nationalist economic policy. Foreign investors would clearly apply whatever international pressure they could to prevent too drastic a change in policy and the reimposition of controls on the economy, but such a turnaround could be accomplished without the institutions of the Indian state being called into question. Despite the efforts on the part of foreign investors to convince themselves that change is irreversible, this will not be the case until state industry has been systematically privatised and dismantled. More problematic would be a situation in which Congress leaders adhered to the programme dictated by the IMF while the domestic bourgeoisie, taking with it a substantial portion of the civil service, swung their support behind the BJP. With their backing the BJP would become a more potent challenge to Congress and could win an election, after which it would be expected to reward its backers by protecting key sectors of domestic industry. Alternatively, Congress could react to the erosion of its support by banning the BJP and its sister organisations and perhaps even suspending parliamentary institutions.

Factionalism in Pakistan is not so pronounced and has not induced ruling class fractions to seek mass support. None has yet been so badly affected by economic reforms as to raise the nationalist banner in opposition to them. Judging by the way in which Bhutto's government has sought to take the edge off reform, it seems unlikely that she would push it so far as to alienate either landowners or the bureaucracy or the army. Pakistan's future is therefore likely to be one of continued bickering among this triumvirate, accentuated by the personality politics of the Bhutto family itself and the rivalry between Bhutto and Nawaz Sharif, rather than a decisive split. If this bickering becomes economically counter-productive in the eyes of the army, which recognises the need for the economy to expand in order to sustain its military competition with India, is it possible that the military would intervene again. Alternatively, if regional conflicts – including the increasingly violent struggle with the MQM and between religious factions in Karachi – were to be seriously inflamed by political mismanagement, the army might act, on the assumption that it was more capable of restoring order and underwriting national stability.

In the Philippines, Ramos's sometimes tentative efforts to impose reform policies have not cut into ruling class interests to the point where any fraction is intent on mobilising mass support against the principle of reform (rather than on particular issues). They are content to obstruct where necessary, while continuing the factional wrangling over state economic patronage. Prospects of military intervention are, for the foreseeable future, slight.

A constitutional reform which replaced the presidential system with a parliamentary one might enable Ramos to win another term as President while taking a more ceremonial role, but there is little reason to believe that the ruling class would find it significantly more difficult to manipulate elections under a parliamentary system. Equally they could accommodate victory for a populist like Estrada or Defensor Santiago in the event that the presidential system remains unchanged. Challenges will probably persist from separatist movements, especially given the disparate regional patterns of growth, and from the rump of the NPA, but neither is likely to be on a scale to threaten the state seriously and draw the armed forces into greater political prominence.

In Sri Lanka, where the armed forces have been much enlarged since the civil war began in earnest, they are unlikely to stake a claim to political power unless there is a major split within the ruling class. Only if an SLFP government were to break with bipartisanship on the war, reject all economic reform measures and return to nationalisation could it alienate powerful interests sufficiently to provoke an authoritarian takeover. While the SLFP will engage in anti-corruption offensives against the UNP and make corresponding populist gestures, policy statements from the new government of Mrs Kumaratunga indicate that it is unlikely to repudiate economic reform or interfere with the lucrative co-operation between local conglomerates and foreign capital. Until his death in October 1994, signals from the UNP's Gamini Dissanayake also implied that bipartisanship should be possible, at least in the early stages, on a policy of ending the war.

Postscript

The first five months of 1995 appeared to confirm many of the trends described in this book. The economic growth performance of the Asian economies remained strong. Yet the effects of that growth on the region's social and political structures continued to be disruptive and unsettling. None of the underlying tensions resulting from growth eased, while some showed signs of forcing their way into the political system.

In China, it became increasingly apparent during 1994 that the economy was still out of control, as inflation exceeded 24 per cent and foreign debt topped US$100 million. The use of direct controls on prices and borrowing continued to yield only shortlived and partial results, leaving large numbers of people excluded from sharing in growing prosperity, or even becoming worse off. At the political level, the manoeuvring within the leadership intensified as Deng Xiaoping's death approached and its ramifications were apparent in the various corruption charges levelled at relatively senior members of the Communist Party. China also became more assertive in its claims over the Spratly Islands and the South China Sea, triggering fears among neighbouring states that its leaders would attempt to divert attention from their internal power struggle by seeking a confrontation with one of the rival claimants to the area. None of the four obvious candidates for leadership – Jiang Zemin, Li Peng, National People's Congress standing committee chairman Qiao Shi or Zhu Rongji – had established a clear advantage or been eliminated completely from the contest, although Jiang made the frontrunning in publicly widening his power base. Savage political infighting is likely to take place against a backdrop of deteriorating economic conditions. Just as during the Cultural Revolution and its aftermath, this kind of intenecine conflict is likely to lead to the neglect of the economy and the worsening of economic problems. The graver those economic problems become, the more difficult they will make the creation of a stable political leadership. Moreover, the longer the conflict goes on, the greater the risk that students, the military, the unemployed and the peasantry will be drawn into it, either through being mobilised by rival political factions or through the damaging effects that economic and political problems have on their own positions.

China provides the most graphic illustration of a market Stalinist economy moving towards crisis. North Korea may be as close to an upheaval as China is, though the workings of its political system remain as opaque as ever. Certainly, there were no clear signs that Kim Jong Il had consolidated his position as the country's leader, nor did North Korea show a consistent willingness to engage with the outside world. There seems little doubt that divided counsels prevail over the risks of opening the economy to foreign trade and investment and thereby breaking the hermetic seal on the country's political time capsule. The longer a decision on this is postponed, the more impoverished the people of North Korea will become and the more turbulent the eventual upheaval which the country is likely to undergo before it disappears as a political entity. In Burma, on the other hand, 'constructive engagement' with the ASEAN states indicated that foreign assistance may enable the SLORC regime to prolong its grip on the country, helped by its military success over the Karen. The continued detention of Aung San Suu Kyi made it clear that SLORC is easily able to weather what little domestic and foreign criticism and opposition there is and that any political change in the near future is likely to be of a purely cosmetic nature.

Meanwhile Vietnam and Laos continued to grapple with the unsettling social effects of capitalist economic growth: rising income inequalities, speculative investment, the downgrading of state industry, corruption and increasing foreign control of the economy. The ruling parties have meanwhile alternated between justifying, ameliorating, reprimanding, sanctioning, or controlling this process depending on the excesses which it spawns and the rumblings within their ranks. Neither is yet close to a political climacteric, although economic and social developments point to a growing tension between one party rule, new social forces and the economic marginalisation of increasing numbers of workers and peasants. In Cambodia, it was clear that the authorities are tightening their controls – over the press in particular – as a way of restricting the criticism of corruption and closing down the country's embryonic political life ahead of a constitutional struggle on Sihanouk's death. Despite some successes in the field against the Khmer Rouge, there is little prospect of political stability or a widespread improvement in living standards until some time after this struggle is resolved.

In the elite democracies, the unsettling effects of economic reform and, where this has resulted, faster growth have accentuated the political trends described in Chapter 7. Populism continues to flourish, most emphatically in India, where N.T. Rama Rao regained office in the Andhra Pradesh state elections partly by unrealistically promising to cut the price of rice nearly in half. Separatism in Kashmir has not abated. The growing popular disillusionment with the consequences of economic liberalisation not only feeds the growth of populist parties but also prompted Prime Minister Rao to urge his finance minister to 'repackage' the economic reforms. That was not enough to prevent a split in the Congress Party. Fearful of losing its electoral appeal and its financial backing yet also wary of alienating foreign investors, Congress is in danger of being stranded without a clear direction to its policy. If its commitment to economic change is seen to waver seriously, foreign investors will hesitate to invest and the economic strategy which relies on their involvement in a number of key sectors will come into question. Yet the political constraints to that change are becoming more and more apparent.

In Pakistan, MQM-inspired violence escalated in Karachi, while Benazir Bhutto's government remained locked in efforts to discredit the previous administration and absorbed by foreign affairs. If the instability apparent during the first five months of 1995 continues, it will damage the chances of attracting foreign investment and increase the possibility of a military intervention to restore order. Pakistan has probably not escaped from the cycle of mismanaged civilian rule alternating with authoritarian military rule. Bangladesh remained equally prone to disturbance, as the opposition continued its campaign of trying to force the BNP government out by mass agitation. A return to military intervention cannot be ruled out in a situation of prolonged instability and contested election results. In Sri Lanka, the election of the People's Alliance provided only a chimerical hope of resolving the conflict with the LTTE, which was soon resumed, dashing hopes of a substantial economic peace dividend. Combined with signs of restiveness in the armed forces, the resumption of conflict makes it unlikely that Sri Lanka can achieve a greater measure of political stability and generate sustained economic growth. In the Philippines, it was apparent that populism and armed protest persisted despite President Ramos' policies. Populists did well in congressional elections, while the armed conflict in Mindanao flared back into prominence. None of the elite democracies indicated that economic growth was providing a resolution of their problems.

In the veiled authoritarian states political pressures continued to be diverted into subcutaneous kind of conflict. Reports of Suharto's ill-health – apparently groundless – set off a fresh bout of speculation about his successor which, in trun, prompted another round of measures against the press. Together with the removal of rebellious members of the legislature for stirring up trouble, this kind of action will push more opposition into informal channels. Labour activism showed no signs of having been curbed and the regime itself appeared uncertain whether to deal with it solely by means of confrontation. Indications that Suharto might be considering a seventh term as president starting in 1998 will only add fuel to the factional manoeuvring between business, the army and the bureaucracy and, if he is successful in extending his hold on power, create a more intense struggle to succeed him early next century. If Suharto remains in power, his favoured close associates are likely to acquire a greater degree of economic leverage but, in doing so, further alienate foreign capital, the army and elements of the bureaucracy, thereby heightening their determination to displace the Suharto clique from office. The longer the succession issue is postponed, the more highly charged it becomes.

In Malaysia, the resounding election victory obtained by Mahathir Mohamad's *Barisan Nasional* in the 1995 polls indicates that formal checks to veiled authoritarianism are likely to remain as weak as before. With the formal political system tightly controlled and the trade union movement weak and fragmented, there are no obvious and immediate checks to the power of capital. Only if increasing labour shortages coupled with infrastructure and technology constraints and a slackening of foreign investment begin to rein in the rate of growth and the rise in incomes – perhaps as per capita income approaches the M$7000 mark – is economic disenchantment likely to mesh with the niggling dissatisfaction at petty restrictions on behaviour. A serious economic downturn could bring to the surface a number of latent conflicts and tensions – those of a racial, regional or religious character as well as those bound up with the growing presence of migrant workers in Malaysia. For the government of Singapore, the collapse of Barings merchant bank at the start of 1995 was not only embarassing but also raised questions as to its ability to regulate the financial system on which its prosperity has come increasingly to depend. The execution of the Filipina maid, Flor Contemplacion, after her conviction for murder raised international concerns about the Singaporean judicial system and caused widespread anger in the Philippines, one of the countries which was expected to play a part in Singapore's economic strategy of 'regionalisation'. These kinds of setbacks have little domestic political resonance, but they do point to difficulties inherent in the country's future economic expansion which, ultimately, may help to bring the existing political system into question.

In the emerging bourgeois democracies, bourgeois parties struggled to make headway in establishing a firm hold over the state. In Hong Kong, concern grew at the likelihood of the Chinese Communist Party ignoring any agreements made with the British and endeavouring to prevent any further concrete changes being implemented before 1 July 1997. China's plans to exclude Hong Kong's Court of Final Appeal from examining 'affairs of state' and to allow review of its decisions gave another indication that the CCP's representatives and supporters in the territory are likely to behave however they see fit once the handover has occurred. There will be little point in bourgeois parties looking to the rule of law for protection of their interests. Taiwan's relations with China meanwhile hinted at closer official economic ties, though the ambivalence of the island's people on the question of mainland relations was demonstrated in the local and provincial elections in December 1994, which saw the KMT retain control of the provincial assembly while losing the mayoralty of Taipei to the DPP. The crucial test of relations with China is yet to come. Like Taiwanese–Chinese relations, those between North and South Korea remained unresolved and potentially profoundly disturbing. At the same time, *chaebol* leaders have continued with their efforts to secure greater independence from the state while Kim Young Sam sought ways to integrate them into the ruling party. The emergence of clearly bourgeois, business-oriented political parties remained in the balance. So, too, in Thailand, where the rise of Thaksin Shinawatra to lead the Palang Dharma Party indicated that it was becoming a more open vehicle for modernising business interests, paralleled by the launch of the Nam Thai party, led by a former banker and deputy prime minister.

While doubts over the long-term prospects for the continued growth of Asia's prosperity remain in the background, it is clear that, in these ways, simmering conflicts, political upheavals and growing social disorder could all lead to an abrupt loss of confidence and associated withdrawal and flight of capital. Whether the 'miracle' of economic growth fractures as a result of these kinds of short-term events or as a result of long-term trends, the inequalities created over the last generation will become more acute and the region's political systems – none of them well adapted to demands for change – will begin to break down. As they do, there can be no simple return to authoritarianism, no easy invocation of traditional values and loyalties and of the 'Asian way' to dampen down conflict. For the process of industrialisation, urbanisation and economic growth has created new social forces that will eventually fashion new political systems in the region.

Notes and References

Introduction

1. J. Gray, 'Rejecting Eastern promise', *Guardian* (4 April 1994).
2. The Asian Development Bank refers to these four economies as the Newly Industrialising Economies, while the World Bank characterises them as 'Tiger' economies and applies the term Newly Industrialising Economies to Indonesia, Malaysia and Thailand.
3. World Bank, *The East Asian Miracle: Economic Growth and Public Policy* (New York: Oxford University Press, 1993) p. 1.
4. Ibid., p. 361.
5. W. H. Overholt, *China: The Next Economic Superpower* (London: Weidenfeld & Nicolson, 1993) p. 59.
6. *Asiaweek* (12 January 1994).
7. W. H. Overholt (ed.), *The Future of Brazil* (Boulder: Westview Press, 1978) p. 45.
8. In C. Dixon and D. Drakakis-Smith (eds), *Economic and Social Development in Pacific Asia* (London: Routledge, 1993).
9. S. P. Huntington, *Political Order in Changing Societies* (New Haven and London: Yale University Press, 1968) p. 41.
10. Shaw Yu-Ming, *Beyond the Economic Miracle* (Taipei: Kwang Hwa Publishing Company, 1989) p. 32.
11. Lee was speaking at the Philippine Business Conference, November 1992. Quoted in 'Discipline vs democracy' (*Far Eastern Economic Review*, 10 December 1992) p. 29.
12. M. Weber, *The Religion of China*, quoted in C. Johnson 'South Korean Democratisation: The Role of Economic Development' in J. Cotton (ed.), *Korea under Roh Tae-woo: Democratisation, Northern Policy and Inter-Korean Relations* (St Leonards: Allen & Unwin, 1993) p. 92.
13. Lu Ya-li, 'Political Developments in the Republic of China' in T. W. Robinson (ed.), *Democracy and Development in East Asia: Taiwan, South Korea and the Philippines* (Washington: AEI Press, 1991) p. 40.

1 Factors in Economic Growth

1. N. Balakrishnan, 'Driving Force', *FEER* (11 March 1993) p. 58.
2. The term was coined by Professor Raj Krishna. See R. E. B. Lucas and G. F. Papanek (eds), *The Indian Economy: Recent Developments and Future Prospects* (New Delhi: Oxford University Press, 1989) Chapter 16.
3. J. Baum, 'Taking the Plunge', *FEER* (22 April 1993) p. 75.
4. *Asian Development Outlook 1994* (Hong Kong: Oxford University Press for the Asian Development Bank, 1994) p. 236.
5. *Asiaweek* (2 February 1994).
6. 'Cambodia: An Economic Report', Asian Development Bank 1991 (unpublished) p. vi.
7. B. Lintner, 'Unfunny money', *FEER* (14 January 1993) p. 51.
8. Preyaluk Donavanik, 'Myanmar: How Bodes Its Future?', *Bangkok Bank Monthly Review*, vol. 34 (June 1993) p. 14.

9. A. Foster-Carter, 'Why North Korea Will Collapse' in *Korean Unification and Its Prospects: A Colloquium of Foreign Journalists*, November 3–4, 1993, The Seoul Foreign Correspondents' Club p. 7.

10. B. K. Martin, 'Intruding on the Hermit: Glimpses of North Korea' (Hawaii, East West Center, Special Reports Number 1, July 1993) p. 16.

11. W. E. Brummit and F. Flatters, *Exports, Structural Change and Thailand's Rapid Growth* (Bangkok: Thailand Development Research Institute, 1992) p. 20.

12. W. Bello and S. Rosenfeld, *Dragons in Distress: Asia's Miracle Economies in Crisis* (San Francisco: The Institute for Food and Development Policy, 1990) p. 81.

13. M. Hart-Landsberg, *The Rush to Development: Economic Change and Political Struggle in South Korea* (New York: Monthly Review Press, 1993) p. 172.

14. Bello and Rosenfeld, p. 186.

15. Gordon White, *Riding the Tiger: The Politics of Economic Reform in Post-Mao China* (London, Macmillan 1993) p. 83.

16. M. Hiebert, 'Fragile Success', *FEER* (28 January 1993) p. 43.

17. *Asian Development Outlook 1993* (Hong Kong: Oxford University Press for the Asian Development Bank, 1993) p. 105.

18. You Ji and Wang Yuesheng, 'China's Agricultural Development and reform in 1990', in Kuan Hsin-chi and Maurice Brosseau (eds), *China Review* (Hong Kong: Chinese University Press, 1991).

19. Mya Than and Nobuyoshi Nishizawa, 'Agricultural Policy reforms and Agricultural Development in Myanmar' and Tin Soe and B. S. Fisher, 'An Economic Analysis of Burmese Rice-Price Policies', in Mya Than and J. L. H. Tan (eds), *Myanmar Dilemmas and Options* (Singapore: Institute of South East Asian Studies, 1990) pp. 89–115 and 145–162.

20. S. Sidhva, 'Most promising export sector', *Financial Times*, 30 March 1994, p. XII.

21. K. Cooke, 'Malaise in the plantations', *Financial Times*, 31 August 1993, p. VII.

22. *Jakarta Post* (18 August 1993).

23. White, p. 109.

24. J. K. Fairbank, *The Great Chinese Revolution 1800-1985* (London: Pan Books, 1988) p. 357.

25. White, p. 109.

26. Shrimps now account for around 10 per cent of Bangladeshi exports. See R. W. Bradnock, 'The South Asian Periphery' in G. P. Chapman and K. M. Baker (eds), *The Changing Geography of Asia* (London: Routledge, 1992) p. 58.

27. R. Broad with J. Cavanagh, *Plundering Paradise: The Struggle for the Environment in the Philippines* (Philippines: Anvil Publishing, no date) p. 78. The death of the Emperor Hirohito suddenly reduced Japanese demand for luxury seafood imports.

28. *The News* (Pakistan) (19 February 1994).

29. M. R. J. Vatikiotis, *Indonesian Politics Under Suharto* (London: Routledge, 1993) p. 35.

30. *The East Asian Miracle*, p. 137.

31. Interview, Nasaruddin Arshad, Malaysian Institute for Economic Research, January 1994.

32. *Financial Times* (30 March 1994).

33. G. C. Gunn, 'Rentier capitalism in Negara Brunei Darussalam' in K. Hewison, R. Robison and G. Rodan (eds), *Southeast Asia in the 1990s* (St Leonards: Allen & Unwin, 1993) p. 114.

34. J. Bartholomew, *The Richest Man in the World* (London: Penguin Books, 1990).
35. M. Hiebert, 'Second Time Lucky?', *FEER* (7 May 1992) p. 64.
36. *International Herald Tribune* (5 March 1993).
37. Martin, p. 4.
38. M. Hiebert, 'Only the brave', *FEER* (9 July 1992) p. 68.
39. C. Goldstein, 'Final Frontier', *FEER* (10 June 1993) p. 54.
40. J. Lowenstein, 'Shell and Chandra Asri resume the olefin race', *Asia Money & Finance* (July/August 1992) p. 45.
41. J. Rigg and P. Stott, 'The Rise of the Naga: the changing geography of South-East Asia 1965-90' in Chapman and Baker (eds) p. 97
42. Broad with Cavanagh, p. 31.
43. 1991 World Bank survey, quoted in *Financial Times* (30 May 1994).
44. M. Craig, *Tears of Blood: A Cry for Tibet* (New Delhi: Indus, 1992) p. 216.
45. R. Tiglao, 'A Long Way to Go', *FEER* (12 May 1994) p. 28.
46. 'Nobody Elects the Press', *FEER* (7 April 1994) p. 20.
47. *The East Asian Miracle*, p. 306.
48. A. R. Khan and M. Hossain, *The Strategy of Development in Bangladesh* (London: Macmillan, 1989) p. 104 for 1985/6 figure; *Financial Times* (9 May 1994) for 1992/93 figure.
49. *FEER* (4 June 1992).
50. Interviews, Rangoon, July 1993.
51. M. Clifford, 'A Rough Fit', *FEER* (26 March 1992) p. 57.
52. L. Bowman, 'Many plus points and one minus', *Asiamoney* ('Sri Lanka' a supplement to Asiamoney, September 1993) p. 3.
53. *FEER* (29 July 1993) p. 14.
54. Hart-Landsberg, p. 181.
55. Ibid.
56. Ibid., p. 184.
57. E. Cheng and S. Mosher, 'Free for all', *FEER* (14 May 1992) p. 26.
58. *The Nation* (Bangkok) (30 January 1994).
59. *FEER* (24 March 1994) p. 59.
60. *Aliran Monthly* (Penang) 1993: 13(4) p. 39.
61. The figures for India are taken from *Asiaweek* (1 September 1993) as is the lower of the estimates relating to the Philippines, which cites a government source on the number of 10–14 year olds in employment. The higher estimate for the Philippines is from R. Pineda-Ofreneo, *The Philippines: Debt and Poverty* (Oxford: Oxfam, 1991) p. 29.
62. Teck-Wong Soon and C. Suan Tan, *The Lessons of East Asia – Singapore: Public Policy and Economic Development* (Washington: The World Bank, 1993) p. 13.
63. *Financial Times* (25 November 1993); *Asian Age* (28 July 1994).
64. S. Mosher, 'Common cause', *FEER* (13 February 1992) p. 21.
65. B. Rhodes, 'Service Without a Smile', *FEER* (4 November 1993) p. 54.
66. A. Higgins, 'In Siberia's Last Gulag', *Independent on Sunday* (London) (26 June 1994).
67. *The Nation* (3 February 1994).
68. Bradnock in Chapman and Baker (eds), p. 54.
69. Bello and Rosenfeld, p. 216.
70. *Aliran Monthly*, 1993: 13 (4) p. 39.
71. Khan and Hossain, p. 169.
72. *Asiaweek* (16 February 1994). His definition was of workers employed for less than 35 hours a week.

73. M. Hiebert, 'Fragile Success', *FEER* (28 January 1993) p. 43. Rural unemployment is estimated at 28 per cent.

74. *Financial Times* (30 September 1993).

75. K. Yoshihara, *The Rise of Ersatz Capitalism in South East Asia* (Oxford University Press, 1988) p. 111.

76. P. Abrahams, 'The dye is cast by growth and costs' *Financial Times* (31 May 1994).

77. *The East Asian Miracle*, p. 135.

78. M. J. Cohen, *The Unknown Taiwan* (Taipei: The Coalition for Democracy and the North American Taiwanese Women's Association, 1992) p. 53.

79. *FEER* (2 September 1993) p. 67.

80. Teck-Wong Soon and C. Suan Tan, p. 2.

81. Interview, Straits Exchange Foundation, Taipei, October 1993. The acknowledged figure is US$3.4 billion, though officials admit privately it is much higher.

82. *Asian Development Outlook 1994*, p. 124.

83. In 1992, 7 per cent of investment in China was foreign and 23.6 per cent linked to it in the form of joint ventures or other co-operative undertakings. See Crosby Research, *Quarterly Economic Review*, Issue no. 1/93.

84. The exact size is the subject of some uncertainty, compounded by the familiar distinction between approved and actual investments. The *Financial Times* (30 March 1994) gives a figure of US$3 billion for Indian approvals in 1993/94, though *FEER* attributes this same figure to the period since 1991 (17 March 1994).

85. P. Cacino, 'New Technology and Labour Relations', *Bangkok Bank Monthly Bulletin* (vol. 34 September 1993) p. 13.

86. *Sri Lanka: Reform and Development 1992/93* (Colombo: Institute of Policy Studies, 1993) p. 12.

87. *Financial Times* (6 April 1994).

88. Ibid. (30 March 1994).

89. P. R. Krugman, J. Alm, S. M. Collins and E. M. Remolona, *Transforming the Philippine Economy* (Manila: National Economic and Development Authority, United Nations Development Programme, 1992), p. 126.

90. *Asian Development Outlook 1994*, p. 248; *Asian Development Outlook 1993*, p. 274.

91. T. Zahid, 'Is the Dollar Coming?', *Diplomat* (Peshawar) February 1994, p. 115.

92. *The Asian Age* (23 June 1994).

93. *Sri Lanka: Reform and Development 1992/93*, p. 2.

94. P. N. Dhar, 'The Indian Economy: Past Performance and Current Issues', in Lucas and Papanek (eds), p. 12.

95. L. Brahm, 'The emergence of China's securities markets', *Asia Money & Finance*, (February 1992) p. 39.

96. Bello and Rosenfeld, p. 4.

97. *Korea Times* (31 October 1993).

98. *The East Asian Miracle*, p. 205.

99. R. Fell, *Crisis and Change: The Maturing of Hong Kong's Financial Markets* (Hong Kong: Longman, 1992) pp. 87–119.

100. Some of the largest business groups in the Philippines – such as Ayala Land – are in the real estate sector and property development in Manila has been one of the most active sectors in the Philippine economy.

101. *Financial Times* (30 March 1994).

102. *Asian Development Outlook 1993*, p. 86.

103. Interview, Malaysian Institute of Economic Research, January 1994. See *Financial Times* (28 February 1994).
104. 'Indonesia', *Financial Times* Survey June 24 1994 p. 11; predictions of investment recovery by Investment Minister Sanyoto Sastrowardyo in *Hong Kong Standard* (15 August 1994).
105. Interviews, Bangkok, February 1994.
106. *Korea Times* (2 November 1993).
107. *Financial Times* (3 June 1994).
108. *Asian Development Outlook 1993*, p. 12.
109. *Financial Express* (Dhaka) (16 November 1993).
110. *Indonesian Observer* (28 August 1993).
111. Broad with Cavanagh, p. 97.
112. Hart-Landsberg, p. 191.
113. P. Bowring, 'Crumbs for the poor', *FEER* (5 March 1993) p. 16.
114. Bello and Rosenfeld, pp. 273–6.
115. Cohen, p. 53.
116. 'A Strategy of Alliances', *FEER* (14 October 1993) p. 44.
117. The figure for Guangdong is from Overholt (1993), p. 124; that for China as a whole from Leung Chuen Chau, *The Lessons of East Asia Hong Kong: A Unique Case of Development* (Washington: World Bank, 1993) p. 21.
118. Estimates made by stockbrokers in Hong Kong vary. S. G. Warburg's report on 'The Economic Miracle of Guangdong Province' (January 1993) gives a figure of over US$18 billion (p. 23). Credit Lyonnais, quoted in the *Financial Times* (2 September 1993), suggests US$11 billion; Peregrine Securities (*Financial Times* 18–19 December 1993) suggests US$7.9 billion.
119. *Financial Times* (27 April 1994).
120. *Financial Times* (12 April 1994).
121. *Korea Times* (2 November 1993).
122. *Financial Times* (8 April 1994).
123. Hart-Landsberg, pp. 253–4.
124. E. Paisley 'Time to Focus' *FEER* (8 April 1993) p. 60.
125. *Straits Times* (17 January 1994).
126. Bello and Rosenfeld, pp. 297–300.
127. G. Fairclough, 'The Knowledge Factor', *FEER* (11 March 1993).
128. *Asian Development Outlook 1994*, p. 119.
129. Crosby Research, 'Malaysian Economic Overview: The Management of Success', October 1992, p. 22.
130. *New Straits Times* (10 January 1994).
131. F. Bartu, *The Ugly Japanese: Nippon's Economic Empire in Asia* (Singapore: Longman, 1992) pp. 68–83.
132. 'Engineering the future', *The Economist* (17 April 1993).
133. *Sunday Star* (Malaysia) 16 January 1994.
134. Chalongphob Sussangkarn and Yongyuth Chalamwong, 'Thailand's Economic Dynamism: Human Resource Contributions and Constraints' (Thailand Development Research Institute, November 1989).
135. Interview, Dr. Hafeez Pasha, Pakistan Institute of Applied Economics, Karachi, February 1994.
136. 'National Economic Outlook' (Malaysian Institute of Economic Research, 1993) p. 10.
137. *Financial Times* (27–28 November 1993).
138. A. Schwarz, 'Looking Back at Rio', citing a World Bank study, *FEER* (28 October 1993) p. 48.

139. C. Goldstein, 'China's generation gap', *FEER* (11 June 1992) p. 45.
140. Krugman, Alm, Collins and Remolona, p. 65.
141. *Muslim Times* (13 February 1994).
142. Hossain and Khan, p. 142.
143. *Social Indicators of Development 1993* (Baltimore and London: The Johns Hopkins University Press for the World Bank, 1993) pp. 27, 153, 187, 255.
144. *Asiaweek* (20 January 1994).

2 Economic Policy

1. Leung Chuen Chau, p. 9.
2. The funding of the East Asian miracle study by the Japanese Ministry of Finance makes this deviation from normal World Bank thinking easier to understand.
3. Lucas and Papanek (eds), p. 6.
4. Fairbank, p. 285.
5. Byung-Nak Song, *The Rise of the Korean Economy* (Hong Kong: Oxford University Press, 1990) pp. 129–135.
6. S. Long, *Taiwan: China's Last Frontier* (London: Macmillan, 1991) p. 89.
7. U. Tun Wai, 'The Myanmar Economy at the Crossroads' in Mya Than and Tan (eds) (1990) p. 23.
8. Mya Than and J. L. H. Tan, 'Introduction', ibid., p. 3.
9. W. Luetkenhorst, 'Industrial Development and Industrial Policy in Myanmar', ibid., p. 178.
10. Interviews, Islamabad, February 1994.
11. H. Luethy, *Indonesia in Travail* (New Delhi: Congress for Cultural Freedom, 1966) p. 65.
12. J. Reinhardt, 'Industrial Restructuring and Industrial Policy in Vietnam' in Mya Than and Joseph L. H. Tan, *Vietnam's Dilemmas and Options* (Singapore: Institute of South East Asian Studies, 1993) pp. 71–95.
13. H. E. Salisbury, *The New Emperors: China in the Era of Mao and Deng* (New York: Avon Books, 1993) pp. 166, 249.
14. R. Manchanda, 'A turn in the south', *FEER* (30 April 1992) p. 13.
15. For an early description of the plan, see *Asiamoney*, July/August 1991. Projects have been scaled back since then: see *Financial Times* (26 June 1994).
16. E. Paisley, 'Kim the broker', *FEER* (4 Feburary 1993) p. 36.
17. Interviews, Taipei, October 1993. See J. Baum, 'Just Too Mucha', *FEER* (21 October 1993).
18. *Financial Times*, 27 July 1993 and 27–28 November 1993 for details of the plans.
19. R. Tiglao, 'Bent over backwards', *FEER* (28 January 1993) p. 47.
20. *FEER* (7 April 1994) p. 12.
21. M. Hiebert and S. Awanohara, 'The Next Great Leap', *FEER* (22 April 1993) p. 69.
22. *Pakistan Times* (13 February 1994).
23. Speech to Asia-Pacific Conference of International Association of Financial Executives 15 October 1993.
24. *Asian Age* (25 June 1994).
25. *Financial Times* (19 May 1994).
26. Teck-Wong Soon and C. Suan Tan, p. 10.
27. D. Tsuruoka, 'Keep 'em coming', *FEER* (11 November 1993) p. 67.
28. *Financial Times*, Indonesia survey, 24 June 1994, p. 11.
29. *Vietnam: The blazing flame of reforms* (Hanoi: Statistical Publishing House, 1993) pp. 145–147.

30. 'Back to basics' in 'Vietnam', supplement to *Asiamoney*, July/August 1993.
31. *FEER* (12 May 1994) p. 73.
32. N. Thayer and N. Chanda, 'Things Fall Apart . . .', *FEER* (19 May 1994) p. 18.
33. *Financial Times* (15 March 1993).
34. *Business Standard* (India) (20 November 1993); H. McDonald 'Capitalist Dialectic', *FEER* (14 April 1994) p. 34.
35. 'A Guide to Investment Opportunities in Pakistan' (Pakistan Investment Board, December 1993) p. 20.
36. K. M. Singh, 'Now come the carrots', *FEER* (17 December 1992) p. 65.
37. Martin, p. 18.
38. *Financial Times* (14 December 1993).
39. Mya Than, 'The Union of Burma Foreign Investment Law: Prospects for Mobilizing Foreign Capital for Development?' in Mya Than and J. L. H. Tan (eds) (1990), pp. 186–209.
40. Long, p. 81.
41. Bello and Rosenfeld, p. 232. Cohen, p. 51, suggests state-owned enterprises account for just 10 per cent of output.
42. *Asian Wall Street Journal* (2 December 1992).
43. Bello and Rosenfeld, p. 232, report that small and medium-sized enterprises received less than 25 per cent of credit in the early 1980s. By the mid-1990s, the proportion had risen to around 30 per cent, according to the DPP's Maysing Yang (interview October 1993).
44. Teck-Wong Soon and C. Suan Tan, p. 8.
45. Ibid., pp. 22–23.
46. PT Morgan Grenfell Asia, 'The Indonesian Banking System: Overview and Outlook' (December 1992).
47. The term was used in the PPP's election manifesto without having been defined. After the election it was left to ministers and civil servants to work out what they believed needed to be nationalised, setting criteria of a capital base greater than rupees 1.5 million. In the process some assets belonging to those close to the PPP escaped nationalisation.
48. HG Asia, 'India Review', June 1993.
49. *Financial Times* (30 September 1993).
50. S. Islam, 'Vote of Confidence', *FEER* (13 May 1993) p. 74.
51. *Asiaweek* (9 February 1994). 1000 enterprises were reported to have been privatised in the 1980s (*Asian Development Outlook 1994*, p. 52).
52. Shipyards have been sold to Singaporean investors, while ARAMCO of Saudi Arabia purchased Petron, the profitable oil sales arm of the state-owned Philippine National Oil Co. The businesses for sale at Subic Bay are also among the more attractive of the Philippines' publicly-owned assets. Philippine Airlines was acquired initially by a consortium headed by Antonio Cojuangco (who controls the near monopoly Philippine Long Distance Telephone) and then by cigarette magnate Lucio Tan.
53. *Asiamoney* (July/August 1992).
54. D. Tsuruoka, 'Switch to industry', *FEER* (16 April 1992) p. 45.
55. Examples include the privatisation of the North–South Highway to United Engineers Malaysia, a company controlled by UMNO. The Sports Toto gambling operation went to Vincent Tan's B&B Enterprises. Tan later received an M$6 billion sewerage contract for his Berjaya Group. The Big Sweep lottery operation went to a group owned by Ananda Krishnan. Ting Pek Khiing of Ekran is handling the Rejang River project.

56. H. Sender, 'The Squeeze Is On', *FEER* (10 June 1993) p. 64.
57. State sector debts were accelerating at the start of 1994, as nearly half the state enterprises went into debt and 'triangular' (inter-enterprise) debts reached US$34 billion. *Financial Times* (26 April 1994).
58. A. McCarty, 'Industrial Renovation in Vietnam, 1986–91', in Mya Than and J. L. H. Tan (eds) (1993), p. 107.
59. M. Hiebert, 'Gains at Risk', *FEER* (23 September 1993) p. 92. Hiebert says the state sector receives 85 per cent of loans.
60. Luetkenhorst in Mya Than and J. L. H. Tan (eds) (1990), p. 175.
61. T. Shale, 'Zhu Rongji's big gamble', *Euromoney* (August 1993) p. 32.
62. *Asian Development Outlook 1994*, p. 82. Other estimates put inflation much higher, e.g. *FEER* (13 January 1994) at 19.5 per cent. The ADB concedes that urban inflation is higher than the average figure, at around 19 per cent (p. 83).
63. *New Straits Times* (14 January 1994).
64. *Financial Times* (31 March 1994).
65. Ibid. (20 September 1993).
66. A Consumer Council report quoted in ibid. (8 March 1994).
67. Interview, Fr. Trisolini, Seoul, November 1993.
68. E.g. Byung-Nak Song, *The Rise of the Korean Economy*, Chapter 6.
69. Hart-Landsberg, pp. 169–70, 235–6; M. Clifford, 'The price of pique', *FEER* (30 January 1992) p. 34.
70. Long, pp. 80–81; Bello and Rosenfeld, pp. 236–7.
71. Vatikiotis, p. 178.
72. *FEER* (16 September 1993), p. 14.
73. E. Paisley, 'Fading Boom', *FEER* (6 May 1993) p. 58.
74. Confidential interview, Taipei, October 1993.
75. R. Tiglao, 'Manila's black hole', *FEER* (23 July 1992) p. 44.
76. Pineda-Ofreneo, p. 91.
77. G. Field, 'Banks refocus on making profits', *Euromoney* (September 1993) p. 253.
78. Interview, Bank Indonesia, August 1993.
79. *Financial Times* (1 May 1994).
80. Vatikiotis, pp. 152–3.
81. *Asiaweek* (2 February 1994).
82. *Independent on Sunday* (24 October 1993).
83. *Financial Times* (5 April 1994); *Aliran Monthly* 1993: 13(4) pp. 2–6.
84. S. Schlossstein, *Asia's New Little Dragons: The Dynamic Emergence of Indonesia, Thailand, and Malaysia* (Chicago: Contemporary Books, 1991) p. 264.
85. C. Lamb, *Waiting for Allah: Pakistan's Struggle for Democracy* (London: Penguin Books, 1992) pp. 175–7.
86. Confidential interviews Bangkok February 1994, citing government sources. See also P. Limqueco, B. McFarlane and J. Odhnoff, *Labour and Industry in ASEAN* (Manila: Journal of Contemporary Asia Publishers, 1989) pp. 44–8 for details of conditions in selected factories.
87. *FEER* (30 April 1992) p. 67.
88. M. Clifford, 'Shades of Capt. Bligh', *FEER* (10 September 1992) p. 55.
89. M. Tully, *No Full Stops in India* (New Delhi: Penguin Books, 1992) p. 263.
90. G. Ogle, *South Korea: Dissent within the Economic Miracle* (London and New Jersey: Zed Books, 1990) p. 76.
91. E. Paisley, 'May Day!', *FEER* (3 February 1994) p. 54.
92. Interview, Pakistan Investment Board, Islamabad, February 1994.
93. W. Wo-lap Lam, 'Governing an Intransigent Society' in Kuan Hsin-chi and Maurice

Brosseau (eds), *China Review 1992* (Hong Kong: The Chinese University Press, 1992) 2.15–2.18; L. Kaye, 'Mayday May Day', *FEER* (7 May 1992) p. 22.

94. L. Kaye, 'Much Talk, Little Action', *FEER* (24 March 1994) 20; A. Bhattacharya and M. Pangestu, *The Lessons of East Asia – Indonesia: Development, Transformation and Public Policy* (Washington: World Bank, 1993) p. 41.

95. Leung Chuen Chau, p. ix.

96. Teck-Wong Soon and C. Suan Tan, p. 17.

97. As of 1981, the private organised sector accounted for 3.3 per cent of employment, the public sector for 7 per cent. 66.5 per cent of the workforce were in agriculture; 15.1 per cent self-employed; and 8.1 per cent in the 'unorganised' sector. *India Review*, p. 5.

98. H. McDonald, 'Boys of bondage', *FEER* (9 July 1992) p. 18.

99. S. Christensen, D. Dollar, A. Siamwalla, P. Vichyanond, *The Lessons of East Asia – Thailand: The Institutional and Political Underpinnings of Growth* (Washington: The World Bank, 1993) p. 11.

100. *Economist* (16 July 1994).

101. 'A symposium on the devaluation of the peso', held at Ateneo de Manila University, October 1993. Indonesia's devaluations are discussed in Bhattacharya and Pangestu, p. 15.

102. Hart-Landsberg, pp. 243–4.

103. Interview, Dr. Ashfaque Khan, Pakistan Institute of Development Economics, February 1994.

104. Edgardo Zialcita of Bangko Sentral at devaluation symposium.

105. *Financial Times* (29 July 1994).

106. P. Dicken, 'The Growth Economics of Pacific Asia in their Changing Global Context' in C. Dixon and D. Drakakis-Smith (eds), p. 37.

3 Dividing the Spoils

1. 40.7 per cent figure given in interview with NEDA, October 1993; 50 per cent is quoted in 'Philippines 2000: An Attainable Vision' (press release accompanying President Ramos' visit to China 25–30 April 1993), also in United Nations Economic and Social Commission for Asia and the Pacific (UNESCAP), note by the secretariat on 'The poverty Situation in Asia and the Pacific' (September 1993) p. 8; 59 per cent is in *Banking With The Poor* (Brisbane: The Foundation for Development Cooperation, 1992) p. 170; 70 per cent is given in Pineda-Ofreneo, p. 13 and R. Tiglao, 'The daunting hurdles', *FEER* (18 June 1992) 20; 21 per cent is the World Bank figure, quoted in the UNESCAP note, p. 10.

2. D. G. Timberman, *A Changeless Land: Continuity and Change in Philippine Politics* (Manila: Bookmark Inc., 1991) p. 159.

3. UNESCAP note, p. 3.

4. Interviews, World Bank and IMF representatives, Dhaka, November 1993, citing International Food Policy Research Institute report.

5. UNESCAP note, p. 10.

6. M. Cohen, 'Sharing the Wealth', *FEER* (28 April 1994) p. 58.

7. *Social Indicators of Development 1993*, pp. 152 (India), 26 (Bangladesh), 254 (Pakistan); UNESCAP note, p. 8 (Nepal and Sri Lanka).

8. UNESCAP note, p. 10. The share of income going to the top 20 per cent rose from 49 per cent in the mid-1970s to 56 per cent in the mid-1980s: see Christensen, Dollar, Siamwalla and Vichyanond, p. 6.

9. *The East Asian Miracle*, p. 29.

10. Bello and Rosenfeld, p. 227.
11. *FEER* (4 November 1993) p. 79.
12. *Guardian* (11–12 April 1992).
13. Vatikiotis, p. 178.
14. The black economy is widespread, in both the developed and less developed economies of the region. Estimates are that it is equal to 25–33 per cent of the formal economy in South Korea, 40 per cent in Taiwan, 20–40 per cent in India, and between 50 and 200 per cent in Pakistan.
15. UNESCAP note 'National Policy Approaches to Poverty Alleviation in Asia and the Pacific'. It singles out West Bengal as an exception. See also M. Tully's account of West Bengal land reforms in *No Full Stops in India*, pp. 200–206.
16. Khan and Hossain, p. 35.
17. *Banking With The Poor*, p. 7.
18. *The East Asian Miracle*, p. 158.
19. Ibid., p. 159.
20. A study by Professor Dani Rodrik of Columbia University, cited in the *Guardian*, 4 July 1994.
21. S. R. Christensen 'Democracy Without Equity? The Institutional and Political Consequences of Bangkok-based Development' (Bangkok: Thailand Development Research Institute 1993 Year-End Conference Report) p. 16.
22. Drawn up in the wake of the 1969 riots that left over 200 people dead. Rigg and Stott in Chapman and Baker (eds), p. 86.
23. Chandra Muzaffar, *Challenges and Choices in Malaysian Politics and Society* (Penang: Aliran, 1989) p. 247.
24. H. Crouch, 'Malaysia: Neither authoritarian nor democratic' in K. Hewison, R. Robison and G. Rodan (eds), *South East Asia in the 1990s: Authoritarianism, democracy and capitalism* (St Leonards: Allen & Unwin, 1993) p. 142.
25. D. Tsuruoka, 'On the golf links' *FEER* (21 January 1993) p. 55 and ibid., 'Politics of golf', *FEER* (12 November 1992) p. 30 on Mara; M. Vatikiotis, 'Prince of patronage' *FEER* (8 October 1992) 28 on Maika.
26. *East Asian Economic Miracle*, p. 159.
27. Leung Chuen Chau, p. 2
28. Ibid., p. 3.
29. P. Bowring, 'Crumbs for the poor', *FEER* (5 March 1992) p. 16.
30. M. Hiebert, 'Wage Revolution', *FEER* (23 September 1993) p. 95.
31. The problem is widespread. Inflation figures in Singapore are disputed by economists despite a government investigation of the accuracy of the statistics. In China, inflation figures are adjusted for political purposes (*Asian Age* 24 June 1994), while in Sri Lanka the Colombo price index in use up until 1993 had not been reweighted since 1952.
32. President Ramos: State of the Nation address July 1993.
33. R. Tiglao, 'Tan's smokescreen', *FEER* (11 March 1993) p. 52.
34. Unpublished World Bank report (1992), cited in J. Hutchison, 'Class and state power in the Philippines' in Hewison, Robison and Rodan (eds), p. 209.
35. Interview with Dr. Hafeez Pasha, Director of the Pakistan Institute of Applied Economics, Karachi and former Commerce Minister, February 1994.
36. S. Ali, 'An Uphill Task', *FEER* (21 October 1993) p. 16.
37. Interview with Dr. Hafeez Pasha; figures on likely yield from *Asian Age* (28 June 1994).
38. V. G. Kulkarni, 'The middle-class bulge', *FEER* (14 January 1993) p. 44.
39. Khan and Hossain, p. 111.

40. *Sri Lanka: Reform and Development 1992/93*, p. 37.
41. Interview Dr Mervyn de Silva MP, Colombo, February 1994.
42. M. Hiebert, 'Wage Revolution'.
43. 'Asia's Welfare', *FEER* (16 December 1993) p. 5.
44. *Economist* (4–10 June 1994).
45. The *Asian Development Outlook 1994* singles out Sri Lanka's record of health care measures, along with those in the Indian state of Kerala (p. 199), as examples of what poorer countries can do to raise life expectancy. The most recent urbanisation figure for Sri Lanka, given in *Social Indicators of Development 1993* is 22 per cent, against 31 per cent in Indonesia, which has a similar level of *per capita* GNP, or 43 per cent for the Philippines, which has a *per capita* GNP 50 per cent higher than Sri Lanka's.
46. 'India Review', June 1993, p. 6.
47. B. T. Montemayor, 'Banking on the poor', *FEER* (11 March 1993) p. 29.
48. Bradnock in Chapman and Baker (eds), p. 53.
49. UNESCAP report, quoted in *China Post* (25 October 1993).
50. *Banking with the Poor*, p. 8.
51. See L. Jellinek, *The Wheel of Fortune* (Sydney: Allen & Unwin, 1991). Similar processes are documented in South Korea (Hart-Landsberg, p. 261), the Klang Valley in Malaysia and in Shanghai to accommodate the Pudong development (*FEER*, 18 June 1992).
52. J. Wintle, *Romancing Vietnam* (London: Penguin Books, 1992) p. 240.
53. *Dawn* (18 February 1994).
54. Pineda-Ofreneo, p. 19.
55. Confidential interview, Rangoon, July 1993.
56. M. Tran, 'Tiger hunters set sights on Vietnam', *Guardian* (4 June 1994).
57. A. Kent, *Between Freedom and Subsistence: China and Human Rights* (Hong Kong: Oxford University Press, 1993) pp. 118 *et seq.*
58. K. Rafferty, *City on the Rocks: Hong Kong's Uncertain Future* (London: Penguin Books, 1991) p. 81. The Hong Kong government began building flats in large numbers in 1954 and was building 40 000 a year by the late 1980s.
59. P. Bowring, 'Crumbs for the Poor'.
60. Teck-Wong Soon and C. Suan Tan, p. 20.
61. The DPP proposal was for an NT$5000 a month pension at age 65.
62. Hart-Landsberg, p. 260.
63. Ibid.
64. *Asian Development Outlook 1994*, p. 58.
65. *ALIRAN Monthly*, 1993: 13 (11) p. 18.
66. *Asiaweek* (19 January 1994). The Philippine figure is open to doubt: the *Asian Development Outlook 1994* (p. 200) puts it at 6570 people per doctor, against over 9000 in Indonesia and barely 1000 in China.
67. 'Politics of Healthcare', *Aliran* 1993: 13 (6)38–40.
68. Bello and Rosenfeld, p. 86.
69. Cohen, p. 54.
70. Pineda-Ofreneo, p. 32.
71. L. Kaye, 'Haves and Have-Nots', *FEER* (2 September 1993) p. 46.
72. *Banking with the Poor*, p. 131. As of April 1992, 11 485 households were involved.
73. D. Tsuruoka, 'Down on the farm', *FEER* (24 September 1992) p. 98. Incomes have been falling on the FELDA estates and tenants are leaving.
74. S. Kamaluddin, 'Lender With a Mission' *FEER* (18 March 1993) p. 38. The Bangladesh Rural Advancement Committee has also been active in lending small sums to 450 000 women (*Financial Times Survey*, 'Bangladesh', 9 May 1994).

75. *Social Indicators of Development* 1993, p. 153, *Asian Development Outlook 1994*, p. 236.
76. R. Tiglao, 'A Long Way to Go', *FEER* (12 May 1994) p. 28.
77. Malaysian figures from Rigg and Stott in Chapman and Baker (eds), p. 91. Thailand from interview, Dr.Scott Christensen, Thailand Development Research Institute, February 1994.
78. B. J. T. Kerkvliet, *Everyday Politics in the Philippines: Class and Status Relations in a Central Luzon Village* (Philippines: New Day Publishers, 1991) pp. 252–8.
79. Jellinek, p. 19.
80. Vatikiotis, p. 114.
81. Broad with Cavanagh, p. 4.
82. R. Tasker, 'Dirty Business', *FEER* (13 January 1994) p. 23.
83. *Financial Times* (1 December 1993).
84. *Asian Age* (23 June 1994).
85. *Economist* (4 June 1994), citing a World Bank study.
86. *Financial Times* (7 April 1994).
87. M. Hiebert, 'Fragile Success', *FEER* (28 January 1993) p. 43; 'Industrial Disease', *FEER* (2 September 1993) p. 16.
88. Overholt, pp. 61, 64.
89. *Financial Times* (31 August 1993), M. Vatikiotis, 'State of siege', *FEER* (18 June 1992) p. 24.
90. G. Chapman, 'The South Asian Core' in Chapman and Baker (eds), pp. 21–28.
91. Bae Sun-Kwang and James Cotton, 'Regionalism in Electoral Politics' in J. Cotton (ed.), p. 184. The verdict on efforts at regional redistribution of activity in South Korea during the 1980s was largely negative: see C. M. Douglass, 'Regional Inequality and regional policy in Thailand: An International Comparative Perspective' (Thailand Development Research Institute Background report no. 3.3 1990) p. 34.
92. Douglass, pp. 24–8; G. Fairclough and R. Tasker, 'Separate and Unequal', *FEER* (14 April 1994) p. 22.
93. M. Hiebert, 'In the Heartland', *FEER* (17 June 1993) p. 58.
94. *Financial Times* (19 July 1994).
95. *Jakarta Post* (28 August 1993).
96. While conducting a series of interviews on the economy with provincial officials and the representatives of central government ministries in East Java, it became apparent that the work of each duplicated and triplicated that of other departments (but without reaching agreement on statistics). Part of the reason for this, I concluded, was to ensure that the central government is better able to monitor the initiatives being taken in the provinces.
97. UNESCAP report quoted in *China Post* (25 October 1993).
98. Hart-Landsberg, p. 265.
99. A. Schwarz, 'Looking Back at Rio', *FEER* (28 October 1993) p. 48, quoting World Bank report.
100. *Time* (11 January 1993).
101. Lamb, pp. 163 *et seq.*; *Banking with the Poor*, pp. 157 *et seq.*
102. G. Wehrfritz, 'Living dangerously', *FEER* (10 December 1992) p. 13.
103. Broad with Cavanagh, p. 36.
104. H. McDonald, 'Closing the Floodgates', *FEER* (15 April 1993) p. 15.
105. H. McDonald, 'Political Tremors', *FEER* (14 October 1993) 18, citing *India Today* estimate.

106. *Financial Times* (30 May 1994).
107. D. Jayasooria, 'Vision 2020 and the Marginalised', *ALIRAN Monthly* 1993: 13 (7) 16.
108. Cohen, pp. 64–6.
109. Tully, pp. 268–97.
110. Broad with Cavanagh, pp. 25–31, 33–34.
111. M. Smith, *Burma: Insurgency and the Politics of Ethnicity* (London and New Jersey: Zed Books, 1991) p. 257.
112. Dato' Hishamuddin bin Haji Yahaya 'Gambling: A Prevailing Social Evil', *Aliran Monthly* 1993: 13 (8) 32. The *Financial Times* (1 July 1994) gives a figure of M$4 billion, M$10 billion in unlicensed activity, equivalent to 4 per cent of GDP.
113. *Asiaweek* (23 February 1994).
114. E. Wachs Book, 'China's Noveaux Riches Flock to Macau', *FEER* (19 August 1993) p. 30.
115. M. Hiebert, 'Long Shot', *FEER* (14 October 1993) p. 58.
116. *Bangkok Post* (31 January 1994).
117. *Asian Age* (19 July 1994).
118. Kent, p. 229.
119. A. Chan, 'The Social Origins and Consequences of the Tiananmen Crisis' in D. S. G. Goodman and G. Segal (eds), *China in the Nineties: Crisis Management and Beyond* (Oxford: Oxford University Press, 1991).
120. C. Goldstein, 'Well-Connected', *FEER* (10 February 1994) p. 54.
121. *South China Morning Post* (1 July 1993).
122. L. Pan, *Sons of the Yellow Emperor: The Story of the Overseas Chinese* (London: Mandarin Paperbacks, 1993) pp. 32–34, 35–36.
123. Vatikiotis, p. 157.
124. M. Vatikiotis, 'Value Judgments', *FEER* (10 February 1994) p. 28.
125. Hart-Landsberg, pp. 272–81.
126. E. Paisley, 'Cut the Fat', *FEER* (9 December 1993) p. 62.
127. *Financial Times Survey* 'Korea' (23 June 1994) p. 2.
128. Cohen, p. 67.
129. In Vietnam, disputes at foreign-invested firms have centred on compulsory overtime, low pay and hectoring by managers. Textile, shoe and garment factories with South Korean, Taiwanese and Hong Kong investment have been the worst affected. See M. Hiebert, 'Industrial Disease', *FEER* (2 September 1993) p. 16.
130. *Asian Age* (8 July 1994).
131. *Independent on Sunday* (29 May 1994).
132. *Asian Age* (8 July 1994).
133. *Asian Age* (29 June 1994).
134. The organisation led by Han Dongfang, for instance, the Workers' Autonomous Federation is little more than a collection of courageous individuals. *Independent on Sunday* (28 July 1994).
135. *Asian Age* (7 July 1994).
136. Chan in Goodman and Segal (eds), p. 107. The following analysis is taken from this essay.
137. C. Goldstein, L. Kaye with A. Blass, 'Get Off Our Backs', *FEER* (15 July 1993) p. 68.

4 Veiled Authoritarianisms: Malaysia, Singapore and Indonesia

1. Schlossstein, p. 20.
2. Muzaffar, p. 105.
3. Ibid., p. 139.
4. M. Clifford, 'Send Money', *FEER* (30 September 1993) p. 72.
5. T. S. Selvan, *Singapore: the Ultimate Island* (Melbourne: Freeway Books, 1990) pp. 17–18.
6. G. Rodan, 'Preserving the one-party state in contemporary Singapore' in Hewison, Robison and Rodan (eds), p. 82.
7. J. McBeth, 'Challenges of Progress', *FEER* (28 April 1994) p. 44.
8. Ismail Muhd Salleh and Saha Dhevan Meyanathan, *The Lessons of East Asia Malaysia: Growth, Equity, and Structural Transformation* (Washington: World Bank, 1993) p. 5.
9. *FEER* (23 January 1992) p. 14.
10. Schlossstein, p. 278.
11. Muzaffar, p. 200.
12. Vatikiotis, p. 95.
13. Ibid., pp. 78, 94.
14. N. Balakrishnan, 'A leg up for friends', *FEER* (14 May 1992) p. 15.
15. In the 1986 elections, for instance, the Chinese comprised 36 per cent of the electorate, but only 20 per cent of constituencies were Chinese-dominated. Muzaffar, p. 285.
16. Crouch in Hewison, Robison and Rodan (eds), pp. 137, 149.
17. Vatikiotis, p. 112.
18. N. Balakrishnan, 'One Horse Race', *FEER* (17 June 1993) p. 31.
19. *FEER* (23 September 1993); Lee Kuan Yew's idea is cited in the *Financial Times* (15 July 1994).
20. Vatikiotis, p. 105.
21. M. Vatikiotis, 'Decline and disorder', *FEER* (1 October 1992).
22. E. T. Gomez, 'Anwar's Friends', *Aliran Monthly* 1993: 13 (9) pp. 35–40.
23. Interview with A. Kadir Jasin, Group Editor, New Straits Times, January 1994.
24. *Independent* (30 May 1992).
25. Vatikiotis, p. 105.
26. See Selvan on Francis Seow, pp. 288–9, and Jeyaretnam, pp. 94–103.
27. N. Balakrishnan, 'Academic Issue', *FEER* (15 April 1993) p. 22. Neuropsychology lecturer Dr. Chee Soon Juan lost his job at the National University for spending S$226 on sending his wife's thesis to the US by courier. Interviews in Singapore in January 1994 indicated that Chee's life was subsequently being made difficult.
28. Muzaffar, pp. 206–11.
29. *Straits Times* (18 January 1994).
30. Raja Aziz Addruse, 'Legalising what is prohibited', *Aliran Monthly* 1993: 13 (6) p. 6.
31. Selvan, p. 37.
32. Jakarta-Japan Club Newsletter, 1 January 1990, quoted in Bartu, p. 50.
33. Sedar, 'Time to Revive Student Activism in Malaysia', *Aliran Monthly* 1993: 13 (4) p. 14.
34. Muzaffar, pp. 130–43.
35. Quoted in Timberman, p. 118.
36. Crouch in Hewison, Robison and Rodan (eds), p. 143.
37. Ibid., p. 150.

38. Robison in Hewison, Robison and Rodan (eds), p. 61.
39. Rosani Projo, chairman of the Indonesian Nationalist Student Movement interviewed in *Indonesian Times* (20 August 1993).
40. Jellinek, p. 133.
41. *Economist* (17 April 1993).
42. See J. Ramos-Horta, *Funu: The Unfinished Saga of East Timor* (Trenton: The Red Sea Press, 1987) on the background to the invasion and the subsequent diplomatic struggle to keep the question of East Timor's independence alive. This struggle was successful in obtaining a UN consensus statement expressing deep concern at human rights violations in East Timor and welcoming the Indonesian invitation for the UN High Commissioner for Human Rights to visit, although the UN has stopped short of a resolution condemning Indonesia which would commit it to some form of action. Independence has not been recognised by Portugal, which in a statement dated April 1994 says that it 'has never relinquished its capacity as administering power of the territory' (Portuguese Embassy, London).
43. R. Osborne, *Indonesia's Secret War: The guerilla struggle in Irian Jaya* (Sydney: Allen & Unwin, 1985) p. 41.
44. For example, the clash over plans to build a resort near one of Bali's holiest Hindu temples. See M. Cohen, 'God and Mammon', *FEER* (May 26 1994) p. 28.
45. Vatikiotis, p. 101.
46. Background to Operation Lalang is given in *The Rule of Law and Human Rights in Malaysia and Singapore* (Kehma-S report on the conference at the European Parliament 9–10 March 1989) pp. 8–14 and 39–54, and in Muzaffar, 149–57.
47. See Rodan in Hewison, Robison and Rodan (eds), pp. 87–9 on the incorporation efforts. Interview with Walter Woon MP, January 1994, on the limits to the nominated MPs' role.
48. Vatikiotis, p. 133; *Jakarta Post* (25 August 1993).
49. M. Vatikotis, 'Hearts and Minds', *FEER* (20 May 1993) p. 32.
50. *Straits Times* (20 January 1994).
51. *Sunday Times* (Singapore) (9 January 1994).
52. *Aliran Monthly* 1993: 13 (9) 5.
53. Ibid., p. 37.
54. Jon Pilger's documentary for Central Television on East Timor (1993) cites other witness accounts which indicate that the total death toll was over 400.
55. Osborne, pp. 109, 146.
56. *Jakarta Post* (25 August 1993).
57. In East Timor, for instance, after the arrest and imprisonment of FRETILIN leader Xanana Gusmao, a new commander, Konis Santana, was explaining his plans for continuing the struggle (*Independent on Sunday* 27 February 1994).
58. A group of students were jailed for six months in 1994 for demanding that Suharto account for his leadership *Financial Times* (24 June 1994).
59. James Cotton, quoted in Rodan in Hewison, Robison and Rodan (eds), p. 101.
60. *China News* (28 October 1993).
61. Robison in Hewison, Robison and Rodan (eds), p. 52–4.
62. M. Vatikiotis, 'The Waiting Game', *FEER* (21 April 1994) p. 20.
63. Crouch in Hewison, Robison and Rodan (eds), p. 148.
64. Interview with Dr. Kua Kia Soong, DAP, January 1994.
65. J. McBeth, 'Third Time Lucky', *FEER* (13 January 1994) p. 24.
66. Vatikiotis, p. 97, a suggestion disputed by Robison in Hewison, Robison and Rodan (eds), p. 63.

5 Market Stalinism: Burma, China, Laos, North Korea and Vietnam

1. G. Evans and K. Rowley, *Red Brotherhood at War: Vietnam, Cambodia and Laos since 1975* (London: Verso, 1990) pp. 28–31.
2. See B. Cummings, *The Origins of the Korean War: Liberation and the Emergence of Separate Régimes, 1945–47* (Princeton: Princeton University Press, 1981).
3. Smith, pp. 59, 65.
4. Ibid., pp. 199–202.
5. N. P. Halpern, 'Economic Reform, Social Mobilization and Democratization in Post-Mao China', in R. Baum (ed.), *Reform and Reaction in Post-Mao China* (London: Routledge, 1991) pp. 46–48.
6. L. M. Stern, *Renovating the Vietnamese Communist Party: Nguyen Van Linh and the Programme for Organizational Reform, 1987–91* (Singapore: Institute of Southeast Asian Studies, 1993) pp. 175–79.
7. *Asian Age* (12 July 1994).
8. *FEER* (10 December 1992) p. 12.
9. M. Hiebert, 'Letting off steam', *FEER* (30 July 1992) p. 10.
10. M. Hiebert, 'House cleaning', *FEER* (15 October 1992) p. 30.
11. Kent, pp. 53–8, 85–8.
12. Craig, p. 223.
13. *S. G. Warburg China Review* (February 1993), p. 17.
14. L. R. Sullivan, 'The Chinese Communist Party and the Beijing Massacre: The Crisis in Authority' in Goodman and Segal (eds), p. 95.
15. P. Handley, 'Making Connections', *FEER* (4 November 1993) p. 28.
16. Aung San Suu Kyi, *Freedom From Fear and other writings* (London: Penguin Books, 1991) p. 276.
17. Fairbank, p. 356.
18. Ibid., p. 357.
19. L. Kaye, 'Congressional record', *FEER* (11 March 1993) p. 23.
20. J. Karp, 'Prime Time Police', *FEER* (21 October 1993) p. 72.
21. *FEER* (9 September 1993) p. 14.
22. *Financial Times* (5 April 1994).
23. M. Hiebert, 'New directions', *FEER* (20 February 1992) p. 20.
24. *Vietnam Investment Review* (1–7 November 1993).
25. G. Segal, 'China Changes Shape: Regionalism and Foreign Policy', International Institute for Strategic Studies Adelphi Paper 287 p. 29.
26. Ibid., p. 30.
27. Chinese suzerainty was recognised by the Tibetans and the British at the 1913 Simla conference, though the Chinese government never ratified the agreement, thereby forfeiting the claim. As Mary Craig points out (p. 37), this was the first time in 700 years that the Chinese had claimed Tibet to be an integral part of China. For the diplomatic and military events leading up to the Simla conference see Peter Fleming's *Bayonets to Lhasa*.
28. Craig, p. 15.
29. Craig's description of the 1979 fact-finding mission from the Dalai Lama's base in Northern India bears this out (p. 208).
30. See *Tibet Facts no. 2* produced by the Tibet Support Group, London. This does not confirm the exiles' claim, but points to an intensification of population transfer since 1992.
31. *Independent* (17 April 1994).
32. Ibid. (16 March 1994).

33. C. Mackerras, 'The Juche Idea and the Thought of Kim Il Sung' in C. Mackerras and N. Knight, *Marxism in Asia* (Beckenham: Croom Helm, 1985) p. 159.
34. L. Kaye, 'Broad Canvas', *FEER* (29 October 1992) p. 12.
35. Stern, p. 177.
36. L. Kaye, 'Mayday May Day', *FEER* (7 May 1992) p. 22.
37. B. Lintner, 'The Generals' New Clothes', *FEER* (25 November 1993) p. 30.
38. Tai Ming Cheung, 'Decimated Ranks', *FEER* (27 February 1992) p. 15. The PAP increased by 20 per cent to 600 000 between 1989 and 1992 while the armed forces were to lose 260 000 after 1992.
39. A. Foster-Carter, 'North Korea in Pacific Asia' in C. Dixon and D. Drakakis-Smith, *Economic and Social Development in Pacific Asia* (London: Routledge, 1993).
40. N. Chanda and Shim Jae Hoon, 'Poor and Desperate', *FEER* (9 September 1993) p. 16.
41. I. Derbyshire, *Politics in China: From Mao to the Post-Deng Era* (Edinburgh; Chambers, 1991) p. 101.
42. Smith, p. 16.
43. Ibid., p. 8.
44. Ibid., p. 371.
45. J. Lilley, 'Freedom of the air', *FEER* (1 October 1992) p. 16.
46. *FEER* (7 January 1993) p. 7.
47. Ibid.
48. *The Nation* (6 February 1994).
49. M. Hiebert, 'More of The Same', *FEER* (10 February 1994) p. 15.
50. White, p. 162.
51. Ibid., pp. 176–7 on an ineffective rectification campaign in the mid-1980s.
52. *Korea Times* (31 October 1993); further repression followed (*Asian Age* 18 July 1994).
53. *Bangkok Post* (7 February 1994).
54. B. Martin, 'Remaking Kim's Image', *FEER* (15 April 1993) p. 36.
55. M. Hiebert, 'Answered Prayers', *FEER* (13 May 1993).
56. M. Hiebert, 'No Middle Path Here', *FEER* (5 August 1993).
57. N. Chanda, 'Vietnam in Post-Cold War Asia' in C. Jeshuran (ed.), *China, India, Japan and the Security of Southest Asia* (Singapore: Institute of Southeast Asian Studies, 1993) p. 248.
58. Smith, pp. 110–8.
59. Ibid., p. 410.
60. Ibid., pp. 374–81.
61. B. Lintner, 'Neighbours' Interests', *FEER* (1 April 1993) p. 28.
62. B. Lintner, 'One More to Go', *FEER* (21 October 1993) p. 32.
63. Kent, p. 129.
64. A. Kuhn and L. Kaye, 'Bursting at the Seams', *FEER* (10 March 1994) p. 27.
65. White, p. 212.
66. M. Hiebert, 'More of the Same'.
67. *Financial Times* (14 July 1994).
68. L. Kaye, 'Bold Blueprint', *FEER* (25 March 1993) p. 13.
69. M. Hiebert, 'Corps Business', *FEER* (23 December 1993) p. 40.
70. B. Lintner, 'Flanking movement', *FEER* (15 October 1992) p. 20.
71. Tai Ming Cheung, 'Serve the People', *FEER* (14 October 1993) p. 64.
72. White, pp. 249–50.
73. Aung San Suu Kyi has reportedly offered to leave, but only if allowed to walk to the airport, confident in the belief that large demonstrations would prevent

her reaching an aeroplane and departing. (Discussion at Foreign Correspondents Club, Bangkok, February 1994.)

74. Thailand is the biggest investor from ASEAN and Singapore the second largest *Asian Age* (29 June 1994).
75. FCC discussion Bangkok. See *Asian Age* (23 July 1994).
76. Chan in Goodman and Segal (eds), p. 127.
77. Transitional leaders in East Germany and Hungary respectively.
78. A. Foster-Carter in Dixon and Drakakis-Smith (eds), p. 215.
79. Evans and Rowley, p. 22.
80. Ibid., p. 99.
81. Ibid., p. 161.
82. Ibid., p. 166.
83. Ibid., pp. 272–8.
84. Ibid., pp. 208–9.
85. M. Hiebert, 'Draining the swamp', *FEER* (11 June 1992) p. 24.
86. N. Thayer, 'Shot to Pieces', *FEER* (20 May 1993) p. 10.
87. N. Thayer, 'Untactical Retreat', *FEER* (5 May 1994) p. 15.
88. N. Thayer and N. Chanda, 'Things Fall Apart . . .', *FEER* (19 May 1994) p. 16.
89. *Financial Times* (8 July 1994).
90. N. Thayer and R. Tasker, 'Voice of the People', *FEER* (3 June 1993) p. 10. At that stage, the Khmer Rouge controlled around 15 per cent of the country.

6 Emerging Bourgeois Democracies: Hong Kong, South Korea, Taiwan, Thailand

1. *FEER* (4 June 1992); *Bangkok Post* (26 July 1992) gives details of those still missing.
2. E.g. Schlossstein, *Asia's New Little Dragons*.
3. Long, p. 73.
4. Ibid., p. 54.
5. Ibid., p. 181. The author of a critical biography of Chiang Kai-shek was, for instance, murdered in California in 1984.
6. M. Hastings, *The Korean War* (London: Pan Books, 1988), pp. 104–5; 279–80. Hart-Landsberg estimates that Rhee killed 100 000 people on being returned to power by the UN forces, p. 131.
7. Shim Jae Hoon, 'Haunted by history', *FEER* (30 April 1992).
8. Hart-Landsberg, p. 54.
9. Ibid., pp. 217–8.
10. Ibid., p. 219.
11. J. J. Wright, *The Balancing Act: A History of Modern Thailand* (Oakland: Pacific Rim Press, 1991) pp. 256–9.
12. See, for example, Hewison in Hewison, Robison and Rodan (eds), p. 176.
13. Ibid., p. 168.
14. Christensen, pp. 9–11.
15. *Asiaweek* (17 November 1993).
16. *Financial Times* (20 July 1994).
17. *Lost Victory* (Seoul: Minjungsa, no date) pp. 116–22.
18. R. Tasker, 'Ascent of angels', *FEER* (24 September 1992) p. 12; Wright, pp. 231–2, 249–50 on the previous entanglements of the Democrats.
19. Long, p. 68.
20. J. Baum, 'Radical Reformist', *FEER* (23 June 1994) p. 22.
21. 'Question of Honour', *FEER* (1 April 1993) p. 11.

22. Patten's exceedingly frosty relations with China arose out of an approach on his part so likely to provoke angry retaliation that it appears quite plausible that he was given a misleading brief by Foreign Office officials in London piqued at seeing their own first choice for the governorship (Sir John Boyd, now ambassador to Japan) overruled and at having former govenor Lord Wilson sacked. No matter how superficial Patten's reforms, the Chinese government saw no advantage in pandering to the ambitions of a defeated British politician after so many years of dealing with supine officials and believing it had reached agreement on the Basic Law, Hong Kong's mini-constitution.

23. Shim Jae Hoon, 'Goodbye to all that', *FEER* (16 April 1992) p. 18.

24. Hart-Landsberg, pp. 300–4.

25. *Asian Age* (5 July 1994).

26. Interview, Dr. Scott Christensen, Thailand Development Research Institute, February 1994.

27. J. Baum, 'Body Politics', *FEER* (28 July 1994) p. 18.

28. J. Baum, 'Democracy Banquet', *FEER* (9 December 1993) p. 21.

29. *Korea Herald* (31 October 1993).

30. For instance, the views of businessmen expressed in the *Financial Times* (2–3 July 1994).

31. The New China Hong Kong Group – linking prominent Hong Kong capitalists, Chinese government ministries, banks and provincial investment bodies, overseas Chinese interests and Western merchant bankers Goldman Sachs – is an excellent illustration of this. See J. Karp, 'The New Insiders', *FEER* (27 May 1993) p. 62.

32. J. Baum, 'Taiwan's Air War', *FEER* (9 December 1993) p. 65.

33. L. do Rosario, 'No Watchdog', *FEER* (7 July 1994) p. 26.

34. *Financial Times* (30 July 1993).

35. Christensen, p. 22.

36. Shim Jae Hoon and E. Paisley, 'Whirlwind Honeymoon', *FEER* (24 June 1993) p. 18.

37. Tai Ming Cheung, 'Company town', *FEER* (18 February 1993) p. 22.

38. A claim denied by the British, who argue that only 14 per cent of the contracts have gone to British firms. See *Guardian* (27 June 1994).

39. Shim Jae Hoon, 'The Battle Within', *FEER* (1 April 1993).

40. E. Paisley, 'Captain of industry', *FEER* (22 October 1992).

41. Crosby Research, 'Quarterly Economic Review', April–June 1991.

42. One of the rumours circulating in Bangkok was that helicopter gunships were to be brought in to clear the streets.

43. The other factions include the Young Turks (or Young Military Officers) and the Democratic Soldiers. Chamlong was a member of the first of these, while the second has been identified with General Chaovalit, deputy prime minister in the Chuan government. See Robison in Hewison, Robison and Rodan (eds), p. 165.

44. A change to the succession law allows her to succeed King Bhumibol as Queen. She would become the first female monarch in modern Thai history.

45. Christensen, p. 6.

46. Hart-Landsberg, p. 122.

47. D. M. Plunk, 'Political Developments in the Republic of Korea' in T. W. Robinson (ed.), p. 111.

48. J. Cotton, 'The Two Koreas and Rapprochement: Foundations for Progress' in Cotton (ed.), p. 293.

49. Ibid., pp. 291–2.

50. US$90 billion is cited in the *Economist* (16–22 July 1994); US$200–300 billion in the *Financial Times* (11 July 1994); US$200–500 billion in Shim Jae Hoon, 'The price of unity', *FEER* (26 March 1992) p. 54. US$2408 billion is given by Professor Eui-Gak Hwang in a paper on 'The Cost of Unification and Its Economic Impact; The Korean Perspective', given at the colloquium of foreign journalists on Korean Unification and Its Prospects, Seoul, November 1993: it includes the total cost of raising living standards in North Korea to those of the South.
51. See, for instance, Lee Hong-koo, 'Unification Through a Korean Commonwealth: Blueprint for a National Community' in Cotton (ed.), pp. 303–12.
52. *Financial Times* (17 December 1993).
53. *Financial Times* (12 October 1993).
54. S. Mosher, 'Gang of forty-four', *FEER* (26 March 1992) p. 13.
55. *Financial Times* (17 December 1993).
56. *Financial Times* (2–3 July 1994).
57. *South China Morning Post* (4 January 1994).
58. The annual jamboree of the rugby sevens competition – an excuse for raucous behaviour by the expatriate community – will be another test. Heavy-handed intereference in its organisation would be regarded by them as a sign that the good times were coming to an end in Hong Kong and that its role as a financial centre was going the way of Shanghai's after 1949.
59. *Asian Age* (21 July 1994).

7 Elite Democracies: Bangladesh, India, Pakistan, the Philippines and Sri Lanka

 1. S. Karnow, *In Our Image: America's Empire in the Philippines* (Manila: National Book Store, 1989) p. 198, pp. 230–8.
 2. S. Seagrave, *The Marcos Dynasty* (London: Hodder and Stoughton, 1990) pp. 330–42.
 3. D. Jayanntha, *Electoral Allegiance in Sri Lanka* (Cambridge: Cambridge University Press, 1992) is a thorough study of the use of different forms of patronage in rural and urban constituencies since independence.
 4. Ibid., p. 161.
 5. M. J. Akbar, *Nehru: The Making of India* (London: Penguin Books, 1988) pp. 250, 281.
 6. R. Gandhi, *Understanding the Muslim Mind* (New Delhi: Penguin Books, 1987) p. 271.
 7. The causes have never been satisfactorily established. Some Pakistanis believe the US was responsible, despite the death of the US ambassador in the crash. General Beg's decision not to board the plane has been regarded suspiciously, but Zia's list of enemies was a long one, including the Soviets, warring Afghan factions, the Indian government and the Al-Zulfilkar terrorist group.
 8. Lamb, p. 290.
 9. S. Ali, 'Soldier's Solution', *FEER* (29 July 1993) p. 15.
10. T. Ali, *The Nehrus and the Gandhis: An Indian Dynasty* (London: Pan Books, 1991) p. 187.
11. Ibid., p. 211.
12. W. McGowan, *Only Man is Vile: The Tragedy of Sri Lanka* (London: Pan Books, 1993) p. 115.
13. Ibid., p. 376.
14. The formation of the Democratic United National Front followed the expulsion of Lalith Athulathmudali and Gamini Dissanayake from the UNP in 1991.

Dissanayake returned to the UNP fold early in 1994, though Athulathmudali's widow continued to lead the DUNF. Dissanayake was assasinated in the run up to the presidential election in October 1994. His widow contested the election unsuccessfully in his place, leaving former Prime Minister Ranil Wickeramsinghe as the UNP's principal standard bearer.

15. Seagrave, pp. 331 *et seq.*
16. Timberman, p. 77.
17. Ibid., pp. 99–101. The killing of Benigno Aquino at Manila's international airport in 1983 brought the violence home to people in the capital.
18. Ibid., p. 207.
19. C. G. Hernandez, 'Political Developments in the Philippines' in T. W. Robinson (ed.), p. 187.
20. R. Tiglao, 'Pride and Privilege', *FEER* (12 May 1994) p. 24.
21. Lamb, pp. 51–6.
22. Ali, p. 203.
23. Broad with Cavanagh, pp. 44 *et seq.*
24. P. S. Jha, *In the Eye of the Cyclone: The Crisis in Indian Democracy* (New Delhi: Penguin Books, 1993) pp. 39–42.
25. Jayanntha, p. 259.
26. R. Tasker and B. Tiglao, 'The jury is out' *FEER* (21 May 1992) p. 14.
27. Timberman, p. 202.
28. Ibid., pp. 226, 280.
29. R. Tiglao, 'Into a corner', *FEER* (11 February 1993) p. 55. The allegations were based on an investigation by a US expert on authorship of English language texts. Justice Hugo Gutierrez resigned shortly after the allegation was made.
30. H. McDonald, 'Abstain and Frustrate', *FEER* (27 May 1993) p. 24. Supreme Court judges can only be removed by a two thirds vote of the Indian Parliament.
31. *India Today* (15 January 1994).
32. *Bangladesh: State of Human Rights 1992* (Dhaka: Co-ordinating Council for Human Rights in Bangladesh, 1993) pp. 17–8.
33. *Guardian* (27 June 1994).
34. As in the 1994 Sri Lankan election campaign, in which independent television stations screened candidate debates for the first time (*Asian Age* 9 August 1994).
35. Ownership of major newspapers is given in H. McDonald, 'Changing Times', *FEER* (24 March 1994) p. 22.
36. For instance, 18 million out of more than 900 million people watch BBC World Service Television News.
37. M. S. Dobbs-Higginson, *Asia Pacific: A View on its Role in the New World Order* (Hong Kong: Longman, 1993) pp. 176–7. A subsequent edition of the book has been retitled *Asia Pacific: A View on its Role in the New World Disorder.*
38. Jha, p. 184.
39. Timberman, pp. 399–400.
40. M. Ram, *Sri Lanka: The Fractured Island* (New Delhi: Penguin Books, 1989) pp. 79–82.
41. R. Tiglao, 'Divine Intervention', *FEER* (30 April 1992) p. 19.
42. UNDP survey, quoted in *Asian Age* (4 July 1994).
43. See *The Chittagong Hill Tracts of Bangladesh: The Untold Story* (Dhaka: Centre for Development Research, 1992) for an account sympathetic to the government's efforts; *Bangladesh State of Human Rights 1992* pp. 88–94 has details of violent incidents in 1992 and of negotiations.

44. J. McBeth, 'Who's in Charge', *FEER* (6 May 1993) p. 28.
45. Lamb, p. 81.
46. H. McDonald, 'Curse of victory', *FEER* (5 March 1992) p. 11.
47. Akbar, pp. 438–52.
48. Jha, pp. 49–50.
49. *Financial Times* (30 September 1993).
50. Estimates by diplomats in Islamabad.
51. Pakistani claim.
52. *Pakistan Times* (20 February 1994).
53. M. J. Akbar, *Riot After Riot: Reports on Caste and Communal Violence in India* (New Delhi: Penguin Books, 1988) p. 147.
54. Ali, pp. 139–40.
55. Jha, p. 51.
56. McGowan, p. 372 on Premadasa's admission of this.
57. Ibid., pp. 215–7.
58. Ali, pp. 178–80. See also R. Ray, *The Naxalites and their Ideology* (Delhi: Oxford University Press, 1988).
59. Karnow, pp. 348–54.
60. R. Tasker, 'Treaty of Utrecht', *FEER* (19 November 1992) p. 12.
61. J. McBeth, 'Attritional Politics', *FEER* (18 March 1993) p. 16.
62. H. McDonald, 'Troubled Tycoons', *FEER* (14 October 1993) p. 18.
63. R. Tiglao, 'Paralysed by Politics', *FEER* (12 May 1993) p. 22.
64. Jha, pp. 132–67.
65. *Financial Times* (30 September 1993).
66. *Morning Sun* (15 November 1993).

Bibliography

Journals and Newspapers

ALIRAN Monthly
Asiamoney
Asiaweek
Asian Age
Asian Wall Street Journal
Bangkok Bank Monthly Bulletin
Bangkok Post
The Economist
Far Eastern Economic Review
Financial Times
Guardian
Jakarta Post
Independent on Sunday
Indonesian Oberserver
Korea Times
Korea Herald
The Nation
New Straits Times
South China Morning Post
Straits Times
Time
Vietnam Investment Review

Books and Articles

M. J. Akbar, *Nehru: The Making of India* (London: Penguin Books, 1989).
—— *Riot After Riot* (New Delhi: Penguin Books, 1988).
T. Ali, *The Nehrus and the Gandhis: An Indian Dynasty* (London: Pan Books, 1991).
Asian Development Bank, *Asian Development Outlook 1993* (Hong Kong: Oxford University Press, 1993).
—— *Asian Development Outlook 1994* (Hong Kong: Oxford University Press, 1994).
—— 'Cambodia: An Economic Report' (unpublished, 1991).
Aung San Suu Kyi, *Freedom from Fear and Other Writings* (London: Penguin Books, 1991).
Bangladesh Manobadhikar Samonnoy Parishad, *Bangladesh State of Human Rights, 1992* (Dhaka, 1993).
J. Bartholomew, *The Richest Man in the World: The Sultan of Brunei* (London: Penguin Books, 1990).
F. Bartu, *The Ugly Japanese: Nippon's Economic Empire in Asia* (Singapore: Longman, 1992).
A. Battacharya and M. Pangestu, *The Lessons of East Asia – Indonesia: Development, Transformation and Public Policy* (Washington: World Bank, 1993).
R. Baum (ed.), *Reform and Reaction in Post-Mao China: The Road to Tiananmen* (London: Routledge, 1991).

W. Bello and S. Rosenfeld, *Dragons in Distress: Asia's Miracle Economies in Crisis* (San Francisco: The Institute for Food and Development Policy, 1990).

B. Bhutto, *Daughter of the East* (London: Mandarin Paperbacks, 1989).

L. Brahm, *Banking and Finance in Indochina* (Hemel Hempstead: Woodhead-Faulkner, 1992).

R. Broad with J. Cavanagh, *Plundering Paradise: The Struggle for the Environment in the Philippines* (Philippines: Anvil Publishing, no date).

W. E. Brummit and F. Flatters, *Exports, Structural Change and Thailand's Rapid Growth* (Bangkok: Thailand Development Research Institute, 1992).

I. Buruma, *God's Dust: A Modern Asian Journey* (London: Vintage, 1991).

R. S. Callanta, *Poverty: The Philippine Scenario* (Manila: Bookmark, 1988).

Chalongphob Sussangkarn and Yongyuth Chalamwong, *Thailand's Economic Dynamism: Human Resource Contributions and Constraints* (Thailand Development Research Institute, November 1989).

D. P. Chandler, *Brother Number One: A Political Biography of Pol Pot* (Chiang Mai: Silkworm Books, 1993).

G. P. Chapman and K. M. Baker (eds), *The Changing Geography of Asia* (London: Routledge, 1992).

S. R. Christensen, *Democracy without Equity? The Institutional and Political Consequences of Bangkok-based Development* (Bangkok: Thailand Development Research Institute 1993 Year-End Conference Report).

S. R. Christensen, D. Dollar, A. Siamwalla and P. Vichyanond, *The Lessons of East Asia – Thailand: The Institutional and Political Underpinnings of Growth* (Washington: The World Bank, 1993).

Christian Institute for the Study of Justice and Development, *Lost Victory: An Overview of the Korean People's Struggle for Democracy in 1987* (Seoul: Minjungsa, no date).

M. J. Cohen, *The Unknown Taiwan* (Taipei: Coalition for Democracy and the North American Taiwanese Women's Association, 1992).

J. Cotton (ed.), *Korea under Roh Tae-woo: Democratisation, Northern Policy and Inter-Korean Relations* (St Leonards: Allen & Unwin, 1993).

R. Cottrell, *The End of Hong Kong: The Secret Diplomacy of Imperial Retreat* (London: John Murray, 1993).

M. Craig, *Tears of Blood: A Cry for Tibet* (New Delhi: Indus, 1992).

B. Crozier, *South East Asia in Turmoil* (London: Penguin Books, 1968).

T. D. S. A. Dissanayaka, *The Dilemma of Sri Lanka* (Colombo: Swastika, no date).

C. Dixon and D. Drakakis-Smith (eds), *Economic and Social Development in Pacific Asia* (London: Routledge, 1993).

M. S. Dobbs-Higginson, *Asia Pacific: A View on its Role in the New World Order* (Hong Kong: Longman, 1993).

C. M. Douglass, *Regional Inequality and Regional Policy in Thailand: An International Comparative Perspective* (Thailand Development Research Institute Background report No. 3.3 1990).

G. Evans and K. Rowley, *Red Brotherhood at War: Vietnam, Cambodia and Laos since 1975* (London: Verso, 1990).

J. K. Fairbank, *The Great Chinese Revolution 1800–1985* (London: Pan Books, 1988).

R. Fell, *Crisis and Change: The Maturing of Hong Kong's Financial Markets* (Hong Kong: Longman, 1992).

P. Fleming, *Bayonets to Lhasa* (Hong Kong: Oxford University Press, 1986).

Foundation for Development Cooperation, *Banking with the Poor* (Brisbane: Foundation for Development Cooperation, 1992).

R. Gandhi, *Understanding the Muslim Mind* (New Delhi: Penguin Books, 1987).

D. S. G. Goodman and G. Segal (eds), *China in the Nineties: Crisis Management and Beyond* (Oxford: Oxford University Press, 1991).

B. Grant, *Indonesia* (London: Penguin Books, 1967).

M. Hart-Landsberg, *The Rush to Development: Economic Change and Political Struggle in South Korea* (New York: Monthly Review Press, 1993).

M. Hastings, *The Korean War* (London: Pan Books, 1988).

K. Hewison, R. Robison and G. Rodan (eds), *Southeast Asia in the 1990s: Authoritarianism, Democracy and Capitalism* (St Leonards: Allen & Unwin, 1993).

H. Hill (ed.), *Indonesia's New Order: The Dynamics of Socio-economic Transformation* (St Leonards: Allen & Unwin, 1994).

S. P. Huntington, *Political Order in Changing Societies* (New Haven and London: Yale University Press, 1968).

Institute of Policy Studies, *Sri Lanka: Reform and Development 1992/93* (Colombo, 1993).

Ismail Muhd Salleh and Saha Dhevan Meyanathan, *The Lessons of East Asia – Malaysia: Growth, Equity, and Structural Transformation* (Washington: The World Bank, 1993).

D. Jayanntha, *Electoral Allegiance in Sri Lanka* (Cambridge: Cambridge University Press, 1992).

L. Jellinek, *The Wheel of Fortune: The History of a Poor Community in Jakarta* (North Sydney: Allen & Unwin, 1991).

C. Jeshuran (ed.), *China, India, Japan and the Security of Southeast Asia* (Singapore: Institute of Southeast Asian Studies, 1993).

P. S. Jha, *In the Eye of the Cyclone: The Crisis in Indian Democracy* (New Delhi: Viking, 1993).

V. R. Jose (ed.), *Mortgaging the Future: The World Bank and the IMF in the Philippines* (Quezon City: Foundation for Nationalist Studies, 1988).

S. Karnow, *In Our Image: America's Empire in the Philippines* (New York: Random House, 1989).

—— *Vietnam: A History* (Lenvan: Pimlico, 1994).

KEHMA-S, *The Rule of Law and Human Rights in Malaysia and Singapore* (Limelette: KEHMA-S, no date).

A. Kent, *Between Freedom and Subsistence: China and Human Rights* (Hong Kong: Oxford University Press, 1993).

B. J. T. Kerkvliet, *Everyday Politics in the Philippines* (Quezon City: New Day Publishers, 1991).

A. R. Khan and M. Hossain, *The Strategy of Development in Bangladesh* (London: Macmillan, 1989).

'Korean Unification and Its Prospects: A Colloquium of Foreign Journalists, November 3–4, 1993' (The Seoul Foreign Correspondents' Club, 1993).

P. R. Krugman, J. Alm, S. M. Collins and E. M. Remoona, *Transforming the Philippine Economy* (Manila: National Economic and Development Authority, United Nations Development Programme, 1992).

Kuan Hsin-chi and M. Brosseau (eds), *China Review* (Hong Kong: The Chinese University Press, 1991).

—— *China Review 1992* (Hong Kong: The Chinese University Press, 1992).

C. Lamb, *Waiting for Allah: Pakitan's Struggle for Democracy* (London: Penguin Books, 1992).

Leung Chuen Chau, *The Lessons of East Asia – Hong Kong: A Unique Case of Development* (Washington: The World Bank, 1993).

P. Limqueco, B. McFarlane and J. Odhnoff, *Labour and Industry in ASEAN* (Manila: Journal of Contemporary Asia Publishers, 1989).

S. Long, *Taiwan: China's Last Frontier* (London: Macmillan, 1991).

R. E. B. Lucas and G. F. Papanek (eds), *The Indian Economy: Recent Developments and Future Prospects* (New Delhi: Oxford University Press, 1989).

H. Luethy, P. Emmanuel and B. Rafael, *Indonesia in Travail* (New Delhi: Congress for Cultural Freedom, 1966).

W. McGowan, *Only Man Is Vile: The Tragedy of Sri Lanka* (London: Pan Books, 1993).

C. Mackerras and N. Knight, *Marxism in Asia* (Beckenham: Croom Helm, 1985).

Malaysian Institute of Economic Research, *National Economic Outlook* (1993).

B. K. Martin, *Intruding on the Hermit: Glimpses of North Korea* (Hawaii: East West Center, Special Reports Number 1, July 1993).

C. Muzaffar, *Challenges and Choices in Malaysian Politics and Society* (Penang: ALIRAN, no date).

Mya Than and J. L. H. Tan (eds), *Myanmar Dilemmas and Options: The Challenge of Economic Transition in the 1990s* (Singapore: Institute of South East Asian Studies, 1990).

—— *Vietnam's Dilemmas and Options: The Challenge of Economic Transition in the 1990s* (Singapore: Institute of South East Asian Studies, 1993).

V. S. Naipaul, *India: A Million Mutinies Now* (London: Mandarin Paperbacks, 1990).

G. E. Ogle, *South Korea: Dissent within the Economic Miracle* (London: Zed Books, 1990).

R. Osborne, *Indonesia's Secret War: The Guerilla Struggle in Irian Jaya* (North Sydney: Allen & Unwin, 1985).

W. H. Overholt, *China: The Next Economic Superpower* (London: Weidenfeld & Nicolson, 1993).

—— (ed.), *The Future of Brazil* (Boulder: Westview Press, 1978)

Pakistan Investment Board, *A Guide to Investment Opportunities in Pakistan*, December 1993.

L. Pan, *Sons of the Yellow Emperor: The Story of the Overseas Chinese* (London: Mandarin Paperbacks, 1993).

R. Pineda-Ofreneo, *The Philippines: Debt and Poverty* (Oxford: Oxfam, 1991).

K. Rafferty, *City on the Rocks: Hong Kong's Uncertain Future* (London: Penguin Books, 1991).

M. Ram, *Sri Lanka: The Fractured Island* (New Delhi: Penguin Books, 1989)

R. Ray, *The Naxalites and Their Ideology* (Delhi: Oxford University Press, 1992).

D. Rees, *A Short History of Modern Korea* (Port Erin: Ham Publishing, 1988).

J. Ramos-Horta, *Funu: The Unfinished Saga of East Timor* (Trenton: Red Sea Press, 1987).

T. W. Robinson (ed.), *Democracy and Development in East Asia: Taiwan, South Korea and the Philippines* (Washington: The AEI Press, 1991).

S. Said, *Genesis of Power: General Sudirman and the Indonesian Military in Politics 1945–49* (North Sydney: Allen & Unwin, 1992).

H. E. Salisbury, *The New Emperors: China in the Era of Mao and Deng* (New York: Avon Books, 1992).

S. Schlossstein, *Asia's New Little Dragons: The Dynamic Emergence of Indonesia, Thailand and Malaysia* (Chicago: Contemporary Books, 1991).

S. Seagrave, *The Marcos Dynasty* (London: New English Library, 1990).

G. Segal, *China Changes Shape: Regionalism and Foreign Policy* (London: International Institute for Strategic Studies, 1994).

T. S. Selvan, *Singapore: the Ultimate Island (Lee Kuan Yew's Untold Story)* (Melbourne: Freeway Books, 1990).

Shaw Yu-ming, *Beyond the Economic Miracle: Reflections on the Republic of China on Taiwan, Mainland China, and Sino–American Relations* (Taipei: Kwang Hwa Publishing Company, 1989).

M. R. Shelley (ed.), *The Chittagong Hill Tracts of Bangladesh: The Untold Story* (Dhaka: Centre of Development Research, 1992).

M. Smith, *Burma: Insurgency and the Politics of Ethnicity* (London: Zed Books, 1991).

Song, Byung-Nak, *The Rise of the Korean Economy* (Hong Kong: Oxford University Press, 1990).

L. M. Stern, *Renovating the Vietnamese Communist Party: Nguyen Van Linh and the Programme for Organizational Reform, 1987–91* (Singapore: Institute of South East Asian Studies, 1993).

Teck-Wong Soon and C. Suan Tan, *The Lessons of East Asia – Singapore: Public Policy and Economic Development* (Washington: The World Bank, 1993).

R. Thapar, *All These Years: A Memoir* (New Delhi: Penguin Books, 1991).

D. G. Timberman, *A Changeless Land: Continuity and Change in Philippine Politics* (Manila: Bookmark, 1991).

M. Tully, *No Full Stops in India* (New Delhi: Penguin Books, 1992).

Van Anh (ed.), *Vietnam: The Blazing Flame of Reforms* (Hanoi: Statistical Publishing House, 1993).

M. R. J. Vatikiotis, *Indonesian Politics under Suharto: Order, Development and Pressure for Change* (London: Routledge, 1993).

J. Wintle, *Romancing Vietnam: Inside the Boat Country* (London: Penguin Books, 1992).

World Bank, *The East Asian Miracle: Economic Growth and Public Policy* (New York: Oxford University Press, 1993).

—— *Social Indicators of Development 1993* (Baltimore: Johns Hopkins University Press, 1993).

J. J. Wright, *The Balancing Act: A History of Modern Thailand* (Oakland: Pacific Rim Press, 1991).

K. Yoshihara, *The Rise of Ersatz Capitalism in South East Asia* (Oxford University Press, 1988).

Index